A Wing...And A Hero!

The Steve Yzerman Story

By Gary L. Morrison

Erin Key (Editor)

© 2002 by Gary L. Morrison. All rights reserved.

No part of this book may be reproduced, stored in a retrieval system, or transmitted by any means, electronic, mechanical, photocopying, recording, or otherwise, without written permission from the author.

ISBN: 0-75965-999-0

This book is printed on acid free paper.

Cover designed by Ryan P. Morrison. All rights reserved. May not be reprinted without permission.

"The information contained herein has not been reviewed for its accuracy or truthfulness by the National Hockey League or NHL Enterprises, L.P. Views expressed herein are not those of, and the inclusion of any information herein does not constitute an endorsement by, the National Hockey League or NHL Enterprises, L.P."

1stBooks– rev. 12/10/01

I would like to dedicate this book to my daughters, son and wife for all the personal struggles we have overcome as a family. I love all of you, and remember to never give up short of your dreams. With love Dad (Gary)!

iv

A portion of the proceeds from this book will be donated to the Make-A-Wish Foundation in loving memory of Marc Marzullo who died of leukemia on July 10, 1999. Marc's life, thoughts and kind words touched the lives of all who knew him. Further donations will be given to Frances Taylor Isbell, age 8, who suffers from Spinal Muscular Atrophy, because to give back to the community one lives in is the right thing to do.

vi

Prelude

For Frances and Marc

Frances Isbell is a third grade student at St. James School. She suffers from Spinal Muscular Atrophy (SMA), a degenerative neuromuscular disease. Frances is truly an angel from above. Most children with SMA die at an early age. Although Frances does not always enjoy life from the top of the mountain, she is rarely seen with out that beautiful smile upon her face. Frances conquers her struggles with bravery, love and hope. Frances will have surgery in September, in Atlanta, Georgia, to correct the curvature of her back.

This book is written about a man who helps children like Frances. The man is Steve Yzerman, captain of the Detroit Red Wings. Steve is a hero for what he does off the ice, and not because he is a star in the National Hockey League. Frances is a hero for all of us, her bright smile should remind us of how fragile life truly is from day to day. To all those who have bought this book, you are a hero, and I thank you in that a portion of the proceeds from this book will be donated to help Frances and to my other hero who died of leukemia in the sixth grade. Marc Marzullo you will never leave the special place in my heart.

Contents

Introduction xi

Heroes 1

Growing Up! From Cranbrook, Bc To Nepean, Ontario 7

Detroit...The City Of Champions? 10

"When Will I See You Again" 17

There Is A New Kid In Town!! 26

Captain Steve...Captain Fantastic! 36

Great Expectations...Great Results??? 45

Okay Captain, Show Us The Way!.. 52

The Bowman Effect!! 61

The Making Of A Champion 70

Heroes: Make A Wish And Change A Life!........................... 79

The Wings Come Alive In 1995! 90

Life Is Not Easy At The Top Of The Mountain 102

Rematch, Respect, And Remember....................................... 129

An Un"Believe" Able Season.. 146

The Captain Pulls Off A Real "Conn" Job... 164

Where Do We Go From Here?.. 175

Captain 2000 Reaches Another Milestone 190

The Humble Hero, Actions Speak Louder Than Words........ 196

INDEX I

x

Introduction

Heroes are people who are admired by society for the positive contributions they make. A hero is a role model not bound by race, sex, size, or occupation. They are quiet, sensitive, giving, caring, responsible, humble and independent thinkers. Heroes are people who we would like to mirror our own character after.

Children, adolescents, and adults seek role models constantly in today's challenging world. We look for heroes who contribute positively to their communities. We respect these people and hopefully we take their leadership qualities with us to make positive contributions to our own communities.

In the 1990's, the hero faded away to a decade made up of violence, hatred and deceit. Once in a lifetime a person comes along to change our lives for the better. Steve Yzerman is one of the special heroes of today.

Steve Yzerman is the captain of the Detroit Red Wings, a National Hockey League team. He is a successful leader, determined, humble, giving, a great family man, and a celebrity. His leadership on and off the ice is what we should represent. Yzerman suffered through humiliation with class and dignity, and believed that hard work and determination would pay off. The way he reached his goal as a professional athlete is unique in the sports world today. However, it is not his fame that makes him a champion.

Steve Yzerman was born in Cranbrook, British Columbia (a suburb of Vancouver), on May 9, 1965. He is the third of five children of his parents, Ron and Jean Yzerman.

Ron Yzerman moved his family to Nepean, Ontario, when Steve was about ten years old. Steve learned how to skate when he was four years old, and began playing hockey at around the age of seven.

As a young boy, Steve Yzerman, idolized Gordie Howe. Later he looked up to Bryan Trottier, number 19, for the New York Islanders. Yzerman wears number 19 today out of respect for his idol, Trottier.

As a child, Steve Yzerman played hockey with older children. Steve played five years in the Nepean hockey system before he moved up the road to play with the Peterborough Petes in the Ontario Hockey League

(OHL). Following his OHL success, he was selected in the first round of the National Hockey League (NHL) draft by the Detroit Red Wings.

After two successful seasons with Peterborough, Steve Yzerman was drafted in 1983. He was selected overall fourth by the Detroit Red Wings in the NHL entry draft. He arrived as a confident yet quiet kid who was only 18 years old.

The newcomer Yzerman had a lot of answers to the Red Wings' problems. At the age of 18, Yzerman thought he was 30, but as time went on he realized he was only 18. He spoke of teamwork right from the start when the Red Wings selected him. Yzerman came to a proud but struggling franchise. He brought with him a glimmer of hope for a Red Wing team that failed to make the playoffs 11 of the past 13 years. The future of the kid known as "Silk" was uncertain right from the beginning as a Detroit Red Wing.

The owner of the Detroit Red Wings, Mike Illitch, had other plans for the beloved future captain, Steve Yzerman. He may have wanted to swap picks with the New York Islanders so that the Wings could land hometown favorite Pat Lafontaine of Waterford, Michigan. Jimmy Devellano, one of the Wings top brass persuaded Illitch to keep Steve Yzerman. Whether Devellano had a hunch or knew Yzerman's full potential could not be known. But the decision paid off for the city of Detroit and the fans in Hockey Town. The amazing roller coaster career would begin and end in Detroit for Yzerman, a true Canadian hero.

Steve Yzerman began his career with the Detroit Red Wings in 1983. He looked up to his experienced teammates for guidance, in particular to Johnny Ogrodnick, and veteran defensemen Brad Park. He brought instant offensive success to his new team. The most impressive thing about Yzerman was that he let his playing on the ice dictate his future.

Yzerman accompanied his team to a suburban Detroit saloon located in Farmington Hills, Michigan. While most of his teammates were recognized at McFrocks Saloon, Yzerman kept to himself and occasionally spoke with his teammates. Some of the patrons at McFrocks wondered about the little kid hanging out with the Red Wings, but it would not take these fans long to recognize Steve Yzerman.

The impact of Steve Yzerman was felt in his first NHL game on October 5, 1983. The slick youngster moved gracefully toward the Winnipeg goaltender and slipped a backhand shot past the netminder to record his first NHL goal. Yzerman also added an assist in his first professional hockey game. The quiet superstar was on his way to the

Hockey Hall of Fame. What he did not realize was how difficult, frustrating, humiliating, aggravating and physically painful the road to the Stanley Cup championship would be.

In his first NHL season in 1983-84, Yzerman knew what it took to become a winner. He was compassionate and confident from the start, and understood that he could not be successful without the help of his teammates. He realized that they had to work on the ice as a team in order for the Wings to be triumphant. As Yzerman progressed in his career with Detroit, he truly became a team player; on the ice and within the community, teamwork became a trademark for Steve Yzerman. His confidence earned him honors as the youngest member selected to the 1983-84 All-Star team.

The youthful Steve Yzerman enjoyed an outstanding rookie season for the Detroit Red Wings, finishing with 39 goals and 48 assists. He was voted to the all-rookie team and finished runner-up to Tom Barasso for the Calder Trophy, the award given to the top NHL rookie. Steve was named "Rookie of the Year" by *The Sporting News* for the 1983-84 season. This wonder boy was off to a great start for the steadily improving Red Wings.

During the decade of the 1980's, the Detroit Red Wings progressed from the blundering team they were in the 1970's. However, the Wings could not match up with the elite teams of the 80's—the New York Islanders and the Edmonton Oilers. The youthful captain, Yzerman, did not have the necessary experience to lead the Red Wings to greatness during the 1980's.

Steve Yzerman had a great deal to do with the Wings' success, and his commitment to charity was quietly making an impact upon the city of Detroit. He never sought recognition for his charitable contributions. He helped others in need out of the kindness of his heart.

At 21 years of age, Steve Yzerman became the youngest player in Detroit Red Wing history to be named captain in 1986, replacing veteran Danny Gare.

As captain, Yzerman, led the Wings to the playoffs every year in the 1980's except for the 89-90 season. Ironically, that was the memorable year that he married his lovely wife Mrs. Lisa (Brennan) Yzerman.

Steve Yzerman suffered numerous injuries in the 80's, leaving some to question his playing ability. In January 1986, the newly appointed captain fractured his collarbone. Then, just two years later in 1988, Yzerman underwent surgery to repair damaged ligaments to his injured right knee. Did the knee injury slow down the NHL superstar to the point where he could not lead his team back to the playoffs in the 1989-90 season? What would the 1990's hold for his questionable health and leadership ability?

The 1990's were a time when violence, corruption and evil were reported on a daily basis in society. Steve Yzerman stepped to the forefront and created an image of hope for the future. Yzerman represented all the good qualities in life to those who felt down and out. He never quit, and he always worked hard to succeed. He often helped others. The 1990's had its fair share of defeat for Yzerman who would be scrutinized by many for his ability to physically play hockey in the NHL, and to carry the team on his back as their leader.

Yzerman led the franchise in the 1980's as the youngest ever NHL captain. He took the blame for the early playoff exits in the 1990's, but Yzerman never complained. The captain held his head high and let his playing on the ice speak for him.

In 1993, Scotty Bowman came to Detroit as the most successful coach in the NHL. Bowman brought with him a defensive system that would direct the way Steve Yzerman would play the game. Thanks to the Bowman effect, Steve Yzerman would become a great all-around hockey player. He would learn to do it all from penalty killing, blocking shots, winning face-offs, playing defensively on the left wing lock system to scoring goals, even though it would not be as many as Yzerman had in his early playing days.

Yzerman bought into Bowman's defensive style and sold his teammates on the system, as he led the way by example on the ice night after night. Once the Red Wings had developed the routine, they became the best team of the 1990's in the NHL.

With Scotty Bowman coaching, and Yzerman's influence on and off the ice, the Detroit Red Wings regained the elusive Stanley Cup. Many of Yzerman's burdens were lifted because of Bowman's coaching strategy. Scotty Bowman and others surrounded Yzerman with great players who had good chemistry. The team grew into a family, sewn together by trust, chemistry, and the desire to win.

Steve Yzerman was fortunate enough to play along-side such remarkable players like Nicklas Lidstrom, Brendan Shanahan, Igor Larionov, Larry Murphy, Chris Chelios, Pat Verbeek, Sergei Federov, just to name a few. Scotty Bowman and management realized that Yzerman was their leader, but they sensibly built the team with key role players that included the Russian Five and the Grind Line. The key to the success of the Detroit Red Wings was their depth.

Yzerman's heroics and behavior on the ice are enough to make him a man of admirable exploits. The quality that truly separates him from other sports role models is the way he spends his time off the ice. He is caring and eager to go out of his way to aid his fans and needy children. His kind heart and humble disposition is what makes him not only a beloved Red Wing - but also a hero.

xvi

CHAPTER ONE

HEROES

Hero, Hero

Hero, Hero, on the ice,
what makes you so kind and nice?
Not the way you score or skate,
but more the way you never hate.
The way you help a child in need,
you take no credit and show no greed.
Now that you have won the ultimate prize,
you still find time to look a needy child in the eyes.
So even when you score zero and do your part,
you will always be a hero in my heart.

Gary L. Morrison
Hero, Hero
July 29, 1998

What is it that makes society look up to certain people as heroes? What are the qualities we look for in a hero? People who stand out from others or people who are successful and rich? Why should any professional athlete care about being a role model for children? The truth is that not all athletes give a second thought to improving society today. A hero is someone who we admire and want to model our own lives after to make a difference in somebody's life.

Athletes have great egos and are very competitive. Some athletes that are embellished today as heroes are in reality celebrities who tend to announce their every good deed. One purpose they fulfill by being charitable and giving is to feed their egos. Do they support charity to be kind, or is it because the team they work for encourages them to do such good acts for the community? Whatever the reason is, it is often publicized or broadcast. On occasion, charitable acts are public relations campaigns.

Who are the heroes of today and where have all the champions gone? Who exactly was the first hero that humans looked up to as an admirable person for future generations to follow? Was it an early religious prophet, or maybe philosophers like Plato, Socrates or Aristotle? Could the earliest hero have been Mother Teresa, Thomas Edison, Martin Luther King Jr., Helen Keller, Abraham Lincoln, Rosa Parks, Babe Ruth or Roberto Clemente? ·

Whoever we commemorate as the first hero needs to be thanked for a lasting tradition that has made a positive difference in people's lives. Heroes today make the world a better place by providing certain deeds to society. We must remember that it is the person, not the job position, that makes him/her a model citizen. A hero does not make a celebrity, but a celebrity can make a hero. A hero can hold any occupation and in some cases be jobless. Heroism is not based upon color, religion, sex, or status. It comes from the heart and from within.

Heroes do things that make a notable, positive impact on our lives. Heroes bring out the best in the world. They are sensitive, caring, humble, and sometimes successful. The accomplishment of a champion is usually a direct result of his/her hard work ethic and charitable contributions to society.

Whatever one gives to his/her community they can expect to get back. Some people give and give and expect nothing in return.

Celebrities compete to win or be the best, but a hero wins by the contributions, time, and love they give to others.

The 20th century has been blessed with numerous heroes and heroines. People like Henry Ford, Thomas Edison, Franklin D. Roosevelt, Winston Churchill, Martin Luther Jr., Mickey Mantle, Gordie Howe, Gale Sayers, Mother Teresa, Steve Yzerman, and others. All of these people were successful and made priceless contributions to better the world we live in.

Henry Ford mass-produced the first automobile, making traveling to visit family faster by shortening the distance between loved ones. Ford never dreamed of the massive expansion of roads and highways throughout the world. Many people saw Henry Ford as a hero for his innovative creation.

One of Ford's good friends made a worthy invention that would change the world for the better. Thomas Edison tinkered with many different ideas in his life, and was constantly busy testing them. He was a compassionate man who would change the way people lived once the sun went down. Thomas Edison invented the light bulb; his modest manner and long hours of dedication made him a 20th century hero people will never forget.

When one thinks of America, what is that comes to mind? The New York Yankees are one common symbol of our great country. Mickey Mantle was one Yankee who was a true American icon. He came from a small town in Oklahoma, bringing the Yankees speed and skill. He could hit a baseball farther than most other players. He symbolized a man who had it all and truly fulfilled the American dream. He was idolized by most Americans, and was seen as a true American hero.

Hockey players have never really stolen the limelight in the media. The most sought after hockey hero was named Gordie Howe—known as Mr. Hockey. Howe brought several championship seasons to the Detroit Red Wings and hoisted the Stanley Cup for the Wings in 1955. It would take 42 years for another Red Wing prized athlete to lift the Cup, and that new hero would skate to glory in 1997. It was a much-deserved award for a truly dedicated athlete. In a four game sweep against the Philadelphia Flyers, the Red Wing captain Steve Yzerman, finally had his moment of glory that he had dreamed about for all of his life.

For any true Red Wing fan, there could be no better justice served than to see Yzerman carry the Stanley Cup around the packed Joe Louis Arena on a beautiful June summer night in Hockey Town. The moment that many had waited to see brought a tear of joy to hockey fans all around the globe. It was only fitting that Yzerman lost his front tooth and smiled for the entire world to see the blank space. When he smiled at the world, Yzerman bore a toothless grin and a heart full of pride. He had lost a front tooth and the monkey off his back. Any questions fans may have had about his leadership abilities were finally answered.

Why did Yzerman deserve this moment of glory? The main reason was his dedication and 14 year commitment to the same team, not to mention all the moments of splendor he gave to suffering children through his compassion, and the exhaustive hours he spent with needy children in need in the Detroit community. Steve had the ability to cheer and bring a smile to a child's face with his magic touch. From Make-A-Wish Foundation to Children's Hospital in Detroit, from the suffering Elysia Pefley, who Yzerman gave his heart and soul to, and for all the children who waited patiently for an autograph, Steve Yzerman was finally re-paid for his kind and caring lifestyle.

Steve Yzerman has paid dearly for his road to glory and fame. He has been roughed up on and off the ice. He has been the subject of trade rumors and injuries, but his daily life of being a good role model to suffering and sick children has never changed. Yzerman has been there for a child in need, his cost of time or money never making a difference.

Did his parents or his peers instill these values in him? Mr. Yzerman apparently was brought up in a close family relationship. His parents did something right when Steve was young to bring up such a caring and concerned young man.

Heroes are like a flickering flame from a forest fire on a clam and peaceful summer night. Brave men have their ups and downs in life and they provide comfort and warmth to those in need. Most importantly, heroes shine an everlasting light upon those that they give to in the way of time, money, and most importantly, love and compassion. Just as the campfire flame lingers in the memory as a peaceful and calming image, so do heroes who remain in the thoughts of the many lives they touch over the years.

Heroism is not simply an act; rather it is a true and sincere attempt to make life better for all people on earth. Heroes care for others because they know they make a real difference for the good in the people's lives they touch.

Many people do great things to help others in their lifetime, but the true hero is the person who constantly helps others and asks for nothing in return.

Children today need to have role models to look up to, in a world that is filled with violence, divorce and other negative influences. Teens especially need to have someone who fills the void of a loving and understanding figure. People need not give up hope because there still are people who are good and caring as we enter the new millennium. Our future depends upon these role models and the hopes that they will shape our future generations to be good, honest and giving members of society.

The world is full of those who are in need, not only financially but also physically and mentally. Tomorrow's adults are in a position where they can make a real difference in giving and family values. The future can burn a bright flame if the heroes of tomorrow learn from the examples being set by the heroes of today.

Good breeds good and bad breeds bad. The human brain is trained to react positively and negatively according to how one feels about himself/herself. However, with the assistance of positive role models, children and teenagers of today can make a difference in the outcome of the world to come. They can lead by example and pass on the caring and compassionate ideology that can be the framework for the next generation.

People must not forget that heroes provide a sense of hope for the future. It is an optimism that creates sunshine through our clouds of doubt, giving us a belief that is a connection to a better tomorrow. When hope diminishes so does the will to remain positive. However, when expectation is kept alive, so is the desire to make the world a better place.

Heroes keep the eternal flame of hope burning so that we may all live in a better world. People who dedicate their time and money to charity give the future generation a true sense of faith. Heroes provide assurance that we may all live together and share a kind of goodness that once was present a long time ago.

The influence that heroism must have upon teenagers today is giving to others is contagious. Being charitable and benevolent to others will create consciences allowing teens to live a more positive life. The little things in daily life will not be as depressing or aggravating as they used to be. Remember that when a person does something kind, the deed done may be tucked away temporarily as a forgotten action; but one day, perhaps when least expected, payment will be bestowed. All charitable contributions seem to find a way of being recycled with a good reward.

Heroes are always repaid for their charitable deeds; it may take a long time, but payday always comes around for those who are giving. Imagine how good the world will be when we all start caring about one another. The process of heroism can be the way of the future that must begin with today's adults and be passed on to their children. The truth is we must never give in to defeat, for if we do, heroism will fade and be a memory that once was.

Why do heroes do good deeds for others? Ultimately it is because they believe in the cause they are supporting. They believe that what they are doing is for the common good of the people involved.

Of course every hero feels a sense of satisfaction, but the feeling of goodness creates positive role models for our children today. The main purpose of heroism is to set an example by instilling positive leadership traits to the children whom so desperately need guidance in today's independent society. With most families having both parents working, kids today need someone to look up to as a role model. It is a busy world in the new millennium, but everybody has someone that they admire and strive to be like...people who are sincere, quiet, humble, and giving, yet display courage and are positive role models.

One person who possesses all the qualities of a hero is the captain of the Detroit Red Wings, Mr. Steve Yzerman. He puts his heart and soul into all that he does, whether on the ice where he makes a living or at home as a father of three lovely daughters. Yzerman is always there to give his best and expects nothing in return. Steve Yzerman realizes that people have good days and make mistakes on the job. He is aware that he is really not different from anybody else. Outside of hockey, Steve Yzerman displays his caring and sensitive demeanor. People like this are who we need to admire and mold our personalities after, so that the world will be a better place for everyone.

CHAPTER TWO

GROWING UP!
FROM CRANBROOK, BC
TO NEPEAN, ONTARIO

Ron and Jean Yzerman are the parents of five children. The most famous and widely known was their third child, Stephen Gregory Yzerman. Stephen's older brother Mike Yzerman is active in his community by helping to coach youth hockey.

Mike works at a hospital full time and still finds time, very early in the morning, to assist high school youngsters with his knowledge and skills of the game of hockey. He is a nice man who respects the privacy of his family. He made it evident that the Yzerman family is close and has great respect for one another. In a brief conversation with Mike Yzerman, it was easy to see that he is a kind man who taught his younger brother, "Stephen" as Mike called him, much about life as they grew up together. It is apparent that Ron Yzerman is very close to his family and serves the best interest of his children, including his famous son, Stephen.

Steve Yzerman was born on May 9, 1965, in Cranbrook, British Columbia, a western providence of Canada. Cranbrook used to be known as a neighboring suburb of Vancouver, British Columbia; that is before it was the birthplace to one of Canada's premier heroes, Mr. Hockey Town and Conn-Smythe recipient, Steve Yzerman.

The Yzerman surname is of European descent and is pronounced (I zer min). While this is not a common name, it has become a legendary name for Steve and his family. A little more than 33 years following the birth of Steve Yzerman, he placed his family name along side hockey's legendary best when he won the Conn-Smythe Trophy on June 16, 1998.

The Conn-Smythe Trophy is awarded to the most valuable player of the Stanley Cup playoffs. As Yzerman was awarded the trophy by NHL commissioner Gary Bettman, he smiled and paused for a moment. He reflected, and at the post-game press conference he spoke. In his own special way, he explained that he was relatively unknown when he joined the NHL. People had a hard time spelling and pronouncing his name. After winning the Conn-Smythe Trophy, Yzerman was proud to have his name on a trophy with great players.

Steve Yzerman may have spoken for his entire family in regards to winning the Conn-Smythe award. On the wonderful night in June 1998, Steve's entire family could be proud to have the surname Yzerman. He is very well known in the hockey world today.

Even though Steve and his family did not live in the Cranbrook, British Columbia, area long, its place in history will be remembered as the birthplace of future NHL Hall of Fame inductee Steve Yzerman. When Steve was four years old he learned to skate nearby Cranbrook. He practiced for a few years before he began playing hockey. Ironically, one of his favorite hockey players was the legendary great Detroit Red Wing, Mr. Hockey, Gordie Howe. Ron Yzerman moved his family to Nepean, Ontario before Steve's teenage years. Steve played five successful seasons in the Nepean hockey system. He played for the Nepean Raiders against kids who were older than he was. The former Sports Complex in Nepean has been renamed The Steve Yzerman Arena in honor of Steve Yzerman who is the proud son of the Nepean hockey system. Nepean is a suburb of Ottawa, Ontario, and is home to Ron and Jean Yzerman. Steve played five years of hockey in Nepean and still remembers his hometown by promoting charitable causes. He returned to Nepean in 1998-99 with Lord Stanley's Cup and his prized possession the Conn-Smythe Trophy. He displayed the Stanley Cup in 1998 at the Nepean Sportsplex, recently renamed The Steve Yzerman Arena. The name was changed to honor the successful graduate of the Nepean hockey system.

Nepean, like Cranbrook, is a suburb. However, Nepean will always be remembered as the place where the legendary captain and hero of the Detroit Red Wings grew up. The people of Nepean can be very proud of Steve Yzerman as a NHL superstar and as a compassionate champion.

While Steve played in Nepean he tried to model himself after his idol.

Steve Yzerman wears number 19 out of respect for his idol Bryan Trottier. Trottier was one of the great leaders of the New York Islanders during their glory years. He led the Islanders to multiple Stanley Cup championships and put up great numbers during his NHL career.

Following Yzerman's success in Nepean, he moved about two hours westward up the road to Peterborough, Ontario. Peterborough is where Yzerman grew up into a young man. He learned the meaning of teamwork and chemistry, not only in high school, but also from the chemistry of his hockey teammates – The Peterborough Petes. It was here that he would develop skills that would make him an improved all-around hockey player.

Steve Yzerman played two seasons for the Petes. With Yzerman present, the Petes showed steady improvement, especially defensively. Peterborough's goals increased both years that Yzerman played with the Petes, and the number of goals allowed as a team decreased during Yzerman's rise to the NHL.

When Yzerman made the big time, the Petes goal production and goals allowed took a turn for the worse. In 1983, these statistics were most likely viewed in respect to Yzerman as a coincidence. However, later in Yzerman's career with the Detroit Red Wings, the same statistics, under the guidance of the legendary Scotty Bowman, would lead the Wings to consecutive Stanley Cup championship seasons. Some of the players that Yzerman had a chance to play with at Peterborough would meet up with him later down the road.

Peterborough Petes teammate Bob Errey played a number of years on opposing teams in the NHL. The two friends were reunited when Errey joined the Red Wings during the Scotty Bowman era in 1995-96. During the 95-96 season, Yzerman and Errey enjoyed hoisting the President's Trophy, awarded to the team with the best NHL regular season record.

During the 1996-97 season, Bob Errey was traded away and did not enjoy the Stanley Cup presentation that signified one shining moment for Steve Yzerman. The Red Wings were the champions, but Errey was no longer a Red Wing. It would be Yzerman, not Errey, who would lead the Detroit Red Wings to the Stanley Cup.

Yzerman has crossed paths with other Peterborough Petes during his tenure with the Detroit Red Wings. Kris King and Terry Carkner were teammates of Yzerman for a short time during their NHL careers. Tie Domi of the Toronto Maple Leafs would meet up with Yzerman and his teammates; some of the Wings wished they had never met Domi. He had proven to be one of the elite NHL tough guys. Chris Pronger, whose family lived in the Detroit area, and who the Wings would be happy to claim, became one of the top defensemen in the league with the St. Louis Blues. Jamie Langenbrunner played with archrival and top contender - the Dallas Stars, a team that chased the Wings for the Cup during the 1990's until finally winning it in 1999.

When Yzerman's Peterborough career ended, he would move on to play in Hockey Town.

CHAPTER THREE

DETROIT...THE CITY OF CHAMPIONS?

Remember the famous line from *The Wizard of Oz*, "Lions and Tigers and Bears – oh my!" The city of Detroit can almost match the famous movie quote with one exception: the chant heard in Detroit goes something like this, "Lions and Tigers and Wings – oh my!" Another sports franchise quite appropriately named the Pistons came to the Motor City and auto capital of the world. The puzzling team is the Red Wings. After all, what is a Red Wing?

Detroit fans have always been great in supporting their teams, whether they win or lose. Detroit sports fans are loyal to their teams and support the rich tradition created by their professional team's players and owners. The tradition of sports in Detroit goes back to the 19th century.

The Detroit Tigers tradition dates back to the late 19th century when players like Ty Cobb were heroes for boys who dreamed of playing in the major leagues. The Tigers played in what was originally Briggs Stadium and is now remembered as Tiger Stadium, since April 20, 1912. The last baseball game played at Tiger Stadium was in the fall of 1999. The Tigers opened the new millennium playing at the new Comerica Park in downtown Detroit.

The Detroit Tigers have always been a loved team by Detroit fans. They have provided many heroes for Detroit, and other fans worldwide. In over a 100-year span, the Tigers have won four world championships. The first title was in 1935, and ten years later the Tigers regained the coveted title. It took the Tigers 23 years to repeat as world champions when they defeated the St. Louis Cardinals in 1968. The latest championship victory happened when the Tigers beat the San Diego Padres in the 1984 World Series.

Every Detroit Tiger's championship team had its differences. All the teams had distinct players with different abilities; however, they shared one similarity, the desire to win.

In 1935, the Tigers were led by first baseman Hank Greenberg...a kind, dedicated player who offered advice to younger colleagues. He was involved in the community and often made it a high priority to visit children in need.

In 1945, Hal Newhouser led the World Champion Detroit Tigers. He was one of the all-time great pitchers in baseball history and fans adored him. Newhouser was a hero in Detroit during his reign on the mound. His competitive spirit and leadership, along with good team chemistry, led the Tigers to their second world championship in 10 years.

The Detroit Tiger team in 1968 may have been the best team ever to wear the old English 𝔇. They were a team that was gifted with many leaders, most notably Al Kaline. The 1968 Tigers came close to winning back to back championships, but they fell a few games short in 1967 to the Boston Red Sox. In 1967 Detroit was in the midst of racial riots within the city. Winning the championship in 1968 helped to heal and unify a city overcome with racial violence, hatred, and turmoil. This team of Tigers was very special in Detroit. The team of black and white heroes signified racial harmony. Willie Horton, Gates Brown, John Wyatt, Earl Wilson, Denny McClain, Norm Cash, Mickey Stanley, and Mickey Lolich were some of the key figures on the 1968 Tiger roster. This team will always be special to Detroit Tiger fans everywhere. Al Kaline led the way with his quiet and humble conduct. The long time Tiger great finally got what he deserved, a World Series Championship.

The 1984 Detroit Tigers was another great team molded by a great manager named Sparky Anderson. Just as Scotty Bowman was brought to Detroit to bring a championship to the Red Wings, Sparky had similar plans for the Tigers in 1979. He hinted that it would take five years to win the championship, and ultimately was true to his word; it was exactly five years that the Tigers became the World Champions once again.

The group was put together from draft picks within the Tiger farm system. Tremendous effort went into this group of men that more resembled a family rather than a team. Close friendships were developed over the years between several players. They stood behind one another through good times and bad. Many players led the way, but the one who stands out was their fearless leader and shortstop Alan Trammel.

Alan Trammel did a lot for the city. He displayed a kind image that was contagious within Detroit. He always found time to speak with the media and his politeness was genuine and sincere. He never said a bad word about anybody.

Trammel was a positive role model for many Tiger fans. He was very business-like; he went to the ballpark and did his job. He played ball and pleased his fans. When the Tigers won the World Series in 1984, it was only fitting that Trammel be named most valuable player in the championship series.

This 1984 Tigers team had character and flare on their roster, but one local boy helped lead the way with his flamboyant personality. Kirk Gibson grew up in Waterford, Michigan, a western suburb of Detroit. As a child, he was better known for his football skills that landed him a scholarship at Michigan State University. Gibson, or "Gibby" as he was called, was blessed with several talents athletically. He had size, power, speed and leadership ability, and was even compared to Mickey Mantle because of his homerun power and strength. Gibby was not shy with the media. Most of the time he would simply tell it like it was. When things were not going well for the Tigers and Gibson, he did not shy away from the media. He tended to represent his team as a leader and spokesman for the Tigers. Kirk Gibson was a clutch performer who lived for pressure situations on the baseball diamond.

Kirk has grown to become a good friend of Steve Yzerman. Both have many similarities in the city of Detroit. Gibson and Yzerman will always be remembered for the contributions they made to their respective Detroit teams. Both will be heralded as good leaders for their teams. They both took criticism from some of the local media but proved the harsh critics wrong when all was said and done. Kirk Gibson is remembered as the celebrity that hit the dramatic game winning homerun for the Los Angeles Dodgers in the World Series when he was playing with a bum knee. He will also be known for saving the Stanley Cup from destruction at an outing at the house of Steve Yzerman. However people may choose to remember "Gibby," he is deemed a good person with a kind heart who has done much for the people he loves.

The Detroit Tigers have retired four numbers in their franchise history: #2 Charlie Gehringer, #5 Hank Greenberg, # 6 Al Kaline, and # 16 Hal Newhouser. Many other players have made a great contribution to the Tiger organization including, Ty Cobb, Mickey Cochrane, Goose Goslin, George Kell, and the famous voice of the Tigers, broadcaster Ernie Harwell. The Detroit Tigers have had three rookies of the year, Harvey Kuenn (1953), Mark "The Bird" Fidrych (1976) and Lou Whitaker in 1978.

The Tigers have put together over a 100-year love affair with the city of Detroit. When baseball season begins, Tiger fans always have the hope that their team will somehow win the World Series, no matter how they seem to be playing.

The Detroit Lions were founded in 1934. They moved from Tiger Stadium to the Pontiac Silverdome on August 23, 1975. The first official game in the Silverdome was against the Dallas Cowboys; and unfortunately the Lions lost their home opener 36-10.

Some outstanding players have come and gone through the doors of the the Lions home, but none seemed to have good, solid team chemistry. The Lions' last official National Football League (NFL) championship was in 1935, they finished first in the NFL in 1952, 1953, and 1957.

The Lions have 15 players elected to the NFL Hall of Fame, and six numbers have been retired by the franchise. Some of the great Lion players include Dutch Clark, Bobby Layne, Doak Walker, Joe Schmidt, Yale Larry, John Henry Johnson, Alex Karras, Wayne Walker and Lem Barney. Two of the most recent Detroit Lions who have made it big are Billy Sims and Barry Sanders.

Barry Sanders will be remembered as one of the best running backs ever to play the game in the NFL. He is second to Walter Peyton in all-time rushing yardage. Surprisingly, as Peyton was dying from a liver disease, Sanders announced his sudden retirement when it seemed certain that he would surpass Peyton as the number one rusher to ever play in the NFL.

Anyone who criticizes Barry Sanders in Detroit should reflect back on all that he did for the Detroit Lions. He was a perfect role model for all people. He did his job and did it well. He never asked to be placed in the spotlight. Barry Sanders led his team silently on the field. Contributing to many wins for the Lions. He *was* the franchise! When Barry Sanders was with the Lions there was hope that they would make it to the Super Bowl.

The Detroit Lions have never been to the Super Bowl. The Lions hold the current longest drought for a championship won by a NFL team. Without the much-needed team chemistry, luck does not fall in favor of the Lions, keeping them out of the Super Bowl running. One day the Lions will win the Super Bowl and the city of Detroit will have a celebration that will be treasured by Detroit fans forever.

The Detroit Pistons joined the National Basketball Association (NBA) officially in 1949 as the Fort Wayne Pistons. They remained in Fort Wayne until 1957. During the 1957-58 season, the Pistons moved to Detroit, and it has been "home" since then. The Pistons arena now stands in Auburn Hills, Michigan, and is called The Palace. During their years in the NBA, the Pistons have been a fairly successful franchise since their inception into the league.

Dave Bing, a point guard from Syracuse University, provided many great and memorable years for the Piston fans. Bing (#21), was voted to the NBA Hall of Fame. Bing was a great leader on the court for the Pistons.

Bob Lanier was another valuable asset for the Pistons for many years. Even with Lanier's great scoring ability; the Pistons came up short year after year. Lanier helped make the Pistons legitimate contenders, but he could not bring the team to the next level to capture the NBA championship.

To say that Lanier could not lead the Pistons to a title is not a fair assessment of Lanier's value to the franchise. When Lanier moved on to the Milwaukee Bucks, the Pistons suffered several miserable seasons. The rebuilding phase for the Detroit Pistons proved to be a long and struggling process. Little by little, the Pistons tried to put together the right pieces to the puzzle that would lead them to the NBA championship.

The Pistons seemed to be one step behind Larry Bird and the Boston Celtics. Once they overcame the Celtics, it was the Los Angeles Lakers and Magic Johnson and company that eliminated the Pistons in seven games in the 1987-88 NBA playoffs. The "Bad Boys" from Detroit desperately hoped that the next season would be the one where all their hard learning experiences would surpass their failures and allow them to grasp the NBA title. The Pistons could not quite cross the threshold that belonged so many years to the elite NBA teams. They were not as good as the Boston Celtics or the Los Angeles Lakers, as most teams could not match up to those great franchises. Occasionally, a team would sneak in and grab a rare championship - teams such as the New York Knicks and the Philadelphia 76ers.

The 1988-89 season would finally put the Pistons, over the top of the mountain. At last, success was awarded to this great group of guys. From Isiah Thomas to Bill Lambier, and from Vinnie Johnson to a sane Dennis Rodman, this Pistons team was like a family. The "father" of the team was their head coach Chuck Daly.

The Pistons played hard every night and truly earned the 1988-89 NBA Championship. They had a great starting lineup that included Isiah Thomas, Joe Dumars, Bill Lambier, Rick Mahorn and Vinnie "The Microwave" Johnson. When the starters tired, Coach Daly replaced them with such noble reserves as John Sallie and Dennis Rodman. The chemistry was perfect for this group of superstars, and Coach Daly knew how to get the most out of them.

The only question for the Pistons next season was, can we win the championship again? Can we win back to back titles? The 1989-90 season would not be a disappointment for the Pistons; they did indeed repeat the championship win, but have not won it again thus far.

When Chuck Daly departed, the team was never the same, and once Isiah Thomas retired, the Pistons had to rebuild. They made moves to try to match the playing ability of the Chicago Bulls, but were not successful. When Detroit drafted Grant Hill, the Pistons were only players away from reaching the top of the NBA again.

Three Detroit Pistons have been chosen to the NBA Hall of Fame: Dave Bing in 1989, Bob Lanier in 1992, and George Yardley in 1996. Today, the Pistons are a consistent playoff team, but they lack the talent to beat the elite teams in the NBA.

Five Pistons have had their numbers retired: Isiah Thomas, Vinnie Johnson, Bob Lanier, Dave Bing and Bill Lambier. The Pistons is the newest professional franchise in Detroit and they have been exciting and successful during their brief history. They lack the long, established tradition of the Detroit Red Wings who are currently the talk of the town in a city nicknamed Hockey Town, USA, removing some of Canada's domination in the sport.

The first professional hockey team in Detroit was founded in 1926 as the Detroit Cougars. In 1930, the team changed its name to the Detroit Falcons. In 1932, the legacy began for the Detroit Red Wings.

In the Red Wings' initial season they were successful and posted a winning record. They compiled a 25-15-8 mark, which is not bad for a new franchise. The winning tradition became contagious for many soon to be Red Wing teams; most of the fans in Detroit fell in love with the team through the good years and the bad.

The Detroit Red Wings have won nine Stanley Cup championships since 1932, more than any other United States franchise. The team won consecutive championships during the 1935-36 and 1936-37 seasons. The Wings were truly a dominant force in the early years of the NHL.

The legendary Jack Adams coached the Detroit Red Wings for 20 seasons.

He led the team to win a third Stanley Cup in the 1942-43 season. The championships, outstanding leadership and great coaching ability landed Jack Adams a place in the NHL Hall of Fame in 1959.

Tommy Ivan replaced Jack Adams as coach of the Red Wings. In the 1949-50 season, Ivan led the Wings to another Stanley Cup championship. The Red Wings fell short of repeating as Stanley Cup champs the next year, but the Cup would return to Motown after the 1951-52 campaign. The highly talented Red Wings just could not seem to repeat as champs in consecutive seasons.

Tommy Ivan entered his final season behind the bench in 1953-54 for the Red Wings. His team consisted of Sid Abel, Ted Lindsay and Gordie Howe, and this trio would make certain that Ivan would not go out as a loser. Once again in alternating seasons, the Red Wings would reign supreme in the NHL by capturing the cherished prize, The Stanley Cup. Could the team finally capture the illusive back to back championship?

A consecutive championship in any professional sport was a difficult goal to reach. To do it with a new head coach on the scene was even more remarkable. The players had to adjust to new line changes and different techniques of each individual coach.

Jimmy Skinner tried to accomplish the task of winning the Cup again as the new head coach for the Red Wings. The novice coach of the Wings in 1954-55 was very fortunate to coach gifted players. His job was simple, win another Stanley Cup and keep the coveted trophy at Olympia Stadium in Detroit, Michigan. Could they hold on to Lord Stanley's Cup for another year? With Terry Sawchuk in goal, and Lindsay, Abel and Howe up front there really was no doubt as to who had the best team in the NHL.

This talented group of Red Wings seemed to love the game, and winning came naturally to the players. They believed they could be champions and had three previous engravings on the Stanley Cup to prove it. The envied prize stayed in Detroit in 1954-55, but no one ever dreamed it would be 42 years until it would return.

CHAPTER FOUR

"WHEN WILL I SEE YOU AGAIN"

Detroit was not only known for hockey in the late 1950's and 60's but also for its singers and musical talent. Nicknamed Motown, it was the home of notable musicians like Smokey Robinson and the Miracles and Diana Ross and the Supremes.

The Three Degrees was a popular group in Detroit, singing the famous song, *When Will I See You Again*. Red Wing fans never imagined that they would have to wait to see the Stanley Cup back in Detroit for what seemed to be an eternity. It would take more than four decades for another Stanley Cup championship to grace the Red Wings. It returned to Hockey Town under the leadership of Red Wing captain Steve Yzerman.

With Gordie Howe on the team, a Stanley Cup championship was always a great possibility, but it would take more than Mr. Hockey to return the Cup to Detroit. The Red Wings struggled through some miserable seasons before they regained the respect they had when Gordie Howe was the driving force for the team.

Gordie Howe had a great career in Detroit. He was the greatest hockey player of his time. Gordie was tough and talented at putting the puck in the opposition's net. He was a great leader who knew how to win.

The Red Wings did continue their winning ways in the 1955-56 season. They went into the semifinals against the Toronto Maple Leafs and defeated the Leafs in five games. Another Stanley Cup was looking promising in Detroit. The Red Wings faced the Montreal Canadiens for the second consecutive year in the Finals. In 1954-55 the Wings defeated the Montreal Canadiens in an exciting seven game series. The Red Wings knew they were in for a tough series with the Canadiens. No one ever dreamed it would be over in five games, but the Canadiens were able to capture Lord Stanley's Cup from the great Detroit Red Wings by winning four out of five in 1955-56. Montreal ended the dominance of the Red Wings and the Stanley Cup.

The Wings returned to the semifinals the next two years, but they only managed one victory in nine playoff games against the Boston

Bruins and the Montreal Canadiens. In the 1958-59 season, the Wings hired a new head coach with a familiar face: Sid Abel. Abel was a member of the famous "Production Line" in Detroit where he played along side Ted Lindsay and Gordie Howe. The Red Wings finished in sixth place under Sid Abel and failed to make the playoffs.

After Sid Abel finished his coaching career, he later became the voice of the Detroit Red Wings. He broadcast games for the local radio station, *WJR* in Detroit. Abel was a pleasure to listen to on the radio broadcast, making it seem as though you were right at rink side. Sid Abel's commentary made for an enjoyable show that was not always provided by some very mediocre Red Wing teams. It was difficult for Abel to cope with the dismal seasons because he could remember as a player the glory days of the franchise.

The 1959-60 season was an improvement from the previous year's disappointing sixth place finish. The Red Wings actually made it to the semifinals of the Stanley Cup playoffs, only to bow out to the Toronto Maple Leafs in six games. The Wings were entering a new decade, and the future looked promising for the resurgent team.

The 1960-61 season was successful for the upstart Red Wings. On November 27, 1960, Gordie Howe assisted on a goal for his 1000th career point. One thousand points in 14 seasons was remarkable during a time when a team played 60 games a year; today, teams play 82 regular season games. The 1960-61 season was not spectacular for Howe alone, as the team returned to the Stanley Cup Finals for the first time since 1956-57.

During the 1960-61 season, the Red Wings finished fourth overall heading into the playoffs. In the semifinals, Detroit met their rivals from Toronto. The Red Wings were able to avenge the previous elimination by the Leafs by ousting Toronto from the playoffs in five games. The Red Wings were returning to the Stanley Cup Finals against the Chicago Black Hawks.

The Red Wings had the talent and the momentum to win the best of seven games in a series against the Black Hawks. The Wings were poised, experienced, and ready to battle the team from Chicago. The Black Hawks surprised the Wings and captured the Stanley Cup for the Windy City. The series loss to the Black Hawks proved to be another of many playoff disappointments to come for the Red Wings.

The 1961-62 season did not have many highlights for the Detroit Red Wings. The team finished with a losing regular season record of 23-33-14. They finished in fifth place and failed to qualify for the playoffs. This was a major disappointment for the Red Wings. The only real highlight of the season was when Gordie Howe netted his 500th career goal on March 14, 1962. Five hundred goals in 16 seasons was an amazing feat for any NHL player. Next season, the Wings were eager to return to see if they could make another run at the prized trophy, the Stanley Cup.

In 1962-63, the Red Wings enjoyed a successful season with a record of 32-25-13, a 17-point improvement over their previous regular season. The Red Wings finished fourth overall during the season and headed into the playoffs ready to take on the Chicago Black Hawks. The Wings eliminated the Black Hawks in six hard-fought games. Once again, the Red Wings were on their way to the Stanley Cup Finals with yet another chance to bring the prized Cup back to Detroit.

The Detroit Red Wings went into the final round confident, yet cautious. They knew it would be a hard checking and physical series against the Toronto Maple Leafs. The Red Wings knocked off the powerful Black Hawks, and only one team stood in the way of the dream prize. The result of the 1963 series was the same for the Red Wings and their fans...disappointing but optimistic that next year would bring a better fate...that the mighty Wings would return the Stanley Cup to Olympia, and the city of Detroit.

The feeling around Detroit for the 1963-64 season was that the Red Wings were going to win it all. The chemistry was right; the team was confident, optimistic and determined. This team was well focused on recapturing the missing Cup. They had been through the wars before and had their sights set on the favored Toronto Maple Leafs.

The regular season was not promising, as the Red Wings finished fourth overall in the league. Their record was only one game over .500. Expectations amongst the fans were cautiously optimistic heading into the Stanley Cup playoffs. The Wings were not the favorite, but anything was possible with the great talent that this team possessed.

The first round was an exciting seven game series for the Red Wings. They defeated the Chicago Black Hawks by winning game seven. Going into the Finals, it looked as though this would be the year that the Red Wings were destined to win the Stanley Cup.

The opponent for the Red Wings in the Stanley Cup Finals was the defending champion, the Toronto Maple Leafs. It seemed as though this team was like a brick wall that stood between the Red Wings and the Stanley Cup year after year. Would this be the year that the Red Wings would finally solve the puzzle to eliminate the Maple Leafs?

The Maple Leafs went in convinced that they could knock off the boys from Detroit just as they had done one year earlier. The Wings believed that they could dethrone the defending Stanley Cup champs. The fierce rivalry had another chapter added to it when this exciting series came to a close. The Red Wings were ready to nail down the series as they headed into game six with a 3-2 lead. One more victory and the Cup would return to Detroit and the friendly atmosphere of Olympia Stadium.

If the Red Wings could win one more game, all that would be left would be the plans for a victory parade in downtown Detroit. The Red Wings were just one win away from capturing an eighth Stanley Cup championship. There was no possible way they could lose two games in a row, or could they?

The Maple Leafs were determined not to lose in game six. Toronto won game six and set the stage for a dramatic comeback. The task ahead of the Leafs would not be easy, but they had to remember to play one game at a time. If they could win the next game, they would repeat as Stanley Cup champions. Momentum was on the side of the Maple Leafs heading into a dramatic game seven.

Game seven was for the Stanley Cup, but for Detroit it represented pride. They had blown a lead in the series and had one final chance to redeem themselves. With a victory, the Red Wings could open the champagne and celebrate the return of Lord Stanley's Cup.

The Red Wings did not want to be remembered as the team who blew a lead in the Stanley Cup Finals. Would they choke under the pressure? Could Toronto really win game seven and snatch the Stanley Cup from the Wings again?

The Maple Leafs won game seven; they did it, and deserve enormous credit. They showed great character, heart and grit, and they wanted the Stanley Cup to remain in Toronto. The Red Wings were depressed and humiliated; they let a 3-2 advantage escape them in the series. They had Toronto right where they wanted but failed to win the one that counted...and it counted dearly in 1964. It cost them the championship!

During the 1964-65 season, the Red Wings failed to return to the Stanley Cup Finals. They lost in the semifinals to the Chicago Black Hawks in seven games. However, 1965 was not a total loss for the Wings.

The 1965-66 season was another hopeful and successful season for the Red Wings. They defeated Chicago in six games, and believed once more that this would be the year. The Toronto Maple Leafs were eliminated but the other team from Canada, the Montreal Canadiens, was the opponent in the Finals against the Wings.

The Wings fought hard and played a good series. The result remained the same as before, and the Canadiens took the series in six games. The Stanley Cup was stationed in Canada once again, but this time in Montreal. The fans still loved their hockey team and believed that somehow they would bring the Stanley Cup back to Detroit where it belonged. With the great Gordie Howe, anything was possible. During the 1969-70 season, the Wings seemed to be back on track. They finished third overall with 95 points. The return to the playoffs was short lived as the Wings were swept in the quarterfinal round by the Chicago Black Hawks. A return trip to the playoffs took even longer for the Red Wings who were without Gordie Howe.

In 1977-78 the Detroit Red Wings finished second in the Norris Division with 76 points. They returned to the playoffs with a record that was under .500. The Wings opponent in the first round was the expansion Atlanta Flames. The Red Wings surprised many hockey fans with an exciting two game sweep of the Flames. The Wings seemed to have found the formula for playoff success in the series with Atlanta. The next series was against a great hockey team, the Montreal Canadiens.

The Canadiens were a powerhouse in the National Hockey League under their head coach Scotty Bowman. They were methodical, and like a machine that was always in sync. The Wings managed just one victory against the Canadiens, which was good for a team that was so overmatched against Montreal. The Red Wings played hard in the series, but Montreal had too many weapons for them to handle.

The 1978-79 season under head coach Bobby Kromm was a disaster. The Wings finished 18 games under .500 in fifth place in the Norris Division. Reed Larson, an excellent defenseman with a great slap shot, led the team.

The Wings' hopes rested on the young prospect selected in the first round of the draft. His name was Dale McCourt. He finished second on the Red Wings' scoring in 1979.

This Red Wings team was struggling to win games and draw fans at Joe Louis Arena. They were still a long way off from contending for the Cup. Rebuilding was taking place, and it would take many good draft picks and nothing short of a miracle to return the Cup to Joe Louis Arena in downtown Detroit.

The 1979-80 season would be the last behind the bench for Bobby Kromm; he was replaced after 71 games. Former Red Wing and Hall of Fame great, Ted Lindsay, was named the official head coach, but Marcel Pronovost worked the duties behind the bench. Even these two hockey legends could not save the season. The Red Wings finished fifth in their division, but they were a long way from matching up with the World Champion New York Islanders.

The Islanders, coached by Al Arbour, were put together with brilliant draft selections and trades, courtesy of a man named Jimmy Devellano. The leader of the Islanders was Bryan Trottier, who was just the type of tireless leader the Red Wings were searching after.

During the 1980-81 season, the Wings went through two head coaches, Wayne Maxner and Ted Lindsay. Together the two coaches could only muster 19 victories and a total of 56 points for the entire season. The Red Wings finished fifth in the Norris Division, and the playoffs seemed a long way off.

The fans were eager to see owner Ned Harkness sell the team. The city was hungry for some new blood and new faces to try to improve the struggling yet proud hockey franchise. A Stanley Cup championship did not even enter the back of the minds for Red Wing fans. At this point, it was hard to imagine that things could get any worse for the Detroit Red Wings.

In 1981-82, the last season that Ned Harkness owned the Wings, the team found a way to finish sixth in the Norris Division. They were two points shy of the previous season with 54 points. The team was in desperate need of help...and they needed it soon.

In 1982-83, a new era began for the Red Wings with a change of ownership from Harkness to Little Caesar Pizza owner, Mike Illitch. Mr. Illitch brought to Detroit the ex-New York Islander genius, Jimmy Devallano. The goal for Devellano was simple – to build the Detroit Red Wings into a Stanley Cup winner.

Success for Illitch and company would take years, and they knew they had to be patient. The first year under the ownership of Illitch, the Red Wings hired Nick Polano as head coach. The Wings under Polano's reign finished only three points better than the previous disappointing season.

Their captain, Danny Gare, who played well with his teammates, led the Red Wings. The team had other quality players, like John Ogrodnick, Reed Larson, Brad Park, Jim Schonfield and goal tender, Greg Steffan.

This team could not match up to the elite teams in the National Hockey League. They needed to rebuild, and they needed a leader, so draft choices were apparently the direction the Red Wing organization needed to pursue.

The 1983-84 draft was loaded with talent, and the Red Wings, having fourth pick, set their sights on a local talent from Waterford, Michigan. The Red Wings were determined to draft Pat Lafontaine and keep him close to home. He was everything that Red Wing owner Mike Illitch was searching for to lead his team back to the playoffs.

The three picks that preceded the Red Wings belonged to Minnesota, Hartford, and the New York Islanders. During the National Hockey League draft, the former Minnesota North Stars selected Brian Lawton first. The second choice went to the Hartford Whalers who selected Sylvain Turgeon. Pat Lafontaine was still available for the New York Islanders, who were already rich in talent, selecting third in the draft. When the Islanders announced that they had selected Lafontaine, Illitch knew he had lost the hometown prospect. Detroit would have to survive without the services of Pat Lafontaine.

Jimmy Devellano, who had a keen sense for selecting and putting together a champion, wanted someone who would provide great leadership...someone who had scoring ability and could make an immediate impact upon the team. Devellano, wanted a player with heart that he could build the team around. He had his sights upon an underage junior from the Peterborough Petes.

On June 8, 1983, the Detroit Red Wings selected a player who had grown up playing against players who were older than he was. The Wings chose a boy with great soccer playing ability who never let his small size interfere with his game.

The youngster selected by the Red Wings looked to be about 15 or 16 years old. Who was this kid and what could he do for the Wings? Was this wonder boy going to be the one to lead the team to the top, or was this another poor selection by the Red Wings in the draft? The average hockey fan in Detroit was hoping for a big name player in this talented group of stars available for the draft. Who would the Wings choose as their selection to build the franchise back to respectability?

The Detroit Red Wings utilized the fourth pick by choosing what would prove to be one of the greatest draft selections in team history. He was 18 years old, and was so small that when they put the famous Red Wing jersey on him following his announcement as their selection, it appeared to be two sizes too big for him. Many Canadians and people who really knew hockey talent knew his name, but within Detroit, his name was not familiar and was very difficult to pronounce.

On May 9,1965 in Cranbrook, British Columbia, a future Red Wing star was born. He was the celebrity who would eventually lead them to their next Stanley Cup championship. His name was Stephen Gregory Yzerman. Though he would not join the team until 1983, when he joined the Red Wings he was a pleasant edition to a team that was known as "The Dead Wings."

Detroit Red Wing owner Mike Illitch did not get who he wanted (Pat LaFontaine), but he got what he hoped for, a franchise player who would one day bring a Stanley Cup championship back to Detroit. The Red Wings chose a quiet, shy and talented goal scorer in Steve Yzerman. Many Red Wings fans read the newspaper the day following the draft and thought that the Red Wings selected a kid named Why-ser-man (actually pronounced I-zer-min). Ironically, this boy wonder would grow and mature to become a wiser man, and painfully lead the Red Wings back to the top to join the NHL's elite teams.

The baby-faced Yzerman was chosen to be the center that would bring a renaissance to hockey in Detroit, a city that was proud of its great hockey tradition. The fans in Detroit were not sure that Yzerman was the answer, but they were willing to give him a chance. Most fans in Detroit were willing to accept a new athlete until he fails to deliver a championship, or display a personality that displays leadership, effort and compassion within the community.

When the Red Wings opened training camp in 1983, they had the new kid in town...a whimsical hockey player who brought vitality to the Red Wings. He was a hard worker and never seemed to run out of energy. Steve Yzerman possessed the gifts of youth, but he also had the talent to accompany his young age.

Yzerman was determined to make an impact and contribute to the Red Wings. He was ready to step into the NHL and play with the big boys, something he had done in his childhood hockey playing days, ever since his father insisted that he play on the same team as his older brother, Mike, at a very young age.

Steve Yzerman did not seek attention from the media; he was quiet and kept to himself. He was not a real "rah-rah type" of player; he let his actions speak louder than his words. The reality of being such a young player with high expectations did not appear to bother Yzerman. He knew he had a lot to learn and nothing to lose. He was having fun, fulfilling a dream, producing, and was extremely likable to his new teammates.

With the new season approaching, Yzerman was eager to get started and advance the Detroit Red Wings. He brought a new sense of teamwork and fun to a team that entered the new season with hopes of returning to the Stanley Cup playoffs. The Red Wing organization felt the team was on the right track and that there would be improvement in the up-coming season. Would the new kid in town make an immediate impact on the Wings in his rookie season?

CHAPTER FIVE

THERE IS A NEW KID IN TOWN!!

On October 5, 1983, the new kid in town, Steve Yzerman got his chance to debut in the honorable Red Wing jersey. He wore number 19 in honor of his idol, Bryan Trottier of the New York Islanders. Excitement was in the air at Joe Louis Arena. Red Wing fans were hopeful during the season, trusting that the new kid, Yzerman, would put up some big offensive numbers.

The Detroit Red Wings had some good veteran players like John Ogrodnick, Reed Larson, Brad Park, Ron Dugay and Danny Gare - the captain. The goaltending was adequate with Greg Stefan, improving with each year of experience. The stage was set for an exciting new hockey season in Detroit; the Red Wings were ready to fly once again.

Steve Yzerman dazzled the crowd on October 5, 1983, by scoring a goal and adding an assist in his first NHL game against the former Winnipeg Jets. Yzerman skated gracefully and seemed much faster than the older players on the ice. It was apparent that this rookie was for real.

He could produce for the Red Wings, who desperately needed a goal-scoring personality. He did not pretend to have all the answers, and he realized there was a lot to learn from the veteran players on his new team. Steve Yzerman looked up to Johnny Ogrodnick and Brad Park for direction, and learned skills from many other experienced players. He listened to them and took their advice. The best part of Yzerman's rookie season was that he did not seek recognition, and he maintained his humble demeanor throughout his first NHL season. Yzerman put up some impressive numbers in his first season as a Detroit Red Wing. Steve played in all 80 games-rather remarkable for a player in his rookie season. More impressively, he led the team in scoring in 1983. He had 39 goals and 48 assists, for a team high of 87 points. He wanted to make an impact, and he used his initial season to do so.

Yzerman did not do a lot of talking off the ice, but he was courteous and polite with the fans and media. He seemed to be enjoying himself with his new team, obliging most fans that wanted autographs, and made his fair share of charitable visits and contributions. At 18, Yzerman was enjoying life to the fullest. He was doing the job that he loved, and having a lot of fun in the process. However, the goal in Detroit was to make the playoffs, not to watch the new kid in town rack up big numbers.

The Red Wings finished third in the Norris Division with 69 points, the team's best finish in over 10 years. The new kid helped the Red Wings advance back into the Stanley Cup playoffs for the first time since 1977-78. This statistic was more important to Yzerman than any of his individual accomplishments by far. He was a team player and worked hard every night to improve the team.

The progression was drastic, the fans were happy to see the Red Wings return to the Stanley Cup playoffs. The Red Wings were no longer the laughing stock of the NHL. They had finally earned some respect in the world of hockey. The Detroit Red Wings were not happy losing four straight games to the St. Louis Blues in the first round of the playoffs. Overall the season was a great improvement from the past, and the Wings had plenty to look forward to in the future.

One pleasant surprise for the Red Wings was the manner in which Steve Yzerman performed in his rookie season. Those who doubted his size or ability to play in the NHL were silenced by the performance of the new kid. Suddenly, the future was looking brighter in Detroit for the Red Wings and their fans.

When it came time to choose the Rookie of the Year, otherwise known as the Calder Trophy, many believed that Yzerman had a legitimate chance to win the award. The top selection in the draft, Brian Lawton, had just 31 points in his initial season with the NHL. The second player selected in the 1983 draft was Sylvain Turgeon, who tallied 73 points with the Hartford Whalers. Mr. Illitch's prodigy, Pat LaFontaine, managed 19 points with the very talent-rich New York Islanders. In all fairness to Pat, he did not get the same amount of ice time that Turgeon and Yzerman did with their respective teams. The fifth player selected in the draft was a goalie playing for the Buffalo Sabres who ended up winning the Calder Trophy.

Tom Barrasso won the Rookie of the Year honors with his brilliant goaltending for the Buffalo Sabres. Barrasso played 42 games in his rookie season and did an excellent job between the pipes for Buffalo. Steve Yzerman finished second in the voting to Barrasso for the top rookie award in 1983-84.

The astonishing numbers that Yzerman put up for the Red Wings were the best in team history by a rookie, a great accomplishment for a team that has such a great hockey tradition. His rookie honors surpassed even those of the great Gordie Howe, Alex Delvechio, Ted Lindsay and Sid Abel. To top these Red Wing legends was like climbing Mt. Everest without a tour guide.

Everything looked promising for Yzerman as he entered his sophomore season. He was runner-up to Tom Barrasso for the Calder Trophy, and he set a rookie scoring record for the Detroit Red Wings with their long and impressive history. He led his team in scoring and was voted Rookie of the Year by *The Sporting News*. After being named to the NHL All-Rookie Team, on January 31, 1984 Yzerman became the youngest player ever at 18 years old to be named to the NHL All-Star Game. He also represented Team Canada in the 1984 Canada Cup at the age of 19. Most importantly to the Red Wings, he was productive in the Stanley Cup playoffs.

With the Detroit Red Wings playing the St. Louis Blues in the preliminary round of the Stanley Cup playoffs, it was important to see how the 18 year old rookie sensation would perform under the playoff pressure. Yzerman handled the pressure like a seasoned veteran. He scored three goals and added three assists for a grand total of six points in four games of the 1984 playoffs.

Jimmy Devellano came across as a genius for selecting Yzerman, and Mr. Illitch was glad that the Islanders selected Pat LaFontaine. Yzerman's first year was a gem, but what would his second year be like for the Red Wings? Were the Wings headed in the right direction or was Yzerman just a flash in the pan? These were some of the questions that needed to be answered in the 1984-85 season for the Red Wings.

With a new season just ahead for the Red Wings they knew that improvements were necessary to become a stronger team. The Wings needed to add some enforcers to the lineup to compliment the offensive talent capable of scoring goals. The Red Wings added five tough guys to the lineup from "pick ups" or drafts.

The Red Wings acquired the services of one of the premier tough guys on skates Dave "Tiger" Williams. Tiger Williams was a role player; it was his job to protect the smaller players on his team. He also shadowed certain players on the opposing team, creating traffic in front of the opposition goalie. The Detroit Red Wings were aware that they had to become a more physical team to compete in the Stanley Cup playoffs. Tiger Williams seemed to be the logical solution to help the Wings become more resilient in the trenches.

Another power forward to join the Red Wings in 1984-85 was Darryl Sittler, a player who enjoyed several successful seasons with the Toronto Maple Leafs. Sittler, a hard working player who gave solid performances night after night, added depth and maturity to the team. Three new rookies broke into the lineup for the Red Wings and would play for many years to come with Steve Yzerman. Shawn Burr, Gerard Gallant and Joey Kocur, was part of the rebuilding process for the resurgent Red Wings.

A big forward with good hands came up late in the season for the Detroit Red Wings. His name was Shawn Burr. He was a power forward who played hard and aggressively against the opposition for several seasons with the Detroit Red Wings. He was a tough player that added a sense of humor to the dressing room. Some fans in Detroit were sorry to see Shawn go when he parted with the Red Wings, as he had become a favorite.

The last two rookies to arrive on the scene for the upstart Red Wings played a big role in the career of Steve Yzerman. These two players protected Yzerman when the opposition tried to rough him up. Gerard Gallant complimented Yzerman as a line mate for several years after their introductory season together in 1984-85. Gerard Gallant played along side Steve Yzerman for eight years in a Red Wing uniform. The two players shared a lot of good times together, and they worked together magnificently on the ice. They were teammates on the ice and friends off the ice.

Gallant deserves a lot of credit; he played his heart out for the Detroit Red Wings. He stood by his teammates and contributed a great deal to the Red Wing organization. As a rookie, Gerard was fifth on the team in penalty minutes, and he provided much needed support for the rebuilding of the Detroit Red Wings; unfortunately he was sorely underrated.

Gallant had a big heart and did a great deal for the Red Wing organization during his playing days in Detroit. He was dedicated to building a contender for the future, and like all players, he wanted to fulfill the dream of one-day hoisting the Stanley Cup over his head. He was an excellent draft choice and a welcomed addition to the Detroit Red Wings. He was committed, and he played hard night in and night out. The Wings knew they would need more muscle up front if they were to contend for the Stanley Cup. When it comes to toughness in the NHL, the answer is to get the ultimate tough guy on your side. The Red Wings were trying to become a physically respected team within the NHL. In the 1984 NHL draft, the Red Wings stole a pick when they selected a rough housing forward named Joey Kocur.

Joey Kocur appeared in only 17 games for the Detroit Red Wings in 1984-85, but he made his physical presence known with 64 penalty minutes; he was an enforcer. As a rookie, Kocur learned about accumulating penalty minutes in defense of his teammates. He also made a statement in regards to what type of player he wanted to be in the NHL.

Joey Kocur was a good prospect for the Detroit Red Wings when he came into the NHL. He played with the Red Wings and Steve Yzerman until 1990-91, and then he was traded to the New York Rangers. Kocur was a key player in helping to rebuild the Red Wings. He went through some rough times and some good times while he was playing in Detroit for six seasons.

Joey was a favorite among the fans, but was feared by the opposition. He was like having Joe Louis on skates. Joey would fight anybody in the league and would almost always come out as the winner of the bout.

When Joey Kocur was traded, many Red Wing fans hated to see him go. In 1993-94, it was good to see Joey get what he deserved: a Stanley Cup championship with the New York Rangers. With Kocur's career winding down in the NHL, it was nice to see such a warrior win the ultimate prize that had eluded him in Detroit.

The championship helped Joey become an inspirational leader in the locker room some years later when he rejoined Yzerman and the Red Wings again, not so much as a fighter, but more as a much-needed leader who had reached the top with the Rangers.

In the 1984-85 season, Yzerman finished two points better in scoring than he had as a rookie, recording 89 points in 80 games. Yzerman finished third in the Red Wings scoring, right behind the improved John Ogrodnick and Ron Dugay. Ogrodnick netted 55 goals, and Dugay pitched in 38 between the pipes. The team overall finished with 66 points, three short of the previous year point total. This was a disappointment for a team that was on the road to rebuilding.

The Red Wings finished in third place in their division and managed to qualify for the playoffs again. This time the opponent was the Chicago Black Hawks. The Red Wings entered round one of the Stanley Cup playoffs as the underdog against Chicago.

The preliminary round of the Stanley Cup playoffs was a best of five series. The Red Wings were hopeful to improve upon the previous year's performance in the first round against St. Louis. The Red Wings had a talented first line, but they lacked depth and could not match up with the Black Hawks. The boys from Chicago won the series in three straight games. The sweep was very disappointing for the Red Wing organization, and the management knew that more changes were needed before the Red Wings could compete in the playoffs.

The Red Wings tried to turn things around by placing a new man behind the bench. Nick Polano was gone and his replacement was Mr. Harry Neale the great *CBC Hockey Night in Canada* announcer. With a new coach, the organization was hopeful that the next season would bring good fortune to the Red Wings.

Steve Yzerman was productive again after the regular season ended. He scored two goals and added one assist in three playoff games against the Chicago Black Hawks. Yzerman went on in 1985 to join Team Canada in the World Championships. He had seven points for Team Canada; he scored three goals and assisted on four others. With the help of Yzerman, they won the silver medal in the 1985 World Championships.

Red Wing owner Mike Illitch would hear from New York Islander owner Bill Torrey, regarding a trade offer. This time it was Torrey who allegedly expressed interest in swapping Pat LaFontaine for Steve

Yzerman. Illitch wisely declined the offer due to Yzerman's two productive years as a Detroit Red Wing. Mr. Illitch could see that Yzerman was the man he needed and wanted to develop his team around. Illitch looked forward to the next season optimistically with a new coach and a franchise player.

As the Red Wings tried to find the right players to mix together for the 1985-86 season, it was evident that management was doing everything possible to produce a contender. In addition to new head coach Harry Neale, the Wings added some new faces to the starting line-up in the 85-86 season, adding a combination of speed and muscle to the team.

The Detroit Red Wings ventured into the European market with the acquisition of a speedy and skilled native from Czechoslovakia, Petr Klima. His expectations were high in regards to scoring goals. Klima was not a big player, but he was lightning-fast, and a really good puck handler. Klima had to learn to play North American hockey, which can be a big adjustment for the European style player. The ice is smaller in North America, and the NHL uses a more defensive style of hockey. Klima fit in well as he ended up fifth in scoring on the team with 19 goals and 41 assists in 74 games. It appeared as though the Red Wings had finally found a much needed set-up man.

The Wings needed play makers to set up scoring chances for players like John Ogrodnick, Kelly Kisio, Gerard Gallant and Steve Yzerman. The addition of Adam Oates brought one such player to the new and improved Red Wings. He added nine goals and 11 assists in just 38 games. Adam Oates was a quiet player who performed very methodically. He was steady but did not log a lot of ice time with the Red Wings.

Down the road, the Red Wings, in what was one the poorest deals the team made, let Adam Oates slip through their fingers. Oates became one of the premier stars in the league and has been a top player in points for several years in the NHL.

Oates was traded to the St. Louis Blues where he played alongside the great Brett Hull. From St. Louis, Oates moved on to the Boston Bruins where he played a key part in their success, then went to play with the Washington Capitals.

Even with Adam Oates, the Red Wings still needed to beef up to protect their high scoring forwards and centers. The Wings knew they needed the type of player that everyone hates to play against, an agitator who always gets under the opponent's skin. The Detroit Red Wings were searching for a valuable player who could create power-play opportunities for the team.

The answer for the Red Wings was none other than Harold Snepts. Harold was an older player who could cause an opponent to drop his gloves, while Harold would skate away with a cynical smile. The Red Wing fans could be heard chanting over and over, "Harooold, Harooold," every time Snepts took the ice. He brought tremendous leadership to the dressing room; he also was a colorful individual and a real crowd favorite in Detroit.

Harold Snepts was not afraid to play in front of the goalie. He took his punishment in front of many opposing goalies as well. However, Snepts was not the true heavyweight in this new group of Red Wings. A talented young forward took on the role of the ultimate protector with scoring ability to go along with his toughness.

Bob Probert crossed the Detroit River from Windsor, Ontario, where he spent many of his junior hockey playing days. Probert was the son of a police officer, so he was naturally tough. Bob Probert was a big player with good hands. He was the ultimate power forward in the NHL and one of the Red Wings better draft choices during the rebuilding process.

When Probert broke into the NHL, the Red Wings believed he would add much needed firepower to the team. They also thought he had the ability to score 20 or more goals a season. Bob proved to be a valuable addition to the Wings.

In 1985-86, Probert showed promise by scoring eight goals and adding 13 assists in 44 games. He was a pleasant addition for the players and the Red Wing fans. With Joey Kocur, Harold Snepts, Lane Lambert, and Bob Probert the smaller players were able to skate and score better. Injuries would hamper the season for the Detroit Red Wings, who failed to make the playoffs for the first time since Yzerman joined the team.

On January 31, 1984, Steve Yzerman appeared in the NHL All-Star game as a rookie. Exactly two years later to the date, Yzerman's season ended quickly with a knee injury. He suffered ligament damage to his right knee and was out for the remainder of the season.

During the 1985-86 season, Steve Yzerman recorded his 200th point in the NHL. This year was his career low with 42 points in 51 games, his lowest average ever. Not only did the Red Wings lose Yzerman about half way through the season, but they also lost their head coach Harry Neale.

Harry Neale was fired and replaced by Brad Park, a former Red Wing player and a great defensemen in the NHL. Park finished the season as the interim coach until the 1986-87 campaign began. The Wings were eager to get started in 1986 to see just where they stood in their rebuilding process.

The Wings were anxious to see how Steve Yzerman would recuperate from his knee injury, and how the team would perform under their new coach. The Red Wing management believed they had put together a strong nucleus, and could legitimately contend for the Stanley Cup. The fans were excited about the new and improved Red Wings.

The Detroit Red Wings hired Jacques Demers as their new head coach for the 1986-87 season. He stood behind his players, acting much like a father figure to many of the young men on the team.

Demers would be the one to give Steve Yzerman his nickname, "Stevie Y" and "Stevie Wonder." Yzerman was like a son to Demers who gave Yzerman an early Christmas present in 1986 by naming him captain of the Detroit Red Wings. Would Yzerman be able to handle his new role as captain at such a young age?

At 21 years old, Steve Yzerman was named the youngest captain ever in club history. The Detroit Red Wings had some teams that included some elite stars through the years that wore the Red Wing sweater. Yzerman had the responsibility of leading a group of veterans that included former captain Danny Gare. From 1986 to date, Steve Yzerman has worn the "C" on his jersey for the Red Wings. He is currently the longest-running captain to play with one team in the NHL among active players, an accomplishment Steve holds in high regard.

The Red Wings had a new look for the 86-87 season. They added a new coach, captain, and several other new faces to the team. The Wings acquired the services of the high scoring Brent Ashton from the Quebec Nordiques. In addition, they obtained Mel Bridgeman from the New Jersey Devils and Dave Barr from the Hartford Whalers. On a sad note, the Red Wings parted with a friend of the captain, John Ogrodnick.

Three new players joined the Red Wings in 1986-87, and if scorecards were not available at the games, it would be difficult to know who was playing for the Wings. One of the newest additions was current assistant coach Dave Lewis. Lewis played 58 games and totaled seven points for the Wings. He was not a real impact player with the team.

The star who played college hockey at Michigan State University was a highly recruited prospect by the Red Wings and other teams in the

NHL. His name was Joe Murphy. He was a forward, predicted to be a high scoring player one day in the NHL, but he only appeared in five games with the Red Wings in the 86-87 season. He had one lone assist for the Red Wings, but the team expected more from Murphy in the near future.

Another valuable addition to this squad was a defensemen named Steve Chaisson. Steve was not a scoring threat, but was highly skilled at playing defense. Every team in the NHL sought after a good defensemen. Steve Chaisson proved to be an important link in the Red Wings' future success.

The biggest breakthrough for this team was the new sense of leadership provided by Jacques Demers behind the bench. The biggest question was the leadership qualities of the latest appointed captain, Steve Yzerman. At 21, the youngster had an enormous burden resting on his shoulders. Would he turn out to be Captain Fantastic, Boy Wonder, or would he fail in his role as captain for the Detroit Red Wings?

CHAPTER SIX

CAPTAIN STEVE...
CAPTAIN FANTASTIC!

Every child who plays hockey in the backyard, on the pond, or indoors, dreams of playing in the NHL. The truth is that very few ever get the opportunity, and if they do, it is because of all the hard work and effort they dedicated to playing the game. It is truly an honor just to be a professional hockey player in the NHL. Once a player is there, he must be a special type of person to be selected as the captain of their respective team.

A captain is chosen to provide leadership for his team on and off the ice. He is the one who the media praises when the Stanley Cup is won, and the one who is to blame when the team fails during the playoffs. The captain's job is to set a good example for his teammates and to be motivating for all members of the team. He is the one to make decisions on the ice and also in the locker room from time to time.

Occasionally, the captain will have input on perspective trades or draft picks. The captain of a team in the NHL has a heavy burden and responsibility to bear. Each year, every team in the NHL dreams of winning the Stanley Cup. However, only one team has the honor of hoisting the Cup. It is the captain of the NHL Stanley Cup champions that is remembered forever in hockey history. It does not matter what the captain did all season long for his team; any sacrifices he made are all forgotten. What most fans remember is which team won the ultimate prize...the Stanley Cup.

The NHL has seen many great leaders who were captains of there team. Anyone chosen for the job has great leadership qualities. They are usually quite experienced in the NHL so that they can help the younger players improve and adjust to the fast-paced world of the new professional athlete. A successful business has excellent leadership, and likewise a professional sports team must have good leadership to succeed. The world of professional sports has had many great leaders throughout its history. Some of the best players in baseball were remembered because their team won the World Series. A few of these men stood out from others because of their great leadership qualities.

The New York Yankees had three men who will be forever remembered as excellent leaders of their team. Babe Ruth was one of the Yankee great forerunners who won several World Series championships during his career. Mickey Mantle was another man who his teammates looked up to when things needed to improve. Mantle led his team to several championships with the Yankees. Reggie Jackson was another extravagant leader who made things happen for the Yankees when they needed it most.

All successful leaders have one thing in common: they are able to deliver in clutch situations. Babe Ruth, Mickey Mantle and Reggie Jackson were all clutch players for the New York Yankees. Whenever something had to be done to win, their teammates could almost always rely upon these men to succeed. The winning ways of these three New York Yankee legends were contagious to the other players on their team. In short, they were born leaders. The leadership they provided was spread out in a positive manner to there teammates. They knew what it took to win, and they committed themselves to being champions. They sacrificed, created continuity and chemistry, and built bonds that in the end resulted in winning championships for the Yankees.

The National Basketball Association (NBA) has had its share of strong leaders. Jerry West led the Los Angeles Lakers, who guided his team to multiple championships during his playing career. Wilt Chamberlain was another dominator for the Lakers. On the court, Wilt ruled with his towering height advantage over the shorter players.

The Boston Celtics won several titles under the leadership of John Havlechek. The great Irish man could shoot with the best; he had a gifted sense of being able to see everything on the court. Havlechek had the ability to plan his next move with excellence. John was one of the best set up players to ever play the game.

Recently in the NBA, another great leader named Larry Bird led the Boston Celtics. Bird, took the Celtics back to the top in the NBA almost by himself. He was a fiery leader, and when the Celtics needed a lift they turned to number 33, Mr. Larry Bird. A short while ago, Larry Bird led the Indiana Pacers to greatness with his brilliant basketball mind as the coach of the Indiana Pacers. Bird, however, had a thorn in his side when it came to winning the NBA championship. That prickly thorn was Earvin Magic Johnson of the Los Angeles Lakers.

Earvin Johnson was a great leader for the Los Angeles Lakers. He led the Lakers to multiple championship seasons during his career with the team. In college, while playing at Michigan State University, Johnson led the Spartans to the NCAA National Championship. His opponent in the finals was none other than the great forward from Indiana State University, Larry Bird.

Earvin Magic Johnson grew up in Lansing, Michigan, and probably attended a Red Wing game in his lifetime. Magic had incredible talent on the basketball court, and winning championships seemed to follow him everywhere he went. Eventually, his magic ran out when he was forced into early retirement from the game he loved due to illness.

The captain Isiah Thomas led the Detroit Pistons, known as the "Bad Boys." Thomas played with the team in some lean years, but he was the type of player who refused to lose. Thomas hung with the Pistons and did not jump ship. He believed that the Pistons could win a championship, and as it turned out he was right. The Detroit Pistons won two NBA titles in consecutive seasons.

Michael Jordan of the Chicago Bulls defined leadership. If leadership is interpreted as teamwork, dedication, commitment and loyalty, then leadership in two words meant Michael Jordan. He was the franchise for the Chicago Bulls, and will be remembered as one of the greatest athletic leaders of all time in professional sports. The greatest thing about Michael Jordan was that he stayed with one team and took his team to the top.

The championships did not begin in Jordan's rookie season. He struggled for a number of years, but when he did reach his full potential as a player, it was like watching a spring flower that had just blossomed into full beauty. Michael Jordan was like poetry in motion on the basketball court; it seemed as though everything he did resulted in success. It will be a long time before another player has the impact that Michael had upon the Chicago Bulls and the rest of the basketball world.

The National Football League (NFL) has seen many great leaders who have taken their teams to the Super Bowl championship. Football is a team sport, but there have been times when one player has stepped up to be the team leader.

Coach Vince Lombardi of the Green Bay Packers was an inspirational leader for his team. He had talent and knew how to motivate his players to get the maximum performance from them. Lombardi led the Packers to the Super Bowl championship on more than one occasion.

Joe Namath played his college football under the legendary coach Paul "Bear" Bryant at the University of Alabama. Namath took what he was taught and his winning attitude to New York where he played for the Jets. Joe was the quarterback who obtained the nickname "Broadway Joe." He took his underdog Jets to the Super Bowl to face the favored Baltimore Colts. Namath went out on a limb and predicted that the Jets would win the Super Bowl game in Miami.

Namath was a flashy leader, but he performed like a field general once the game started. He was determined and confident, and like most successful leaders, he was focused. Namath was flawless in the Super Bowl as he led the Jets to the championship, just as he had promised to do.

The next Joe to come along was also a quarterback, but this one was no ordinary Joe. He played his college ball at the University of Notre Dame. His name was Joe Montana, and he was born to be a leader. Montana took Notre Dame to the National Championship in his senior year with the Fighting Irish. The San Francisco 49ers drafted Joe Montana following his collegiate playing days.

During Joe Montana's career in San Francisco, he became a franchise player and one of the greatest quarterbacks to ever play the game. Joe seemed to have radar on the football field; his passes were not always pretty, but they usually found their way to his receivers. He was the master at the late game or two-minute drill...he definitely knew how to win.

Some great leaders have not been recognized for their abilities because their teams have not won the championship game. Dan Marino, Jim Kelly, and Barry Sanders were great leaders who will be sure to make the NFL Hall of Fame. Players like these men who stay with one team their whole career and never win the Super Bowl pay a dear price.

John Elway of the Denver Broncos was one of these players, but his name was removed from the list in 1998 when the Broncos defeated the Green Bay Packers in the Super Bowl. Elway and the Broncos repeated as champions in 1999 with a victory in the Super Bowl over the Atlanta Falcons. In Elway's final two seasons, he lifted the label of loser off his back with consecutive titles. Elway was known for his late game heroics, but for a long time he, like Marino, had the label of coming up short. John Elway was always on the losing end of the Super Bowl game until 1998, when the Broncos won. Most people felt the joy on Elway's face, which had a look of total satisfaction and relieved frustration. At last he was a champion in the NFL.

The prize in the NHL is the Cup, named after Lord Stanley Baldwin of Great Britain. It is what every player longs to achieve, but it is so difficult to win. Dynasties come along rarely in hockey because the playoffs are so grinding. Teams must have healthy players, luck must be on their side, and they must have the leadership and determination to stand alone when the final buzzer sounds.

The team that wins sixteen games in the Stanley Cup playoffs owns the prized trophy for a one-year period until the next champion is crowned. Occasionally, some teams have been able to put together a string of consecutive championship seasons. Today, with more teams in the NHL, it is almost unheard of. Hockey is one sport where leadership is a key in winning the Stanley Cup.

The success of the Detroit Red Wings in their early years was because of their superior guidance. They established a dynasty with such greats as Ted Lindsay, Gordie Howe, Alex Delvecchio and Terry Sawchuck.

The influence of these men provided seven Stanley Cup championships for the Detroit Red Wings. During the 1970's, it was the Montreal Canadiens who dominated the NHL with their prominent leaders.

Henri "Rocket" Richard, Jean Belliveau, Yvan Cornoyer, Gump Worsley, Ken Dryden and their head coach, Scotty Bowman, led the Canadiens. The Montreal teams were very disciplined and businesslike on the ice. Together, they were like a machine that was well maintained and never in need of repair. The Canadiens were not always a flashy and exciting group to watch, but they knew how to win.

The Boston Bruins were the next team to become untouchable with players like Bobby Orr, Wayne Cashman, Derick Sanderson and Phil Esposito.

The fun-loving Don Cherry coached this successful group. The Bruins won because of the great effectiveness on the hockey team.

The next dominant team in the NHL won with good direction and by placing fear into the enemy. The Philadelphia Flyers had great guidance in their captain Bobby Clarke. Clarke was well protected with such players as Dave "Hammer" Schultz who was like a police officer on skates. The Flyers were not afraid of anyone, and they proved it by chasing the Russian Red Army machine off the ice in a slugfest resulting in the Russians leaving during the game.

This Flyers team brought a new rough style of hockey to the game that started teams believing that in order to be successful in the NHL, goons had to be present on the ice. Size was substituted for speed and grace. The question was not how many players could put the puck in the net, but who was standing when the final buzzer sounded.

The 1980's brought back defense, speed and skill to the NHL. The team of the early 80's was the New York Islanders. Mike Bossy, Bryan Trottier and Billy Smith led the team; the coach was Al Arbour, who did an excellent job of maintaining focus and discipline with this gifted group of stars. The Islanders won the Stanley Cup an unprecedented four straight years from 1980-1984.

It seemed as though the Islanders would dominate the 1980's...that is, until "The Great One" joined the NHL with the Edmonton Oilers.

During the middle of the 1980's, the NHL was blessed with a dream team.

If ever there was a group constructed having all the tools to dominate, it was the Edmonton Oilers. Compared to most of their opponents, they seemed to be in a league of their own.

The Oilers had a real hockey genius behind the bench named Glen Sather. On the ice, they had the perfect mixture of speed, skill, toughness, goal tending and defense. This team was untouchable because the players could score almost at will.

The Edmonton Oilers lost in the Stanley Cup Finals to the New York Islanders in their first year, but what they won was valuable playoff experience that would last for several years to come. This team would win the Stanley Cup in 1984, led by one of the greatest gentlemen and hockey players of all time.

He was called "The Great One," but his real name was Wayne Gretzky. Gretzky dominated the game, encouraging the players around him to be intense as well. The likes of Mark Messier, Jarri Kuri, Kevin Lowe, Paul Coffey, and the goalie, Grant Fuhr, surrounded him. No other matched this tandem in hockey, and they could light up the crowd and the scoreboard with ease. Edmonton won the Stanley Cup five out of seven years from 1984 till 1990.

The Oilers won because of the guidance provided by a group of young players like Gretzky, Messier and Kurri. Wayne Gretzky was the captain who led this team by his actions on the ice. He was not the type to stand up in the locker room and give a big pre-game speech; he led by example and had fun at the same time while playing hockey. While Gretzky played with the Edmonton Oilers, opponents tried to key on him, only making his teammates more dangerous in respect to scoring goals.

The early years of the 1990's were led by the next sensation to come along and lead his team to the Stanley Cup championship. The team was the Pittsburgh Penguins, and their captain was Mario Lemieux. Mario had the ability to make players around him play well with his enormous talent. He was also very fortunate to have a great line mate like Jamr Jagr.

Lemieux and Jagr were in the top in scoring statistics in the NHL when they played together. Winning was easy with these two putting pucks in the opposing nets. The Penguins dominated the NHL for two years, until Lemieux left the team with an illness. He returned in the 2000-2001 season as a player/owner and had a significant impact upon the Penguins success.

The team of the 1990's was the Detroit Red Wings, who had a good core of youthful and veteran players in 1993. The Wings also had the legendary coach, Scotty Bowman, behind the bench. When Bowman came to Detroit, he knew he had great talent, but it was discipline that had to be enforced by Bowman before the Red Wings could contend for the Stanley Cup.

The Detroit Red Wings were anxious to get started in the 1986-87 campaign with Steve Yzerman leading the way as captain. Yzerman was only 21 years old, but he was without a doubt the leader and the future of the Detroit Red Wings. He became the youngest captain in team history, which was quite an honor with all the tradition the Red Wings have passed on throughout their history. The responsibility of captain for the young Canadian-native Yzerman was yet another role that he would accept in hopes of leading the Red Wings back to the Stanley Cup championship.

Under Yzerman's leadership, the Red Wings improved drastically in 1986-87. They doubled the number of wins they had in the previous season with 34, and almost doubled the number of points in the standings, increasing from 40 points in 1985-86 to 78 points in 1986-87. Steve Yzerman, like any good captain, led his team in scoring with 90 points; he scored 39 goals and added 51 assists. His real leadership would be tested in the Stanley Cup playoffs. Was Steve Yzerman the man for the job in Detroit?

With the Red Wings finishing second in the Norris Division, they received a good seed in the playoffs. Their first-round opponent was the Chicago Black Hawks. Finally, Detroit was a legitimate contender instead of a pretender. The road to the Stanley Cup would still be through Edmonton, but at least the Red Wings had a decent chance of getting to Edmonton.

It would take the Red Wings 16 wins in the Stanley Cup playoffs to recapture the prized Cup from the Edmonton Oilers. The Wings were paired off against the Chicago Black Hawks in round one, and it took the resurgent Red Wings only four games to eliminate the Black Hawks – a team they matched well against. The Red Wings were confident going into the second round where they would play for bragging rights against the Toronto Maple Leafs for the Norris Division title.

The Maple Leafs were ready for the Red Wings, and may have been a slight favorite against Detroit. The series was extremely physical and whichever team did survive, they knew they would have to face the up-hill climb encountering a well-rested Edmonton team in the Western Conference Finals. The Red Wings gained respect in this series by winning in seven games, and were pleased to be headed to the Western Conference Finals.

The Oilers were the best team in hockey and were the team to beat to capture the Stanley Cup. They were the defending Stanley Cup champions, and were the favorite likely to repeat. To get to the final round, the Oilers had to beat the new and improved Detroit Red Wings. Edmonton did not take the Wings lightly. They knew the Wings were on the rise and had earned the right to play in the Western Conference Finals.

Edmonton ended the Red Wings' season in five games, but Detroit felt they were moving in the right direction. They needed 16 victories in the playoffs and got nine; they were more than halfway there. They needed good coaching and got it from first-year coach, Jacques Demers.

The Detroit Red Wings needed good leadership and got it from their new captain, Steve Yzerman. Steve had 18 points in 16 playoff games, proving he was mature enough to lead this team back to glory. This captain was different from other captains in the NHL. Steve Yzerman won the hearts of the fans in Detroit at 21 years old.

At last, the Red Wings had a leader who put everything he had into the game. He cared about his teammates and he cared about the fans in Detroit. He was a pillar of the community and to the city of Detroit. He was just what the team needed, a soft spoken, genuine, dedicated, humble and caring human being. Detroit finally had what it wanted: a hero for the rest of the world to admire. Yzerman gave people from the Detroit area a sense of hope and pride.

A television station in Detroit (WXYZ) broadcast lyrics to set the mood for the new theme to take pride in the city of Detroit. The theme song had a catchy tune, explaining the importance of Detroit dignity. People of Detroit needed to stand up for each other as one community, and believe in each other to be successful.

The tune was popular in Steve Yzerman's early years as captain of the Detroit Red Wings. He may have heard it, or he may not have heard it, but he sure did live it. Yzerman could have had this song written just for him. He reached out to the fans and to the community. His middle name is Gregory, but perhaps it should be changed to charity. When it comes to a child in need this guy, Steve Yzerman, was "the class act."

CHAPTER SEVEN

GREAT EXPECTATIONS...
GREAT RESULTS???

Steve Yzerman left little doubt that he was a good choice for captain of the Detroit Red Wings in 1986-87; he was the building block for the Illitch franchise. He was the first draft selection chosen by Jimmy Devellano, who was very proud of his decision. The coach of the Red Wings, Jacques Demers, was also delighted with his choice to name Yzerman captain of the improving Red Wings. The only question now was what the Red Wings would do in 1987-88 with all of the valuable playoff experience they gained in the past season.

The Detroit Red Wings entered the 1987-88 season with great expectations to improve upon last season, which brought them within one round of playing for the coveted prize, The Stanley Cup. Edmonton was still the team to beat, but the Red Wings started to believe they could play with the highly talented Oilers. Besides, Detroit was one of the better young teams in the NHL.

The Red Wings did not make many changes to the roster in 1987-88 since they had good blending the previous year. At last they had a core of key players to build their team around. With Steve Yzerman, Gerard Gallant, Bob Probert and others, all Detroit needed was to bring in some good young players to solidify the roster.

The latest cast to strengthen the team was in the way of more muscle, speed and skill. The Red Wings added Kris King to the lineup in 1987-88. He was a tough player who the team could rely on to create traffic in front of the opposition's goalie.

The other player added to the Wings was Adam Graves. He was a quiet kid when he first joined the team, but he was fast and had good scoring skills in junior hockey. Graves was not a real big guy, but he fit in well with his new team. He was a fine example of the total team player: he worked hard and did what was asked of him. He was a good addition to the new-look Red Wings.

The Red Wings were confident going into the season, because they now had two legitimate scoring lines that could produce in the NHL. They also had a captain who took off in scoring in 1987-88. Yzerman scored 50 goals and added 52 assists to top the 100-point total for the first time in his career. He also aided in the improvement of his teammates.

Gerard Gallant, who played on the same line as Yzerman, had 34 goals and a total of 73 points for the season. Petr Klima had 37 goals, which was second best only to the captain. The real surprise was in the production provided by Bob Probert. He scored 29 goals and showed everyone that for a big man, he could do more than just fight. Bob had good hands and good scoring skills and he proved it during the 87-88 season.

The 1987-88 season was rolling along for the Red Wings with whispers of beating the Oilers circulating in Detroit among some of the faithful fans. The Red Wings had become one of the elite teams in the NHL, and some believed that with a little luck they could return the Stanley Cup to Detroit. As a team, Detroit finished first in the Norris Division with 93 points. However, one night in February, the Red Wings season took a roller coaster ride from high to low.

The Wings' season literally came to a crashing halt when Steve Yzerman went down in a game that was highlighted by him scoring goal number 50. In Yzerman's second season as captain he was enjoying his role as team leader during the 87-88 season. Steve was named to the NHL All-Star team for the second time in his career. Head coach Jacques Demers called him "Stevie Wonder", and on the ice he truly was a wonder.

Shortly after Steve Yzerman scored goal number 50, his season came to an abrupt ending. Yzerman was taken down by an opponent while skating in on goal. In a flash, his right knee smashed up against the goal post, and Yzerman was helped off the ice, the crowd was silent and still. The Red Wing fans knew that without Yzerman, there would be no playoff run for the Stanley Cup. That night, he was very happy to reach the milestone, but became frightened due to the injury.

Knee injuries have ruined many careers in the NHL, and the ligament damage done to Yzerman's knee was one such injury that required surgery to possibly repair the damage. Steve Yzerman was lost for the remainder of the regular season, but his returning for the Stanley Cup playoffs was still questionable.

Miraculously, Steve returned for the second season, thanks to modern medical procedures. He had the choice to play or wait until the next year, but he decided that he would go for it. His loyalty was with his team; he felt that he had helped advance his team to the playoffs, and he should help them when they relied upon on him most. Yzerman did not see as much ice time as he did during the regular season, but his presence helped carry the team to success during the playoff run.

The Red Wings' opponent in the first round was their archrivals, the Maple Leafs. The Leafs wanted nothing more than to derail the Red Wings in the first round of the Stanley Cup playoffs. Toronto knew that Steve Yzerman was not 100 percent and were poised and ready to knock off the favored Red Wings. Detroit had different plans in mind; they were determined to return to face the Edmonton Oilers for a rematch in the Western Conference Finals. The first round of the playoffs went to Detroit with relative ease as they eliminated the Maple Leafs in six games.

The next opponent for the Red Wings was the St. Louis Blues, another comparable opponent for Detroit. The Blues also knew that Yzerman was not at the top of his game and would be tentative after returning from a knee injury. This group of Red Wings was made up of determination and character, and was not going to let their captain down. St. Louis was gone in five games, and the long awaited rematch was next.

For the second straight season, Detroit was the Norris Division Champion, and collected another banner to hang from the ceiling of Joe Louis Arena. The real goal was to win the Stanley Cup, and in order to do so they had to eliminate the highly powered Edmonton Oilers, led by Wayne Gretzky.

It was no fluke that the Red Wings got to the Conference Finals for the second straight year, but the odds of them winning with Yzerman playing at only 75 percent were not in their favor. The Wings gave everything they had, but once again, the Oilers outplayed the Red Wings and went on to win another Stanley Cup.

This time, the blame went to Steve Yzerman, who gave his heart and soul to his team by playing injured. Without Yzerman, the team probably would not have made it to the Conference Finals. Some people questioned whether Yzerman should have played after having such a severe knee injury. He had only four points during the Stanley Cup series, and he took the blame for the team losing again in the playoffs. Placing the blame with Yzerman was unfair, but he accepted the criticism with grace and dignity. Many wondered whether Steve Yzerman would ever be the same following his knee surgery. To Yzerman, the hovering doubt strengthened his willpower and drive to come back better than ever.

Steve worked very hard in the off season at rehabilitating his right knee. He lost respect of some media, but he never lost his dignity as a man. His comeback during the next season was crucial in making or breaking his career as a hockey player.

The focus for the 1988-89 season was on Steve Yzerman and whether or not he could be productive again following his knee surgery. As captain of the Detroit Red Wings, Yzerman, had his sights set upon winning and contributing to the team.

The Red Wings enjoyed another successful regular season finishing first in the Norris Division with 80 points. Thanks to several players on the team, the 88-89 regular season was quite gratifying. Gerard Gallant finished the year with 39 goals and 93 points, a career high for Gallant.

Another key to the good fortune of the Red Wings was the emergence of Adam Oates. He scored 16 goals and added 62 assists, second on the team only to Yzerman. Oates played 69 games with the Red Wings in 88-89, and accounted for remarkably 78 points. He was emerging into a great playmaker and a good team player.

One bitter note for the Wings that season was the loss of Bob Probert, who was arrested at the United States/Canadian border for possession of cocaine. His teammates and fans dearly missed him especially during the Stanley Cup playoffs. The arrest of Probert shook the team and fans, but people knew that deep down Bob Probert had a good heart. It just took him a little longer to mature and adjust to the lifestyle of the NHL.

The 1988-89 regular season was full of surprises: Gerard Gallant and Adam Oates put up big numbers, Bob Probert had personal problems and was arrested at the border. The real question this season was how Steve Yzerman would perform following major knee surgery?

Yzerman quietly worked hard behind the scenes conditioning and rehabilitating his right knee. He knew he would be ready for the upcoming season. He was determined to come back and play better than ever.

Steve Yzerman silenced many of his critics with the best season of his already impressive NHL career. He finished third overall in scoring in the NHL, behind Mario Lemeiux and Wayne Gretzky respectively. Steve Yzerman scored 65 goals and added 90 assists. His point total was 155 points, the most ever by a Detroit Red Wing. He finished second in goals in the NHL, but he scored 11 more goals than the great Gretzky, who had 54 goals during the regular season.

He was by far the most valuable player for the Red Wings that season. While this was not a big surprise to the fans, it was most satisfying to Yzerman, who overcame his injury. Nobody expected Yzerman to put up numbers like that. Steve returned to the NHL All-Star game for the second consecutive year. He was also rewarded with the Lester B. Pearson Award, given to the league's most outstanding player. All of these accomplishments and awards were victories for Steve, but he had one other trophy in mind...the Stanley Cup.

The Detroit Red Wings entered the Stanley Cup playoffs, confident they would return to the Conference Finals and hopefully make it to the last round, the Stanley Cup Finals. The first round opponent in the playoffs was the Chicago Black Hawks. The Black Hawks had the physical strength, and the Red Wings would dearly miss the services of Bob Probert, their strongest physical player.

The Red Wings had a disappointing first round of the playoffs in 1988-89; they bowed out to Chicago in six games. Some players performed well, but others could not match their regular season playing ability.

Once again, Steve Yzerman performed well in the Stanley Cup playoffs. He scored five goals and added five assists for a total of 10 points in six playoff games. Even after his great season, Yzerman again had his leadership questioned by some of the media, but he never retaliated with negative comments. He decided to 'do what he did best, and let everyone else see the rest'.

In 1988-89, Steve Yzerman not only came back from a serious knee injury, but he did it in grand fashion. He rewrote the scoring numbers for the Detroit Red Wings during the regular season by recording a team-high 155 points. He also set a club record with his 28 game scoring streak from November 1, 1988 to January 4, 1989. On March 15, 1989, Yzerman set a career high point total for one game with six points. Once again, he led the team in scoring.

On the international level, Steve Yzerman represented Canada at the 1989 World Championships. Canada took the silver medal, thanks in part to the strong play of Yzerman; he was named to the tournament All-Star team. After the season, Yzerman knew the previous knee injury might slow him down, but his determination allowed him to have a noteworthy season.

The Detroit Red Wings hoped to return to the top of the NHL and make a run at the Stanley Cup in the 1989-90 season with a couple of new faces, in Bernie Federko and Jimmy Carson. Both players were ranked among the top in scoring for the Red Wings during the regular season. Federko finished third on the Wings in scoring with 57 points in 73 games. He was a quick and skilled player who knew how to score. Federko was a good role player for the Detroit Red Wings.

Jimmy Carson was a local talent that Detroit wanted for quite some time.

Carson grew up not too far from Joe Louis Arena in nearby Grosse Pointe, Michigan. He was scouted heavily as a youngster and was one of the top players to be drafted. Before joining the Red Wings, Carson played with the Los Angeles Kings and the Edmonton Oilers. He was part of the deal that brought Wayne Gretzky to Los Angeles.

The Red Wings gave up a great deal of talent for Jimmy Carson when they traded Petr Klima, Joe Murphy, and Adam Graves to Edmonton for Carson and Kevin McClleland. The three youngsters who left Detroit later help Edmonton to win another Stanley Cup championship. Carson had very high expectations that he never did live up to. He was an average player who scored in streaks for the Red Wings, but Carson was not enough to put Detroit over the top in their bid for the Stanley Cup.

Detroit went from first place to last place in a one-year period. The chemistry never came together as a team and they could not seem to get on track.

Once again, it was the captain, Yzerman, who led the team in scoring. He did not match his incredible numbers that he had the previous season, but he finished third in the league again in scoring behind Lemeiux and Gretzky. Yzerman scored 62 goals and added 65 assists for a total of 127 points, turning out another great season for the captain.

The 89-90 season was a memorable one for Yzerman even though the team failed to make the playoffs. In 1990, Steve married Lisa Ann Brennan, and the distraction of his lovely wife may have been on his mind a time or two during the regular season. This was the only year that the Detroit Red Wings failed to make the playoffs with Yzerman as their captain.

The year was not a total washout for Yzerman, who appeared in the NHL All-Star game for the second consecutive season. He also set a club high record with his nine goal-scoring streak from November 18, 1989 to December 5, 1989. Yzerman returned to the World Championships with Canada in 1990.

On the international scene, the Canadian-born Yzerman was picked for a second consecutive year to represent his country in the World Championships. In 1990, Yzerman led all players with nine goals and 10 assists, for a total of 19 points in the tournament. He was also named the best forward of the tourney, and he was an All-Star for the second time in two years at the World Championship games.

Even though 1989-90 was not a good year for the Detroit Red Wings, it was a very memorable year for Steve Yzerman. He married his lovely wife Lisa, and he made a name for himself in the hockey world. Entering the new decade of the 1990's, Steve Yzerman was refreshed and felt confident about the future of the Detroit Red Wings.

The captain was at ease at the beginning of the 1990-91 season. He felt he could focus on the team and provide the leadership that the Red Wing organization was looking for in a captain. Would the 1990's be the decade for the Red Wings to recapture the Stanley Cup? Would it be Steve Yzerman to lead the team down the long road to hoist the Stanley Cup in Detroit again?

CHAPTER EIGHT

OKAY CAPTAIN, SHOW US THE WAY!

After failing to make the Stanley Cup playoffs in 1990, the Red Wings believed that it was time to make another change. Head coach, Jacques Demers, who was a fan favorite in Detroit, was gone. Some claimed that he was too nice of a man and was not tough enough on his players.

The Detroit Red Wings hired Bryan Murray to replace Demers for the 1990-91 season. They also added some new ingredients to hopefully provide the much-needed firepower the team seemed to be lacking. The Wings needed more scoring personnel to help take some of the pressure off Steve Yzerman.

The Detroit Red Wings added four key players to the roster in 1990-91 in order to try to improve upon the previous season's failure to make the playoffs. The new faces that joined the Red Wings were Sergei Federov, Bobby Dollas, Keith Primeau, and Paul Ysabaert. All of these men would develop into very gifted hockey players later in the NHL. They were a welcomed surprise to the pool of talent the team already had. With Bob Probert back, the Detroit Red Wings did not have to worry about being pushed around in 1990-91. The Wings had their fair share of enforcers to join Probert in the likes of Joey Kocur, and the new big guy in town, Keith Primeau. Primeau was not only big, he had soft hands and a keen scoring touch.

Keith Primeau was a Canadian born player who dreamed of one day being a star in the NHL. Primeau was blessed with good size and the gift of being able to put the puck in the net. In his rookie season with the Red Wings, he played on a limited basis in 58 games. Primeau had 15 points, but more importantly, he was adjusting well to the team and the league.

Bobby Dollas joined the Red Wings as a defenseman. He was not spectacular, but he showed talent and was reliable in the limited action he had on the blue-line for the Red Wings. Eventually, Dollas became very reliable later in his career. He never became a superstar in the NHL, but he was a valuable asset to any team in the league.

Paul Ysabaert was acquired in a trade from the New Jersey Devils in 1991. Ysabaert was another dependable addition to the team. Coach

Murray had his own ideas of what players matched up well together, and was trying to develop good chemistry within the team.

The next player that was added to the Detroit Red Wings in 1990-91 would become one of the best to wear the uniform for the franchise. This man took a lot of pressure off team captain Steve Yzerman. His name was Sergei Federov.

Federov was born in Pskov, Russia, on December 13, 1969. He played in 77 games and ended up second on the team in scoring. Federov had 31 goals and 48 assists for a total of 79 points. The Red Wings knew they had a legend in the making. Federov not only could score goals, but he was lightning fast. He brought the European style of hockey with him to the NHL, but adjusted quickly to the NHL.

Sergei Federov missed his family when he came to the Detroit Red Wings. Eventually his parents, Natalya and Viktor, moved along with his younger brother Fedor to the Detroit area. Fedor Federov signed with the IHL Detroit Vipers, a minor league hockey affiliate. Sergei is a close friend of the Russian born tennis star Anna Kournikova.

Imagine how difficult it was on Federov when he first joined the Detroit Red Wings. He was no longer playing with the Central Red Army, and he had to adjust to a foreign culture. Federov did not speak fluent English in 1990-91. The Red Wings were not concerned with his language barrier, but rather delighted in his playing ability. The Detroit Red Wings now knew they had stolen a pick in the 1989 NHL entry draft.

Steve Yzerman welcomed Federov to the Detroit Red Wings, knowing that the more talent the team had, the better the chances were of winning the Stanley Cup. Yzerman and Federov played well together in 1990-91 as new teammates. With the addition of Federov, the Wings seemed once again to be headed in the right direction.

Under the leadership of captain Steve Yzerman, the Red Wings finished third in the Norris Division in the 1990-91 regular season and returned to the playoffs. Yzerman led the team in scoring again, as he had done ever since he was promoted to team captain in 1986-87.

Steve Yzerman topped the 100-point mark for the fourth consecutive season. In 1990-91, Steve scored 51 goals and added 57 assists for a total of 108 points. After a one-year layoff from the Stanley Cup playoffs, the Red Wings returned to the second season. Their first round opponent in the playoffs was the St. Louis Blues.

The Red Wings were eager to display their new look in the playoffs, but no one knew how this new group would hold up under the pressure of the Stanley Cup playoffs. What seemed to be a recent trend for the Wings was that they kept changing the chemistry of the team, a tactic often done when teams do not succeed in the playoffs. The problem was that the new players never had a chance to gain valuable playoff experience together as a team.

The Red Wings were confident going into the first round against the Blues and hoped that they could return to the Conference Finals as they had three years earlier against the Edmonton Oilers. The series between St. Louis and Detroit was hard fought and came down to an exciting game seven. Unfortunately, for the Red Wings, the Blues won it.

In 1991, trade rumors were circulating involving Yzerman. He played well in the Stanley Cup playoffs with three goals and three assists. After the season, he was up for grabs to two different teams. In the first proposed offer with the New York Islanders, the Wings featured Yzerman in a deal that tried to get Pat LaFontaine again. The second deal was with the Quebec Nordiques, hoping to acquire the services of Eric Lindros, who was not reporting with the Nordiques. Yzerman let it be known that he was not interested in being traded to either team. Ironically, Murray would depart down the road and Yzerman remained with the Detroit Red Wings.

Steve Yzerman survived the criticism for another year. Once again he took the blame for the team being knocked out of the playoffs. He was a respectful leader who was just as tired as all Red Wing supporters of the continuous early exits in the playoffs year in and year out. He never gave up the hope that one day he would lead the Red Wings to another Stanley Cup celebration that had been missing for so many years in Detroit.

The Wings looked to the 1991-92 season for hope. They made several changes from the previous season in hopes of improving the team to be able to make a run in the Stanley Cup playoffs. The Red Wings added two new goalies, two new forwards, two new defensemen and one new center to their talented team.

Detroit signed Ray Sheppard as a free agent in 1991. Sheppard was not flashy, but he could light up the scoreboard. During the regular season, Sheppard scored 36 goals and added 26 assists. He provided a much-needed scoring touch to the Red Wing roster.

The Red Wings acquired two new goalies during the season, hoping to give Tim Cheveldae some rest during the long season. Greg Millen played eight games in goal for Detroit; he won three, lost two, and tied three games. The other goalie had stoned the Wings one-year earlier in the playoffs when he played with the St. Louis Blues.

Vincent Riendeau was traded from St. Louis during the 91-92 season to the Red Wings. He only played two games in goal, but he won both. Riendeau was seen as a valuable back up to Cheveldae for the Stanley Cup playoffs.

Defense was a big void for the Red Wings. It was one area that needed a great deal of help, and Detroit got help from the European market. The Red Wings management chose the 221st player selected in the 1989 draft, Vladimir Konstantinov, who played seven years with the Central Red Army hockey team. He was a different generation player than Federov was in the Russian hockey system.

Konstantinov was a true gladiator from Murmansk. He played the game like a robot. He always played hard and with reckless abandon at times. His stone-faced expression never changed on the ice. "Vladdy," as he was called later, was the terminator on ice in the NHL.

The other defenseman that was added to the Red Wing roster during the 91-92 season from Sweden, was Nicklas Lidstrom. He was selected in the third round in the 1989 draft, bringing a strong resume with him to Detroit. At the age of 19, Lidstrom played with the Swedish Elite League, and also represented his country in the World Junior Championships in 1990.

In Lidstrom's first season as a Detroit Red Wing, he finished sixth on the team in scoring. Nicklas Lidstrom had 11 goals and 49 assists, for an amazing first year total of 60 points. More importantly, he kept the opponents' stars off the scoreboard with his excellent defensive play.

Lidstrom was a smart player who played defense with the best in the NHL. He was an excellent point man to have on the power play, because of his blistering slap shot that has beaten many goalies during his career with the Wings. He is likely assured a spot in the NHL Hall of Fame whenever he retires.

The next addition to the Red Wings during the 1991-92 campaign was a Canadian forward by the name of Martin Lapointe. He was chosen by the Detroit Red Wings as first choice in the 1991 draft, tenth overall in the NHL draft. Marty was charted as a tough guy who could score goals. He came up late in the season, but his dividends paid off down the road for the Red Wings.

The final blockbuster addition to the team during the 91-92 season was another European player, Slava Kozlov, another Russian forward with great potential. He was the Red Wings' second choice in the 1990 NHL draft. Kozlov learned to play hockey under the Russian great hockey legend, Khimik Novoplotltsk, when he was 15 years old. He played 11 games with the Central Red Army team before he left Russia to join the Detroit Red Wings in the early 1990's.

Nobody knew exactly how Kozlov would fair in the NHL. He was involved in a serious car accident in Russia that left some doubt if he would be as great as the Red Wing organization had planned. In the 91-92 season, Kozlov never had a chance to completely develop or prove himself. He played only seven games with the Red Wings his initial season in the NHL.

With all of the new additions to the Red Wing team, the foundation was set for the making of a great hockey team. Ray Sheppard, Nicklas Lidstrom, Vladimir Konstantinov, Slava Kozlov, and Marty Lapointe would hang around to lead the Red Wings to the top of the pack in the NHL during the early to mid 1990's. They also helped during the 91-92 season to elevate Detroit to the top of the Norris Division.

The Detroit Red Wings finished first in the Norris Division with 43 wins and an unbelievable 98 points, the most by a Red Wing team in exactly 40 years. The last Red Wing team to equal 98 points or better in a season ended up winning the Stanley Cup.

In 1951-52 the Detroit Red Wings ended their regular season with 100 points in just 70 games, capturing the Stanley Cup for the city of Detroit. The fans were hopeful 40 years later that their team would bring the long lost Cup back to Detroit.

During the regular season, the Detroit Red Wings were led by their captain, Steve Yzerman. Steve finished the regular season with 45 goals and 58 assists, 17 points better than Sergei Federov did. Yzerman topped the 100-point mark again with 103 points overall.

Steve Yzerman appeared in his fifth straight All-Star game, and he recorded his 900th career point during the regular season. Year after year, it was getting easier to see who was the leader of the Wings on the ice. It was Yzerman, but with all of this new talent and his playoff experience, the question again was, whether Yzerman and the Wings could go over the top to capture the Stanley Cup?

The new look Red Wings had put together a group of players who had a great regular season and would have a real chance of winning back the elusive Stanley Cup. Heading into the playoffs, the Red Wings were confident that their captain would provide the leadership necessary to have a successful run in the Stanley Cup playoffs. With the regular season concluded, the Red Wings were looking forward to the second season, the Stanley Cup playoffs.

The first round opponent was the Minnesota North Stars. Detroit was favored to defeat the Stars and advance into the second round of the playoffs rather easily. The series proved to be far from easy for the Wings who once again faced a game seven in the first round. The seventh game was exciting and this time the Red Wings came out on the winning end. However, this series took a great deal out of the Wings physically, and their next round opponent was an extremely physical team.

In the second round of the Norris Division Finals the Detroit Red Wings faced the Chicago Black Hawks. The Black Hawks knew that Detroit had just come off a seven game series with the Minnesota North Stars. Chicago knew that if they played physically they had a good chance to win the series against Detroit. What they did not know was that they would wind up sweeping the series in four games. A surprise that left the Red Wings scratching their heads, and staring blankly off into space following the series finale.

Another season had ended in disappointment, and now it was time for the organization to evaluate just where the void was that kept them from the top teams in the NHL. Frustration was brewing with the Red Wings management, they wanted answers, and they wanted them now. Some suggestions were that a big name goalie was needed and could be landed in exchange for Steve Yzerman.

Yzerman was once again being questioned about his leadership when playoff time came around. He should have had enough experience in the playoffs by now to take the team up to the next level, some thought.

The 1992-93 Stanley Cup playoff season was not the best for Steve Yzerman, but it was not due to a lack of effort. He played hard every shift that he was on the ice, just as he always did. Yzerman scored three goals and had five assists in 11 playoff games.

Following this season, Yzerman felt that in 1992-93, he had to shine a little extra and prove that he could indeed take the Red Wings to the promised land. He was feeling the pressure that so many athletes have felt from the Detroit media.

Detroit was an impatient sports town, very demanding about winning; they expected a chance to win the championship year after year, and with the Red Wings they had every right to be impatient. It had been four decades since the Detroit Red Wings had hoisted the Stanley Cup in celebration of a championship.

The Red Wings felt coming into the new season that they needed experienced playoff veterans who previously had a taste of winning. They acquired the services of three offensively talented players and one defensive specialist who belonged in a Red Wing uniform. Detroit traded for another defenseman in somewhat of a blockbuster deal.

The latest forward was the kind of player that fans hated when he was on the opposing team. He hounded the goalie, and was a tireless worker who took his lumps for the team. His name was Dino Ciccarelli.

Dino was a nemesis to the Red Wings in the playoffs when he played for the Minnesota North Stars. The Red Wing organization felt that Dino was the type of player they needed badly. He was tough and experienced in the Stanley Cup playoffs, an overall great team player.

The next player Detroit added to the team was Dallas Drake, a forward with good goal scoring ability. Drake added speed to the team and had a good season as one of the Wings top ten offensive players. Drake was young and regarded as a player of the future who could help the team in years to come. He was a good and talented prospect for the Red Wings.

The Red Wings brought back fan favorite Johnny Ogrodnick. The people in Detroit loved "Johnny O," as he was known. Ogrodnick played for several bad teams with the Red Wings and the team felt it was time to give him one more chance to reach the top. He added veteran experience to the Red Wing locker room, and was admired by his teammates.

The Red Wings added two valuable defensemen to the team in 92-93. The first was the son of the Red Wing great, Mr. Hockey, Gordie Howe. Mark Howe played several years with the Philadelphia Flyers. He, like Ogrodnick, brought valuable experience to the Red Wings. Just having the presence of a Howe on the Wings was inspiring. Mark Howe was talented and steady at defense, but he had lost a step or two with age. The second defenseman was acquired in a major trade, he was the type of player they needed badly. He was tough and experienced in the Stanley Cup playoffs.

A little better than halfway through the season, the Red Wings decided they needed more experience in the playoffs. They felt they were a little weak on defense and needed the help of a crafty veteran. Detroit made a risky trade that some felt was not a good deal for the Red Wings. The team worked hard to get Jimmy Carson. He was steady for the Red

Wings, but never developed the potential that the team felt he had. The chemistry and the leadership never really blossomed for Jimmy Carson in Detroit. The Red Wings felt that it was time to get all they could for Carson.

The Red Wings dealt Jimmy Carson to the Los Angeles Kings for Paul Coffey and his teammate Jim Hiller. Several other players were involved in the trade, but Coffey and Carson were the main participants for their new perspective teams.

Paul Coffey brought an offensive-minded defense with him to Detroit, but most importantly, he brought playoff experience to his new team. Coffey won the Stanley Cup three times with the Edmonton Oilers, and was voted best defenseman of the year on more than one occasion. He could lead a rush up the ice better than most defensemen in the league.

Paul Coffey played 30 games for the Red Wings and finished with 30 points, an average of one point per game. He finished fourth on the team in scoring with 87 points. Most importantly, Paul Coffey added depth and talent on the blue line for the Wings. He was an excellent teacher for the younger defensemen on the team. Paul Coffey added leadership to the Red Wings that took some of the pressure off of the captain Steve Yzerman.

The 92-93 season ended with the Red Wings finishing with 103 points, which was good enough for second place behind the Chicago Black Hawks, coached by Mike Keenan. Detroit finished fifth overall in NHL in total points.

The scoring leader on the team again was Steve Yzerman. It was the seventh year in a row that Yzerman had led the Wings in scoring.

Yzerman finished with 137 points, 58 goals and 79 assists. The next closest player to Yzerman was forty points behind in the likes of Dino Ciccarelli. In 1993, Steve Yzerman reached a milestone in his NHL career.

On February 24, he recorded his 1000th point in his NHL career with an assist. Numbers did not mean a whole lot to Yzerman; it was winning and getting the monkey off his back in the playoffs that stood first and foremost. The Detroit Red Wings entered the playoffs as one of the teams that had a good chance of winning the Stanley Cup.

In the first round of the playoffs in 1993, the Red Wings felt they had the talent to go a long way. They had experienced playoff veterans in the likes of Paul Coffey, Dino Ciccarelli, Mark Howe, Gerard Gallant and Steve Yzerman.

Detroit was a solid contender going into the opening round against the Toronto Maple Leafs.

The Detroit Red Wings finished four points ahead of their rivals from Toronto during the regular season. Detroit knew they were in for a tough series in the first round against the Maple Leafs. The Red Wings outscored the Leafs 30 to 24, but they lost in games, with Toronto winning four games and the Red Wings winning three. This series proved to be another seven game failure for the Red Wings in the first round.

Yzerman had another steady performance in the playoffs with seven points in seven games. Still, when the press had to point a finger at some one, it was Yzerman, who accepted the blame once again for the team's early departure from the playoffs. He never gave up; he just kept playing hard every night, whether he was being criticized or was the subject of trade rumors.

This season was the last one behind the bench for Bryan Murray...he accepted a position in the front office.

CHAPTER NINE

THE BOWMAN EFFECT!!

When the Detroit Red Wings went out and hired Scotty Bowman as head coach in 1993-94, management stated that they were determined to bring the Stanley Cup back to Detroit at any cost. It was rumored that General Manager, Bryan Murray, placed Steve Yzerman back on the trading block in an attempt to land a top-notch goalie for the upcoming season. A goalie that had experienced winning the Stanley Cup. It was the area Murray felt the Red Wings needed the most help with in order to win the Stanley Cup. Fortunately for Detroit, the deal never took place and "The Captain" remained in a Red Wing jersey.

Under the new coach, the Red Wings learned to respect Scotty Bowman and play the way he demanded. Unlike a lot of NHL coaches, Bowman never had the opportunity to play in the NHL. Although he probably understood the game better than any active NHL coach, he was certainly welcomed in Detroit when Jimmy Devellano engineered the deal to acquire Bowman as head coach of the Detroit Red Wings.

With Scotty Bowman behind the bench, it was apparent that the Red Wings' management was serious about winning the Stanley Cup. After all, it had been almost four decades since Detroit last earned the right to display the Stanley Cup in Detroit. It had been a long time indeed; many changes had taken place since the Red Wings last won the Stanley Cup. The team now had eight different general managers, 21 coaching changes, and they moved from Olympia Stadium to Joe Louis Arena. The team shifted ownership from the Norris family to the Illitch family. The league had gone from six teams to 26, and the World Hockey Association (WHA) had come and gone.

Bowman's playing days ended in Junior hockey when Jean-Guy Talbot unleashed his stick on Bowman's head. It was rumored that Bowman had a plate put in his head because of the serious injury. The incident ended any chances Scotty may have had of moving up to play in the NHL. Bowman did not hold any resentment towards Talbot because of the accidental mishap.

Scotty Bowman began his coaching career with the expansion of the St. Louis Blues in 1967-68. He guided the Blues to the Stanley Cup Finals against the Montreal Canadiens, who were heavily favored and defeated Bowman's Blues. The Canadiens were coached by Scotty Bowman's idol, the legendary coach Toe Blake, winner of eight Stanley Cup championships.

The 1968 season was a bittersweet year for the city of St. Louis. The Cardinals played in the World Series against the Detroit Tigers. The Blues were in the Stanley Cup Finals against the Montreal Canadiens. The baseball Cardinals lost the World Series against the Detroit Tigers in seven games.

On the ice, the Blues were given no chance against the awesome Montreal Canadiens. The Canadiens were first overall, and the Blues were the eighth seed. Toe Blake was the coach of Montreal. He had won more games than any coach in the NHL had. The Blues had the youngest coach in the league named Scotty Bowman. Bowman was 32 years old when he led his team to the Finals. The Blues lost in four straight - two games in overtime, and the other two games by just one goal. This was an outstanding performance by Bowman's underdog Blues.

With Scotty behind the bench, the Blues were in three consecutive Stanley Cup Finals. However, they failed to win one game. The Montreal Canadiens swept the expansion Blues in 1968 and 1969, and in 1970, it was the Boston Bruins who eliminated the Blues in four games. In 1971, the Blues lost in the quarterfinals to the Minnesota North Stars in six games.

After losing in the 1971 Stanley Cup playoffs, Scotty Bowman lost his job as coach of the St. Louis Blues. The Montreal Canadiens needed a new coach for the 1971-72 season and Scotty Bowman was the man chosen for the job. Bowman agreed to coach the Canadiens.

When Bowman came to Montreal in 1971, he faced adversity right from the start. He lost John Beliveau and John Ferguson to retirement, and goalie Rogie Vachon wanted out of Montreal. Scotty took charge immediately in Montreal with his new team. The Canadien players had no doubt who was in charge of the team when Bowman stepped behind the bench.

Bowman was like a police officer when the team played on the road. He had a master key to the players' rooms and would search the rooms for alcoholic beverages. He would wait in the lobby for curfew violators, and once, he even had Canadian customs check the teams' luggage. Bowman was an intimidating coach for the Canadiens, keeping them off balanced. He had to be this way, since he spent his first years in the shadow of Toe Blake; it became a successful tactic to get the most out of his team.

During his coaching days in Pittsburgh, he was nicknamed "Rain Man," because he was like a computer hard drive with statistics. As a coach, he was a student of the game; he watched televised games and studied constant footage of opponents. Bowman even included his players in his learning process by asking them questions.

Bowman was a strategic coach; sometimes his own players did not know what to expect, therefore, the opposition never knew what Bowman had planned. He could match lines with the best NHL coaches in the game. Jimmy Devellano believed that Bowman was still the best at running the bench. Bowman had the ability to get his players to come out and play hard every night. He is a legendary figure behind the bench; one hockey fans can admire. One never knows when watching from the stands just what Bowman is thinking behind the bench because his facial expression rarely changes unless he is provoked or agitated.

The first Stanley Cup championship won under the leadership of Scotty Bowman belonged to the 1972-73 Canadiens. Bowman's team, thanks to the great goaltending of Ken Dryden, won the Stanley Cup Finals in six games. The next year, the Canadiens lost Dryden because of a salary dispute. Ken Dryden won the Conn-Smythe Trophy for the Canadiens in the 1971 Stanley Cup Finals and truly was the most valuable player on the Montreal Canadiens. Without Dryden's spectacular saves, the Canadiens' fate may have been much different. Scotty Bowman admired Ken Dryden, comparing him to Hall of Fame goalie Glenn Hall, who Bowman coached in St. Louis when he coached the expansion Blues.

The absence of Dryden would prove to be crucial to the Canadiens' quest to repeat as Stanley Cup Champions in 1973-74. The Canadiens were well coached by Bowman in 1973-74, just as they had been in the previous year when they reigned as champions of the NHL. The odds of repeating were not overwhelming for any great team, and the loss of Dryden would be deeply felt in the playoffs.

The Canadiens advanced to the quarterfinals where the upstart New York Rangers awaited their arrival. The Rangers knew that without Dryden in goal, they had a chance to beat the defending Stanley Cup champs. When it was all over, the Rangers took out the Canadiens in six games.

The following season in 1974-75, Dryden returned to the Canadiens. He was welcomed back with open arms by Scotty Bowman and his teammates. The Montreal Canadiens failed to win the Stanley Cup, as the Philadelphia Flyers reaped the award, thanks to the stellar play of their goalie, Bernie Parent, who incidentally won the Conn-Smythe Trophy as most valuable player of the 1975 Stanley Cup playoffs.

In 1975-76, the Canadiens, who were led by Bowman, returned the Cup to Montreal with a team that consisted of players who primarily were bred from within the system. One exception was Pete Mahovolich, who was acquired in a trade with the Detroit Red Wings. Bowman took his team to the Stanley Cup Finals in 1976, and his Canadiens were poised and ready to face the "Broad Street Bullies," – the Philadelphia Flyers.

Some people found it difficult to believe that Scotty Bowman did not win the Jack Adams Award for coach of the year in 75-76. The award that Bowman did win was more self-gratifying; he added another Stanley Cup ring to his collection when the Canadiens defeated the Flyers. With next season approaching some folks wondered if the Montreal Canadiens would emerge into a full-fledged hockey dynasty under Scotty Bowman.

The 1976-77 Montreal Canadiens were the first NHL team in history to record 60 wins in a regular season. With this accomplishment, Scotty Bowman received the Jack Adams Award in 1977, recognizing him as coach of the year. It was apparent that he knew how to lead his team to victory in the NHL.

Scotty Bowman did not show favoritism toward his players; in his eyes, they were all equal. Occasionally he challenged his players by cutting their ice time. At times, he manipulated players, opposing coaches, and referees into situations that favored his motives. Outside of hockey Scotty Bowman was a different man.

Scotty Bowman is a caring and peaceful man when he is not engaged in the battle of a NHL activity. Bowman's family lives in Buffalo, New York. He is a father and husband who cares a lot about his family; they come first before hockey and anything else in the world.

During the 1977-78 season, Bowman had his players contending seriously for a third consecutive Stanley Cup title. It was very difficult to win one Stanley Cup championship in the NHL. The Montreal Canadiens under the leadership of Scotty Bowman had already won the Stanley Cup the past two years, but to win it again would have been a difficult accomplishment.

The Canadiens repeated as champions under the outstanding play of Conn-Smythe winner Larry Robinson. It is rare to see a defenseman win this prestigious honor as the most valuable player during the Stanley Cup playoffs, but Robinson was most deserving. The question going into the next season was whether or not the Montreal Canadiens could win a fourth consecutive Cup. Winning the Stanley Cup requires several ingredients: experience, talent, healthy players, good coaching, and a bit of luck. The Stanley Cup playoffs are not like the regular season. The playoffs are a grinding, physical, mental, and courageous episode added on at the end of a long season for teams that qualify.

If a player in the NHL wins the Stanley Cup, he will have to pay a price physically during the long stretch run to glory. It takes a certain kind of mentality for a player to remain focused for the playoff season. The men who hoist the Cup take a physical beating during the playoff season.

Acquiring the Stanley Cup takes a good committed organization. The coach must match opposing lines, rotate players in out of a game, and rest his stars by including the proper mix of excellent role players. A role player in the NHL is equivalent to the sixth man in the NBA. The role players have made Scotty Bowman a successful coach in the NHL; he realizes that the role player is a must to any Stanley Cup contender.

During the 1978-79 season, Bowman had his team in the Stanley Cup Finals again for the fourth straight year. This is a remarkable task for any team in professional sports. Yes, the Canadiens were talented, but it takes more than mere talent to win the Stanley Cup in the NHL. The Canadiens' opponent in the Stanley Cup Finals was the New York Rangers. The Canadiens won their fourth Stanley Cup championship in a row, and reigned as a hockey dynasty during the 1970's.

When Bowman went to Montreal, he wanted to be the coach and the General Manager. He did not want to spend his life behind the bench. Following the 1978-79 season, he made it clear that he wanted out as a NHL coach. He had hoped to stay with the Montreal Canadiens' organization as there General Manager, but the deal never came from the Canadiens at that time. Bowman entertained the idea of coaching at the collegiate level, and he had his mind set on either Notre Dame or Michigan State University.

Scotty Bowman was determined to land a job as a General Manager in the NHL, and at last he had three separate offers on the table. He had opportunities with the Toronto Maple Leafs, Washington Capitals and Buffalo Sabres. Finally, the Montreal Canadiens decided to join the group and make an offer to Bowman for the General Manager position. It took

Bowman only a number of days to decline the offer with the Canadiens as he accepted an offer from the Buffalo Sabres. He was leaving Montreal to shuffle off to Buffalo for the 1979-80 season.

The Stanley Cup followed Bowman to New York, but not by way of the Buffalo Sabres. The Sabres offered Bowman a five-year contract worth roughly one million dollars. He was given complete control of operations as General Manager, Coach and Director of Personnel. It was a difficult decision for Bowman to leave Montreal, and he left with mixed feelings, claiming that his players in Montreal made him the coach he'd grown to be.

Scotty Bowman knew how to pick his spots when it came time to move on in the NHL to another city. He chose Montreal because of the talent, and as a result, he won five Stanley Cup titles. He chose Buffalo because they were talented and on the way upward.

Scotty went to Buffalo to build another dynasty as he had in Montreal, but this time he failed. He created a .500 hockey team, and was plugged as a coach who was no longer capable of winning. Roger Nielson, former coach of the Philadelphia Flyers, indicated that players under Bowman were motivated by fear and did not know what to expect from him. The Buffalo Sabres fired Scotty Bowman in 1987.

During the next two NHL seasons, Bowman worked as a color commentator for *Hockey Night in Canada*. He was not the greatest broadcaster to work there, but he knew his hockey. Bowman was somewhat careful in his commentary because he knew he would one-day want to return to management or coaching in the NHL.

After his time in the booth with *Hockey Night in Canada*, Bowman returned to the NHL with the Pittsburgh Penguins. He came back as the Director of Player Development and Recruitment with Pittsburgh. Eventually, Bowman would be forced to return behind the bench where he did what he did best: coach. He was an important part of the Penguins success story.

In 1983-84, Pittsburgh selected the prospect of the decade; a 19-year-old Canadian named Mario Lemeiux (no relationship to the notorious Claude Lemeiux of the Phoenix Coyotes). Mario Lemeiux was given the nickname of "Super Mario" or "The Next One," in reference to Wayne Gretzky – "The Great One." Mario Lemeiux had a major impact upon hockey in Steel Town, PA.

In 1987-88, Mario won the NHL scoring championship, but the Penguins were a one-dimensional team that lacked key role players. All of these problems changed with Scotty Bowman in the organization. He was not the type of competitor to sit back and watch things develop.

Bowman was hired in Pittsburgh as a scout that was working out of his home in Buffalo. He did a good job for the Penguins; in 1990, Pittsburgh selected Jaromir Jagr in the draft. Jagr played with the Czech Republic before his playing days in the NHL.

The Penguins opened the 90-91 season with talented players like Mario Lemeiux, Tom Barrasso, Paul Coffey, Bob Errey and Mark Recchi. They also had an American-born coach who was involved with the "Miracle on Ice" United States gold medal winners during the 1980 Olympic Games.

Craig Patrick of the Penguins hired Eddie Johnson as head coach. Johnson was fortunate to have a host of talent when he came aboard. The Penguins added experience when they signed Bryan Trottier who had won four Stanley Cups with the New York Islanders in the 1980's. They also added two quality veterans on the blue line: Gordie Roberts and Larry Murphy.

Mario Lemeiux was out till March of 1991, and without him, the Penguins struggled to remain above .500. Prior to the Stanley Cup playoffs, the Penguins made some trades with the help of Scotty Bowman. They added Ron Frances, Ulf Samuelson and Grant Jenning. Ron Frances was a good play-making center that played in Sault Ste. Marie, Ontario, and was very sound defensively for a center.

The 1991 season was a special one for the Pittsburgh Penguins; Scotty Bowman was elected to the NHL Hall of Fame, and the Penguins made it to the Stanley Cup Finals. Coach Johnson and the Penguins were up against the Minnesota North Stars in the Finals. The Penguins proved to be too much for the North Stars, and as a result, Eddie Johnson was the first American coach to win the Stanley Cup since Bill Stewart in 1938. Tragically, Johnson coached his last full season with the Penguins when they won the Cup.

Eddie Johnson had a malignant tumor removed from his brain in 1991. Shortly after his operation, a second tumor developed. Johnson underwent radiation treatment, causing him to lose his speech. His bad health left the Penguins without a coach for the upcoming season.

Craig Patrick turned to his ace in the hole. Scotty Bowman was named interim head coach of the Pittsburgh Penguins in the absence of Johnson. Sadly, Eddie Johnson died on November 26, 1991. Toe Blake was a difficult act for Bowman to follow in Montreal, but following

Johnson was even harder. The Penguins' players were motivated by the loss of Eddie Johnson. Scotty Bowman did the best job he could considering the circumstances. Scotty Bowman took over the coaching duties behind the bench in Pittsburgh, along with his assistant coach Barry Smith.

The number one problem for Bowman to face was Mario Lemeiux's back problems, which caused him to miss several games during the regular season. Bowman did not care for the end to end wide-open style of play of defenseman, Paul Coffey. He traded Coffey to beef up the offense in exchange for scoring threat, Rick Tocchet.

Bowman led the Penguins to a third place finish in the Patrick Division. Before the start of the Stanley Cup playoffs, Adam Graves unleashed a wicked slash upon Mario Lemeiux, knocking him out of the second season. Without Mario, the team's chance to repeat as Stanley Cup champions were seriously diminished.

The Penguins met adversity head on and went forward in the Stanley Cup playoffs with confidence. They were determined to win for Eddie Johnson. Somewhere up above Johnson smiled as the Penguins repeated as Stanley Cup champions.

In January of 1991, the Ottawa Senators offered Scotty Bowman a management job, an offer that Bowman declined. After all, he was in the midst of a possible dynasty with the Penguins. The next offer he received he did not refuse. He made another wise decision to move on.

When Mike Illitch purchased the Detroit Red Wings, he was determined to win a championship. He bought a team in need of serious help, but it was obvious that Illitch was not afraid to make the moves to build a champion in Detroit. He hired Jimmy Devellano, a mastermind when it came to building championship teams in the NHL. Devellano helped build three Stanley Cup winners with the New York Islanders in the 1980's. Devellano had been acquainted with Scotty Bowman earlier in his career with the St. Louis Blues.

Jimmy Devellano played a key role in acquiring the services of Al Arbour to coach the Islanders when he was in New York. In 1981-82, the Detroit Red Wing owner, Mike Illitch, hired Jimmy Devellano as his General Manager. Devellano inherited a complete mess known as the "Dead Wings." He felt that some of the players on the Red Wings were not capable of performing successfully in the NHL.

Jimmy Devellano had a plan to build a winning team in Detroit. It all began with his brilliant draft choice in June 1983, when he advised the

Red Wings to select Steve Yzerman as their first pick in the draft. Devellano knew what he was doing when he selected Steve, and to this day, he is not shy to admit that Yzerman was his baby.

In 1993-94, the Detroit Red Wings were in need of a coach after Bryan Murray moved on. Mike Illitch contacted Mike Keenan, but Jimmy Devellano was opposed. Jimmy's first choice was Al Arbour, whom he had worked with in St. Louis and later in New York. His second choice was Scotty Bowman whom he also worked with in St. Louis. When Arbour turned the job down, the Red Wings offered Bowman the job as coach. He would be paid $800,000 a year in addition to a signing bonus. Bowman accepted the job and the rest is history for the Red Wings.

Scotty Bowman developed the Detroit Red Wings into a legitimate playoff contender, his impact was immediate in nature. He was not always well-liked as a coach, but certainly would be well-respected by the Red Wing players.

CHAPTER TEN

THE MAKING OF A CHAMPION

With Scotty Bowman behind the Red Wing bench, the fans had a good reason to believe the Stanley Cup would be back in Detroit soon. Bowman and Devellano had proven that they knew how to build a champion. Why should the result be in any different in Detroit?

The 1993-94 season brought several new faces to the Red Wings. Four of the new players were added to the team, two on offense, one defenseman, and one became the goalie of the future. This group of newcomers had a positive impact on the future of the Red Wings.

Offensively, the Red Wings added depth to their already-potent offense. Detroit added Greg Johnson, a speedster who could put the puck in the net. Johnson played 52 games as a Red Wing in 93-94, and he tallied 17 total points for the season. He was a nice addition to an already-talented hockey club.

The next offensive weapon added to the arsenal was Tim Taylor. Taylor was a small player with good speed. He only played in one game in 1994 and in that game, he scored a goal. Taylor would have to wait till the next season to prove that he belonged on Scotty Bowman's team.

Detroit added another small offensive force in the likes of Kris Draper. Draper was a determined and gritty character that gave all he had on the ice. Draper was fast and tough for his size, and he did not back down to anyone in the NHL. In Draper's initial season in 93-94, he played in 39 games; he scored six goals and added seven assists.

The next man the Red Wings added became a fan favorite in a short period of time. He added humor and character to the team, and provided more than his share of community service for the Detroit Red Wings. His name was Darren McCarty. He was a natural in the Red Wing uniform.

In McCarty's first season as a Detroit Red Wing, he played 67 games and totaled 26 points for the year. More importantly, McCarty brought an energized sense of chemistry to the Red Wings. He was a big tough guy who stuck up for his teammates. He was not afraid to tell the media what was on his mind. McCarty brought a family atmosphere to the Red Wings, and he took some of the media pressure off the shoulders of his captain and friend Steve Yzerman.

McCarty had good hands for a big man. He was not as graceful on the ice as Yzerman and Federov, but was an achiever. When he set out to do something, McCarty did not quit until the job was finished. Darren McCarty was a winner!

The Detroit Red Wings added some defensive help to their roster with the addition of Aaron Ward. Ward played his collegiate hockey just down the road from Joe Louis Arena, in Ann Arbor, Michigan, with the University of Michigan. He learned to play defense at Michigan under former Detroit Red Wing great and head coach of the Michigan Wolverines, Red Berenson. Ward was a good defensive player who was not afraid to mix it up with the opposition. He played just five games with Detroit in 93-94, and he scored one goal in his brief stint with the Wings.

The next player added to the Red Wings was a goalie whose name was Chris Osgood. Osgood was groomed to be the goalie of the future. He was very talented and a real competitor between the pipes.

In his rookie season in 1993-94, he played in 41 games with the Red Wings. Osgood posted a record of 23-8-5 in his rookie season, and led the Red Wing goalies in shutouts with two. It was starting to look obvious that Osgood would replace Tim Cheveldae within time, which in fact he did during the season when Cheveldae was traded to the Winnipeg Jets.

Under Scotty Bowman, the new look Red Wings finished first in their division with 46 wins, one less than the previous year under Bryan Murray's leadership. Bowman looked to make his players more than just scoring machines. He had his work cut out for him.

Bowman wanted the likes of Federov, Yzerman, Sheppard, Kozlov, Primeau, and others to become complete players. Bowman liked role players, but with the Red Wings, he had to teach his players all facets of the game. He taught them to play defensively, win face-offs, block shots, and do all the little things it took to win.

When the legendary Jack Adams coached the Red Wings, he ruled them with an iron fist. He had many bachelors on his team, and if they wanted to hang out all night during the playoffs, they paid the next morning. Adams would hold early morning practice sessions the next day.

Scotty Bowman did not treat his players a harshly as Adams but he was not concerned outwardly with his player's feelings toward him. Bowman understood that it is his responsibility to make his players play well. He expected to make his players the best that they could be. He also demanded that his players play as hard as they could all the time. All he was concerned with was winning when it came to hockey. He stressed over achievement to his team. His philosophy during the playoffs was that the players had to play better than they did during the regular season in order to be successful.

Bowman learned to rely upon role players from Dick Irvan, a former Montreal coach, who believed that it was the secondary player who delivered in the big games. Bowman was a master at hiding these role players all season long, allowing them to blossom during the playoffs.

Bowman believed in preparing his team well in advance for big games. He was not one to stand up and give the big speech before a game, he merely cautioned his players to be careful as to how they conducted themselves off the ice, and especially with the media.

Bowman realized that Detroit was a real hockey town shortly after his arrival. There was no fooling the fans about how the team was playing; great hockey tradition thrived in Detroit, and the fans were not shy when the Red Wings faltered. When the number one seeded Red Wings entered the 93-94 playoffs, the fans did not expect them to lose in the first round against the expansion San Jose Sharks.

Scotty Bowman knew better than to take the Sharks for granted in the first round. They had to play hard all season in order to have the right to face Detroit in the playoffs. Furthermore, a defensive specialist in Kevin Constantine coached the Sharks. The Sharks played well defensively night after night during the regular season, which was a cause of concern for Scotty Bowman.

The Detroit Red Wings had the upper hand offensively, but their stars had to perform in the Stanley Cup playoffs. Detroit needed production from Sergei Federov, Ray Sheppard, Steve Yzerman, and the other big gunners on the team. They had to get production from their marquee players, or they would be in for a long series.

The big question for both teams focused on the goalies. The Red Wings had two inexperienced goalies: Bob Essena and Chris Osgood. The Sharks duo had no prior playoff experience between Jimmy Waite and Artes Irbe.

The Detroit News offered two different opinions as to what would be the outcome of this series. Of course, both polls picked the Red Wings, the team that was the overwhelming favorite. Cynthia Lambert, who writes for *The Detroit News,* chose the Red Wings to win in five. Keith Gave, from *The Detroit News* staff predicted that the Red Wings would advance to the second round by beating the Sharks in seven games. The fans in Detroit did not want another seven game series to end like it had the previous year, with an overtime defeat in game seven against the Toronto Maple Leafs.

Game one of the series began with a bit of mystery. Where was the Red Wing captain and what was wrong with him? How long would Detroit have to play without Steve Yzerman? Who would step up in the absence of Yzerman and lead the Wings to victory against the expansion San Jose Sharks?

The first game of the series had a total of nine goals scored. With the Red Wings' high-powered offense, it only seemed logical that game one belonged to Detroit. However, just the opposite happened when game one went to the Sharks. Not only did the Sharks win 5-4, but they also won in Detroit and proved to the Wings that they were a formidable opponent in the Stanley Cup playoffs. Heading into game two, Detroit sensed that improved goal tending was a must to survive the Stanley Cup playoffs.

Detroit remained sworn to secrecy in regards to the injury preventing Steve Yzerman from playing in the series against the Sharks. Bowman did not want to let the opposition in on what was wrong with Yzerman, who was not at liberty to discuss his injury with the media. Yzerman was apologetic for not elaborating on his injury; he insisted that management could provide the press with answers. He did not want the media and fans to look down upon him because of his inability to discuss it. During the playoffs, it was best not give the opposition an edge regarding injuries to key players.

It was believed that Yzerman was bothered by one of his previous injuries that hampered him in past Stanley Cup playoffs. Perhaps, it was the knee injury of 1988, a wrist injury from 1993, or the herniated disc in his neck that kept him out for part of the 94 regular season that was bothering him.

The San Jose Sharks knew that Detroit would be ready to play in game two with or without Steve Yzerman, but the Sharks had to feel a bit more confident with him out of the lineup. Yzerman watched game two from a distance at Joe Louis Arena. Game two suddenly became a must win for the Wings.

Detroit knew the series would be all but over if they had to go to San Jose down 2-0 in the series. Following game one, Scotty Bowman let his team know they had to play better defensively to have a chance in game two. He reminded them that they had given the Sharks 17 scoring chances in the first game. The Detroit Red Wings realized the importance of winning the next game against San Jose.

Detroit knew they had a critical situation early in the series. San Jose had played well defensively all year, but in game two, it was the Red Wings who threw a shutout when they needed it most. Detroit seemed to take the series back in command with a 4-0 whitewashing of the Sharks in game two. The series was all even heading out west to San Jose, but the Red Wings were still without the services of their leader, Steve Yzerman.

Game three was decided by a one-goal margin. Once again it was defense that made the difference. The Red Wings prevailed by a 3-2 score and seemed to be in command of the series with two impressive back-to-back victories against the Sharks. It was the Red Wings who played strong defensively in game three. If the Red Wings could win game four, the series would be all but over for the Sharks. Game four was going just the way that the Red Wings had planned; early in the second period, Detroit had a 3-1 lead over the Sharks.

At the end of the second period, the Red Wings were holding on for their playoff lives. The Sharks struck quickly with two goals to tie game three at 3-3 going into the third period. The Red Wings had let a two goal lead slip away. The third period proved to be a critical one in this series;

both teams played well defensively. One goal made the difference in this game. At 6:35 of the third period, Sergei Makarov of the Sharks scored to put his team in a deadlock against the heavily-favored Red Wings in the first round of the Stanley Cup playoffs.

During the first four games of the series against the Sharks, the Red Wings' top six offensive players had failed to put one puck in the net. Federov, Sheppard, Coffey, Kozlov, Primeau and the injured Steve Yzerman had not scored once in the first four games. In order to win the series, Detroit knew they had to get goals out of their top gunners.

Game five was pivotal in the series for Detroit. With a victory, they needed just one more victory to ice the inexperienced Sharks. San Jose seemed to be enjoying the series, and the crowd support at the Shark Tank was in hysteria for this pivotal game. The theme music to *Jaws* that played in San Jose seemed to be eating away at yet another Red Wing opportunity to win the Stanley Cup.

Whether or not Steve Yzerman would return in the series was still questionable heading into game five. He seemed healthy in practice after skating for the first time in 10 days. Yzerman tried to put some spark in his team by indicating that when the game was closely played, he felt confident with a guy like Federov on his team. The captain did not hope the series would be tied at 2-2, but he knew it would not be an easy task to eliminate the Sharks.

Steve Yzerman returned for game five, but whether or not he was 100 percent was questionable. As team captain, he had an obligation to try to inspire his team to rally together and eliminate the pesky Sharks. The return of Yzerman meant more offensive punch for the already-potent Detroit Red Wings.

Prior to game five of the series, Yzerman was the Red Wings playoff-scoring leader among active players. Yzerman added experience and a positive attitude when it came to the subject of comeback victories. He explained that many of his teammates had come from behind before, most recently against the Minnesota North Stars, when they came back from a three game deficit to win the series. He reminded his team that many of the same players who went through that experience were still around in 1994.

Yzerman added two assists for his team, but it was not enough to win the critical game five for the Detroit Red Wings. They had plenty of opportunities in the game, but seemed to be pressing on the power play. They tried too hard to make the right play, instead of just letting things happen. The only thing in the Wings favor now was the fact that they were returning home to Joe Louis Arena for game six, and hopefully, game seven.

Game six proved just how much character the Detroit Red Wings had as a team. They could both come back and eliminate the underdog Sharks, or they could fall victim to another embarrassing upset in the Stanley Cup playoffs. Once again, Steve Yzerman had not given up on his teammates. The captain still believed that his team could come back and win the series against the Sharks.

Game six was ready to begin, and it was do or die time for the Detroit Red Wings. They had to win to advance to game seven in the series, or else they would have to hang up their skates and head for the golf course. This was a situation they did not want to be faced with. After all, these Red Wings were the number one seed. Now it was time to see just what they were made of as a team. Fortunately for Detroit, the saying 'there is no place like home' held true. The Wings had an outstanding record at Joe Louis Arena, and they had the greatest hockey fans in the world behind them.

If game six was a gut check for the Red Wings, they passed with flying colors. They never looked back. This was what the Detroit fans had expected from the boys all series long. The Wings crushed the Sharks convincingly 7-1. Game seven was up next and momentum was now with the Red Wings. Detroit had been here before, but it was the first ever Stanley Cup playoff experience for the San Jose Sharks.

Game seven was played at Joe Louis Arena in Detroit. Before the puck was dropped to signal the start, the crowd was loud and supportive of the Red Wings. Detroit had all the momentum and seemed to be a team on a mission to stave off a first round elimination again.

The season before, they had lost to the Toronto Maple Leafs in the first round. This season there were no more excuses. Time was up for these Red Wings. It was time to put up or get out of town.

The Red Wings went into game seven with a new goalie, Chris Osgood; a young superstar named Sergei Federov, who had yet to score a goal in the series, and a captain who could easily be sitting in a wheelchair, had his desire to win not been so powerful. Yzerman looked like hell going into game seven...cuts and bruises covered his face, a black and blue swollen lip that was stitched together, and two bum knees. All of this meant nothing to him. His yearning to win was measured next to none.

Before game seven, Yzerman took time to reflect upon a moment that he remembered most during the past playoffs. He sat by his locker after one practice and looked around the dressing room reflecting back to 1987, when the Wings were preparing for their semifinal game against the Edmonton Oilers. There were three familiar faces left around him that he could share the memory with Shawn Burr, "Probie" (Bob Probert), and Steve Chaisson. He recalled being one of four teams remaining in the Stanley Cup playoffs. Even though they were eliminated, this was Yzerman's proudest moment to date in his illustrious career with the Detroit Red Wings.

Hockey fans everywhere had to feel for this great warrior. Yzerman had poured his heart and soul into his team year after year. He had been disappointed every year.

Steve Yzerman could be grouped in the same company with Mario Lemeiux and Wayne Gretzky when it came to scoring, but there was one area Yzerman would have gladly traded away: and that was to carry the Stanley Cup around the ice. In a column written by Mitch Albom, *Detroit Free Press*, April 30, 1994, Yzerman responded in regards to Lemeiux and Gretzky when he said, "they can retire, because they've already accomplished what they want. I'm still chasing my dream." (© Tribune Media Services, Inc. All Rights Reserved. Reprinted with permission.) It was evident that all the early playoff exits had finally taken a toll on Steve Yzerman.

Following the loss in seven games to Toronto in 1993, the captain, who was the subject of trade rumors, spoke his mind. He finally broke down and revealed his inner thoughts when he said, "I decided I'll try to be a good player, a good person, and good things should happen. I tell myself I have lots of hockey left. That's how I live with it" (Albom, *Detroit Free Press*). (© Tribune Media Services, Inc. All Rights Reserved. Reprinted with permission.)

Game seven against the Sharks was a hard-fought tough battle. The loss in game seven to the Sharks was far more devastating than the previous year, which was humiliating. Yzerman felt the team was not moving in the right direction following the loss to the Sharks in the opening round.

It was time for the Red Wings to place the defeat behind them and look forward to the next year. Yzerman and the Wings could not dwell upon the loss to San Jose. The captain was disappointed with the result, but Detroit had learned a lesson by being humbled by the San Jose Sharks in round one of the Stanley Cup playoffs.

Even with the great Scotty Bowman, the Red Wings were handed another early playoff exit. Changes would be needed for this team to win the Cup. Changes would be made for the upcoming season. The team would be balanced and the players would play all aspects of the game or else they would not be around much longer in a Red Wing uniform.

CHAPTER ELEVEN

HEROES: MAKE A WISH AND CHANGE A LIFE!

Marc Marzullo

Breanna Morrison

Frances Isbell and her father

The things that Steve Yzerman does on the ice for his career are truly appreciated by hockey fans everywhere, but the other things he does for children and charity go beyond his call of duty. Steve has never sought outside recognition for his good deeds. He does it to give something back to the community, and most notably to children.

With all of the disappointment in the Stanley Cup playoffs, Steve still found time to visit children in the hospital. He met Elysia Pefley in 1992 at St. John's Hospital in Detroit. Elysia suffered from Ewings Sarcoma, a form of bone cancer. Yzerman was very busy at the time with all of the responsibilities of a husband and a career hockey player. He visited many children at hospitals, just as he had done since he joined the Red Wings. On January 30, 1992, his visit brought hope, love, and great joy to Elysia's life.

Steve was a special person to Elysia Pefley. Steve will never forget the moments he shared with Elysia and she always remembered what he did for her.

Elysia Pefley had a special bond with Yzerman, and Steve had a special place in his heart for her. As busy as Yzerman was, he found time to spend with her and talk to her.

His relationship with Elysia Pefley came out of his desire to help those who are not as fortunate as he is. Elysia took a liking to Yzerman the moment she met him. She had the fortunate opportunity to meet other giving Red Wing players besides Steve.

Former Detroit Red Wing, Keith Primeau shared time with Elysia. Her mother recalls that Elysia would talk to Keith, but she became shy and stargazed when in the presence of Steve Yzerman. Elysia was so likable that even opposing goalie and a caring gentlemen, Patrick Roy, handed his goalie stick to Elysia following a Wings and Montreal Canadiens game.

Steve went out of his way to bring happiness to the life of his favorite fan, Elysia Pefley. Steve brought her to practice, visited her at her home, rode with her on the Zamboni, and he enjoyed a skate with his favorite fan, Elysia. He gave Elysia a reason to fight for her life. She simply wanted to be in his presence. Steve likewise wanted her to be a part of his life. He shared time between his wife, new daughter (Isabella), and Elysia.

In 1994, Elysia underwent a bone marrow transplant in Ann Arbor, Michigan. She had to see her man Yzerman in a Stanley Cup playoff game that evening. She endured great pain to get to the game, but it was worth it to her. In 1996, Steve Yzerman showed his feelings toward Elysia at the Fox Theater when he was voted Michigan Athlete of the Year. Elysia presented the award to Steve on this memorable occasion. He proudly stood at center stage with her, and in a moment that truly should have been his, he shrugged off the award by letting the audience know who the real winner was; Miss Elysia Pelfley. Steve let Elysia and the gathering know that she was the one who was brave and tenacious. It was moments like this that made Yzerman a hero. It was the genuine kindness in his heart that bonded him with his community. He did not seek recognition, but he surely deserved it.

When Elysia turned 11, Steve Yzerman gave her a gold heart-shaped locket. Only Steve and Elysia knew what was inside the locket; it was a secret between the two buddies, and was very sacred to Elysia. She wore it the rest of her young life.

On March 17, 1996, Elysia died. She was watching a televised Red Wing game against the Calgary Flames. About the time of her passing, the lights on the Joe Louis scoreboard flickered without any explanation. Elysia wore the priceless locket that Yzerman had given to her as a special gift.

Steve Yzerman is always doing so much for children; from promoting the Make-A-Wish Foundation, signing autographs for children, giving time and money to charity, and helping raise money for his fallen teammates, Vladimir Konstantinov and Sergei Mnatsakov (who were injured in a severe auto accident in 1997). He expects so little in return from his contributions, yet he gives so much – a fine quality that everyone should practice more frequently.

Why do so many children admire Steve Yzerman? Is it because of his play on the ice, his involvement with the community, his visits to the hospitals, his face on a cereal box, or because Mom and Dad say he is a good guy? It is a combination of the previously mentioned reasons. For one little girl, he is a special man who refused to quit, and he motivates her in everything she does.

Breanna Morrison, my daughter, was born with a quarter-sized hole in her bladder. Her birth misfortune caused her a great deal of pain as an infant, and she lived with the pain for the first four years of her life. She did not complain terribly when she had a bladder infection, because her pain tolerance was so high.

While moving from Michigan to Alabama, in the summer of 1993, Breanna suffered a bladder infection. The move was interrupted by a brief stop to the emergency room in Bowling Green, Ohio. After a trip to a nearby pharmacy, Breanna had her medication and was ready to travel on down the road.

Once she arrived in Alabama, her bladder infections became more frequent. As a result, tests were conducted to find out exactly what was wrong, putting Breanna in extreme pain and discomfort. The news came in and it was not what any parent wanted to hear.

Surgery at the age of three is not fair for any child, but when it is your own child, it really hits home. This poor girl had no idea what lie ahead for her, and there was not an easy way to explain to her what was going to happen. She knew that when the operation was over she would not have as many problems as she had in the past.

Breanna went to the hospital for her surgery in April 1994, to have her bladder repaired. It is difficult when your child has any type of surgery. As a parent, it eats away at your heart. It makes you realize how fortunate people are who have healthy children.

At the age of three, Breanna knew she was going to have surgery, but she had no idea what to expect. She was carefree and happy. She trusted that Mom and Dad would not let anyone harm her, making things that much harder on a parent.

When Breanna woke up from her surgery, she looked up at Mom and Dad with disappointment in her big eyes, and painfully asked, "Why did you let them do this to me?" All we could do was sit and cry. Recovery was not easy for Breanna, because she was so little and it was so difficult to move her around. Her dog (Geronimo) ran away, but returned and made her recovery a little easier when he appeared outside her hospital room window.

The surgery was over and all was well for little Breanna. Her life was back to normal as she watched and cheered her favorite hero, Steve Yzerman. All she would talk about was number 19 as she sat back and watched the television in awe, dressed in her very own Red Wing jersey.

However, Breanna's trouble was far from over. She returned to the hospital for a routine post-surgery check-up, only to find that one of her kidneys had shut down. The doctor did not want to reveal the likely possibility that more surgery would be needed to correct the removal of scar tissue that had formed during her initial operation.

As parents, we waited and waited for what we hoped would be good news. Three months following her first operation, the decision to go in for a second operation was finalized. How do you tell your child that they have to do another operation? The nightmare had returned for Breanna, but this time she knew what surgery meant. We could not guarantee this would be the last time. We did not want to break our little girl's heart again.

Breanna spent July of 1994 in Michigan enjoying a family vacation with her cousins, uncle, and grandparents. It was difficult to enjoy this vacation as a parent, knowing that when we returned to Alabama in August, a second operation awaited our lovely daughter.

Steve Yzerman and his Red Wing teammates bowed out painfully in the first round to the San Jose Sharks, but they still had one of their best fans hopeful and confident that they would win the Stanley Cup in 1995. Breanna loved the Detroit Red Wings, and clearly Steve Yzerman was her favorite. She idolized Yzerman, and could relate through her own struggles what Yzerman was going through in her own little imagination. Just as Yzerman would face next season with confidence, Breanna went into her second operation brave and confident that she would live a normal, healthy life following this setback.

The second operation was easier and went a lot smoother than the first. The results were positive following her second operation. Everything seemed promising as the scar tissue that had formed was at last removed. The post-operation results were positive and everything was going well for Breanna.

Early in September 1994, Breanna became very sick and suffered from a high fever while visiting relatives in Tennessee. She was taken to an emergency room in Cookeville, Tennessee. Tests were taken at the hospital to determine what was causing the fever.

Upon returning to Alabama, Breanna's fever grew higher and higher. When she arrived home, she returned to the hospital in Centre, Alabama. She had developed a rare infection called pseudomonis, and the only treatment for a child as small as Breanna was through using an intravenous. She was so dehydrated that it was nearly impossible to find a vein to administer to her the proper medication. Little Breanna was exhausted, but she continued to fight and hang on for her life. She was listless as she lay in the hospital bed for the third time in five months.

Breanna understood what it meant to be tough and to not give up until your dreams come true. She is a fighter, leader, and a champion, just like her idol, Steve Yzerman. Breanna came home before her fourth birthday on September 13, 1994. It looked as though her trouble was at last behind her.

Soon after she came home, Breanna had become re-infected with the rare infection that is very difficult to eliminate. She was not going back to the hospital. This time they sent home health care services at our request. We had become exhausted with all the trouble this poor kid had to endure. Her birthday was going to be at home with her parents.

Breanna received injections daily in her fight to get better. She remained friendly and polite with the nurses. The bottom line was she was happy to be home. She never gave up and kept fighting day after day. About two months later, in November 1994, Breanna finally had beaten the odds. On Thanksgiving Day, she had one of the proudest days of her life - a moment we will never forget.

At the age of four, Breanna began her running career in Fort Payne, Alabama. Her first race was almost three months following her second operation. She was happy just to be able to run at all. Breanna ran the one-mile fun run with her sister, brother and father. After finishing the race, participants went inside to receive awards for placement. The top three in each age group won a trophy.

As the trophies were presented for the one mile fun run, the announcer said, "First place in the one mile fun run for age group 4-5 goes to Breanna Morrison." Breanna had a smile and look of amazement on her face. She looked at her parents and said, "I won, I really won!" It brought a tear to our eyes as our young warrior went up to the center stage to claim her prize. It was Breanna's shining moment for all she had been through in the past year.

Breanna had run in 5K races from 1994-1998, and currently competes against girls two years older than her on her track team. She has won a total of 31 trophies, one medal, and several ribbons. Just like Steve Yzerman, Breanna has overcome many obstacles to earn the title of a champion. She can relate to Steve and all the problems and criticism he went through during his career in the NHL. She has seen Yzerman through good and bad times, but she is aware that he never quit chasing his dream – The Stanley Cup.

In many things Breanna does, she thinks of Steve Yzerman and his refusal to give up. She idolizes and relates with him, and she admires his courage and kind heartedness. Her goal was to one-day meet Steve Yzerman face to face.

She had the opportunity to meet her hero recently in Nashville. Breanna had rehearsed what she would say to him. When her opportunity came, however, she was speechless. Breanna just stood in awe as Steve Yzerman signed her #19 Red Wing jersey. Her hero looked her in the eye and signed the back of her jersey. What a great day for Breanna – the happiest of her life!

Breanna loves hockey and there is no doubt that her favorite player and hero is Steve Yzerman. Part of her competitive drive to succeed at all she does comes from him. She can not help but admire the work that Steve does for children and charity. She knows that not only is he a great hockey player, he is also a good person who cares about others.

Making a wish carries a different meaning for all people. When a child makes a wish, it is usually one of a simple nature. When an athlete makes a wish, it is usually attainable. Wishes are possible taking for granted that the people involved have the luxury of good health. Sometimes health restrictions hinder all of our dreams, or at least place them on hold until another day or time.

A youngster like Steve Yzerman may have wished for a new pair of ice skates as a child. Although this wish may have meant a lot to him, it had a great chance of coming true. As Steve grew older, he may have dreamed of being a professional hockey player in the NHL. As he improved his skill level and ability, even this wish had a relatively legitimate shot at becoming a reality. Of course, that is if he were blessed with good health and could remain injury free.

When Steve was a child he idolized Bryan Trottier and wished that one-day it would be him carrying the Stanley Cup around center ice. Even this wish was within the parameters of reality, because Steve had a future in hockey due to his skills and outstanding health. When he became a Detroit Red Wing, another wish was fulfilled: the wish of playing in the NHL. In 1983, Yzerman knew that his chances of winning the Stanley Cup soon with the Detroit Red Wings was unlikely, but not impossible...at least physically.

As children we do not know how fortunate we are to be healthy and free of disease and sickness. For children who suffer from disease and illness, not only are their dreams altered, their whole way of life is altered. They must learn to adjust and be thankful for what they have. One charitable organization has brought happiness to children throughout the United States.

The Make-A-Wish Foundation of America began in 1980, when a seven-year-old boy with leukemia wanted to be a police officer. The boy was from Phoenix, Arizona. The Arizona Department of Public Safety made the youngster's wish a reality. They custom made a uniform, helmet, and badge for the young boy. It inspired volunteers to form the Make-A-Wish Foundation Chapter.

Today, more than 50,000 wishes have been granted to children who suffer from a serious illness. The wishes are granted from $3,000 to $5,000 per wish. The Make-A-Wish Foundation is the oldest, largest and most-respected wish granting organization in the world.

Many wishes are granted through the 82 chapters in the United States, Puerto Rico, and Guam. The purpose of Make-A-Wish Foundation is to fulfill wishes of children under 18 who have a life-threatening illness. The rule is that one child must identify one wish they would like to fulfill. All wishes are cleared with the child's physician for the safety and protection of the child.

Make-A-Wish Foundation assigns two volunteers per child, and they ask the child what wish they would like most to come true. Once the dream is approved, the teams set out to make the dream a reality. The volunteers try to include the immediate family to share the dream with the child to provide the child with memories that will last forever.

There are many dreams that have been fulfilled through the Make-A-Wish Foundation. One child dreamed of being an astronaut and was sent to the Space Camp at the Space and Rocket Center in Huntsville, Alabama. Many famous people have contributed to the Make-A-Wish Foundation to help children in need. Some of the most notable helpers are Michael Jordan, Jeff Gordon, Janet Jackson, and the Detroit Red Wings captain, Steve Yzerman.

The Make-A-Wish Foundation has brought joy to many children around the world. Marc Marzullo, a sixth grader from North Carolina was one child who spoke highly of the Make-A-Wish Foundation. Marc was a special child in his school, and was thought of every day at Our Lady Grace School.

Marc suffered from leukemia, a disease he described as "cells that go to the bone marrow, and kills white blood cells." In an interview conducted with Marc on April 22, 1999, he was in good spirits. He said he first became aware of his illness in March 1995. Marc was a very brave boy who described his treatment that includes chemotherapy as "not painful, it's just liquid."

Marc was happy with his life because his leukemia was in and out of remission, but he noted that he could not do some things that other healthy children could. Marc said, he "couldn't run, and do other physical stuff." Before Marc knew he had leukemia in March 1995, he enjoyed playing sports.

Marc covered his head with his favorite hat, a New York Yankees baseball cap. I am sure that Marc's father (Peter Marzullo) was proud of Marc for being a Yankee fan. Marc commented that when he was younger he was "basically the only one in his family who played sports regularly." On the day of our interview, Marc added "I still like playing baseball," and when questioned if he still did play, Marc proudly and confidently assured me that he "still plays."

When asked about heroes, Marc Marzullo could not single out one person. He said he had "some sports heroes who donate to charity." He commented on the actions of one athlete he viewed as a hero, Steve Yzerman. Marc reflected about all the charity events and contributions Steve has devoted so much time to. Marc thought for a moment and said in regards to Steve Yzerman's contributions, "I think that's good. That's a hero!"

Marc remembered when he was involved with the Make-A-Wish Foundation, a memory he treasured for the rest of his life. He reflected back, and added, "When I was sick in 1997, they (Make-A-Wish Foundation) contacted me and explained that they wanted me to make a wish. Most people make a wish to meet Michael Jordan, or to go to Disney World. They always succeed, or most of the time."

He explained his story as a unique one. Marc explained, "It's kind of a funny story, Michael Jordan, Jeff Gordon, Disney World is what the volunteers expected." When the volunteers asked Marc what his wish was, they said, "Okay Marc, what is your wish?" Marc did not hesitate, he said proudly, The Pope, to meet the Pope in Rome. They almost fell out of their chairs. They never had a wish like that." Marc added with a snicker.

Marc commented about his wish experience. "It was a really good experience, a really nice experience." Marc's immediate family was able to join him, and that was special for he and his family, a memory they will treasure together forever.

Marc was very close to his family and said that the people he loved most were "my Mom, my family, my Dad." Marc said that he remembered that, "he (Pope John Paul II) kissed my head, and I had my picture taken with him." He added with excitement in his voice that "my parents were there and they got to kiss his ring."

Marc was special because he realized the importance of his family. He related to his sports heroes and appreciated all the work that they do for children and charity to support those who are less fortunate. To Marc, this is what made Steve Yzerman a hero. It was not a double overtime goal in game seven, or winning the Stanley Cup. In Marc's eyes, it was his relationship with Elysia Pefley and other children that Steve spends his valuable time with.

When asked about his future, Marc Marzullo assured me that he was "optimistic." He added that his condition was "pretty good, and I will be having a bone marrow transplant." As far as a cure to Marc's condition, he added that he would be experiencing "something new." He assured me that a "bone marrow transplant back then, from a healthy to a sickly person has to match." He added, "It was successful."

What Marc was to undergo he described to me as "a new thing started a few years ago called a cord cell." He said, "They freeze the umbilical cord of a baby, it is recommended, and is all fresh and new." About two weeks following the interview with Marc, he was to undergo a bone marrow transplant in New York City at Columbia Presbyterian Hospital.

In regards to the operation, Marc said he was "pretty nervous, but confident." Marc was extremely brave for a young boy his age. He had grown to be a true hero himself. Thanks to his parents, Nancy and Peter Marzullo, who did a wonderful job raising Marc.

Marc was an incredible person...optimistic, confident, and happy in spite of his illness. Marc asked me before we parted for the last time on April 22, 1999, "Could you please get me an autograph from Steve Yzerman when you meet him!" I assured Marc that "Mr. Yzerman would be happy to give Marc an autograph once he became aware of his situation." Marc had a smile from ear to ear with the thought of getting an autograph from him. Marc never saw the photograph signed by Steve Yzerman that pictured Marc and me. Steve signed the picture while boarding the team bus before a game with the Nashville Predators.

Marc Marzullo died on Saturday July 10, 1999. He will be remembered as a polite young man, who spread love everywhere he went. He will be dearly missed by all those who had the joy to have known him. His classmates who shared loving memories with Marc planted a maple tree in front of the school in his memory.

Marc Marzullo's condition was similar to that of Elysia Pefley. On the other hand, Breanna Morrison's condition was bad but not as bad as Marc's and Elysia's. Steve Yzerman may have suffered early playoff exits and criticism from the media, but his condition was not as bad as Marc's, Elysia's, or Breanna's. Maybe that is why Steve Yzerman is so willing to help children in need. He is a man who really cares about others.

Perhaps it is children like Elysia, Breanna and Marc that drive Steve Yzerman to give back to the community. He is aware of the gifts he has, especially his good health. Winning or losing hockey games is meaningless compared to the life and death struggles sick children go through on a daily basis. That is what makes Steve a true hero; he does his job well and still finds time to reach out to those in need. It would be easy for him to sit back and do his job and not worry about others, but that is not heroic.

Steve Yzerman is not concerned about being a hero. He simply tries to be himself and has not changed his lifestyle since he first joined the Detroit Red Wings in 1983. He does not seek recognition for what he does for children, fans, and charity. Steve Yzerman is the captain of the Detroit Red Wings, but the fact remains that he is still the Steve Yzerman he has been all of his life.

CHAPTER TWELVE

THE WINGS COME ALIVE IN 1995!

After being eliminated by the San Jose Sharks in the 1994 Stanley Cup playoffs, the Red Wings realized it was time to get a big name goalie. Not only did they concentrate their efforts on a veteran goalie; they sought out help to solidify their defense. When the strike-delayed season began in 1994-95, the Red Wings had added seven new key players to their roster throughout the season.

Detroit added another enforcer to compliment Darren McCarty and Vladimir Konstantinov. Although he only played in 11 games for the Red Wings in 94-95, Stu Grimson helped protect his valuable teammates. Grimson was an intelligent man who had a good sense of humor in the dressing room.

The Red Wings added an American born player to their roster: Doug Brown. He was a good role player just the type Scotty Bowman liked to have on his bench. Brown was also a good all around player who gave 100 percent every shift he played. He finished in the top 10 in scoring on the Red Wings with nine goals and 12 assists for a total of 21 points.

Brown played well with Sergei Federov, and as a third or fourth line man for Bowman and the Red Wings. He seemed to come alive during the playoff season. He played his best hockey after the regular season ended.

Doug Brown was drafted by the expansion Nashville Predators in 1998-99, but he was reluctant to leave the Red Wings. Detroit was not going to let someone as valuable as Brown get away. They reacquired his services from the Predators by trading some future draft picks to Nashville.

In 1994-95, Detroit was determined to beef up on defense. They went out and signed four quality defensemen. Mike Krushelnyski was not a superstar, but he was a smart hockey player who knew how to position himself well.

Mike Ramsey was another excellent defenseman who played a key role in the success of the Red Wings in 1995. Ramsey played in 33 games with Detroit in 94-95. He helped bolster down a defensive core that was bringing success to the team. Ramsey was a smart player who knew how to cut off the angle of on-rushing opponents.

Bob Rouse was very welcome in Detroit, because he was such a thorn in its side for so many years when he played with the Toronto Maple Leafs. Rouse was a veteran who had plenty of playoff experience. He was a defenseman who was not afraid to "mix it up." He produced many retaliatory penalties during his ice time, and added leadership to the Red Wings; most importantly, he was one of those guys who could easily get under the opponent's skin.

The next addition the Red Wings made to the defensive unit may have been the best. They added the Russian Red Army warrior, Slava Fetisov. He was called "Papa Bear" by his teammates. Fetisov played with Russian hockey stars Sergei Makarov, Alexi Kasatonov, Igor Larionov and Vladimir Krutov. These Russian superstars played together in the glory days of hockey in the Soviet Union in the 1970's.

Fetisov began his NHL career with the New Jersey Devils, and his crafty defensive style had an impact immediately on the NHL. Fetisov had been through everything as a player in Russia. He was a genius when it came to defense, which was crucial because he was not as young as he used to be. Fetisov adjusted to the new style of hockey in the NHL. He was an extremely intelligent hockey player and teacher of the game for the younger defensemen. Fetisov also provided great leadership, especially for the other Russian players on his new team the Detroit Red Wings. He was like a father figure to Kozlov, Federov, and Konstantinov. Fetisov blended in perfectly with his new teammates. He was very tough and gave all he had on the ice during his shift, providing a fine example for the other players on the team.

When Scotty Bowman replaced Bryan Murray as director of player personnel, he proposed an immediate solution to the Red Wings' playoff woes. He realized that the team needed a goalie that had Stanley Cup playoff experience, but he also needed a veteran who could help Chris Osgood develop. He looked to the man who had not only won the Stanley Cup, but captured the Conn-Smythe Trophy as well. Bowman's answer was Mike Vernon of the Calgary Flames.

Mike Vernon was born in Calgary and learned how to play hockey in his hometown. He was 31 years old when he joined the Red Wings as a veteran goalie. The Red Wings traded Steve Chaisson to Calgary in exchange for Vernon. Calgary was resting their hopes on a young goalie named Trevor Kidd.

Mike Vernon seemed to be the answer to the Red Wings' problems. They now had a veteran of nine seasons and a goalie with substantial playoff experience.

During the 94-95 season, Mike Vernon played in 30 games compared to 19 games for "Ozzie". Vernon posted a record of 19-6-4. His goal against average was an impressive 2.52. "Ozzie" posted a remarkable record of 14-5-0, and had a goal against average of 2.26. At last, it looked like Detroit had got rid of the beast that had plagued them for so many years in the past...the goal-tending enigma.

During the Stanley Cup playoffs, there were some goalies that rose to the occasion to carry their teams to the championship. The Red Wings felt that Mike Vernon was the one who could finally get them over the top. Going into the first round, Detroit was focused on their opponent, the Dallas Stars.

The Red Wings ended the lockout-shortened season with 70 points in just 48 games. They finished first in the Central Division, earning them home ice advantage in the playoffs. Detroit opened the first round of the Stanley Cup playoffs in the familiar surroundings of Joe Louis Arena.

Steve Yzerman did not produce as much offensively, but he was quickly learning how to lead his team with his overall contributions on the ice. He was killing penalties, winning face-offs, blocking shots, and becoming more of a play-maker on the power play. Most importantly, he was leading his team to play better defensively, which was critical to the Red Wings' success in 94-95.

Heading into the first round against the Dallas Stars, this Red Wing team had no fear of their opponent. Detroit was confident, and they knew in order to survive in the Stanley Cup playoffs, they had to eliminate the first round opponent quickly.

Game one at Joe Louis Arena was a close hard fought battle. It was basically a must-win for Dallas; it was also a critical game for the Red Wings. With a victory, Detroit could erase the past playoff nightmares and get on with their business. Detroit won game one by a 4-3 count.

A win in game two would send the Red Wings to Dallas with a two game lead in the best of seven series. Game two was also crucial for the Red Wings. The final score was 4-1, the Wings were the victors. They seemed to be dominating the series, and their power play had a lot to do with their success. Detroit was 5 for 10 on the power play in the first two games of the series.

Game three moved the series back to Dallas in a game that the Stars had to win in order to have any realistic chance against the Red Wings. Game three was all Detroit as the Wings won convincingly 5-1. The Red Wing fans were hoping for a sweep.

In game four, Dallas was not about to roll over and give up the series to Detroit. The Stars dominated game four and came out on top with a 4-1 victory. The Red Wings needed to get rid of their first round opponent as soon as possible.

Detroit left Dallas with no intention of returning for a game six. The Wings were poised and ready to wrap up the series on home ice. Game five went just as the Red Wings had planned.

The Red Wings were heading to the second round, but their opponent was none other than the San Jose Sharks, the team that had eliminated the Wings in an embarrassing first round one year ago. One thing was certain, Detroit would not take the Sharks lightly this year.

The second round of the Stanley Cup playoffs opened at Joe Louis Arena against San Jose. Game one was important for the Red Wings to win in order to avoid a collapse that they had suffered in the previous year against the Sharks. In the first game Detroit received no challenge from them, and the Red Wings won convincingly by a 6-0 score.

Detroit knew that it was important to win at home in the playoffs, and if they could get up two games to none, they would have a huge advantage over the Sharks. The Red Wings came out in game two beaming. Another easy win in a convincing manner would boost the confidence of the Red Wings.

Game two went Detroit's way as they dominated the Sharks by a score of 6-2. The Wings were right where they wanted to be going into game three. The pressure was now on the Sharks. They had to win the next game, which was held at the Shark Tank.

In 1995, the Red Wings were anxious to sing along with the famous song – *Do You Know the Way to San Jose*. After the first two games, Detroit was expecting an exhausting effort from the Sharks. The Red Wings knew they had to step up to the next level to defeat them in game three.

Detroit came out flying in game three, and the result proved that this team had decided that it was time to get serious about winning the Stanley Cup. The Wings had a 36-12 advantage in shots on goal in game three. San Jose could not get anything going against the Red Wings, and the Sharks power play was almost non-existent. Detroit did not rely upon its superstars to provide the scoring. The system that Scotty

Bowman had implemented was working; his players were starting to buy into the system. The Red Wings got two goals out of Slava Kozlov and one goal apiece from Ray Sheppard, Sergei Federov, Dino Ciccarelli and Darren McCarty.

The Red Wings were well focused going into game four. The team had a different attitude in the 1995 Stanley Cup playoffs. Steve Yzerman had a new outlook on the playoffs. He knew that winning the first round was not the ultimate goal. Steve knew that it would take 16 playoff wins to accomplish the Wings hidden desire – The Stanley Cup.

Detroit stayed focus on eliminating the Sharks. The task was to win one game at a time and move one step closer to winning the championship in the NHL. During the first 10 minutes of the game, Detroit was aggressive again. They jumped out to an early 4-0 lead, but the second period brought bad news to the Wings.

The scene was all too familiar and it was a nightmare Red Wing fans had hoped they would not have to witness again. During the second period of the four game sweep by the Wings, their captain Steve Yzerman twisted his right knee and had to be helped to the dressing room by teammates, Kris Draper and Keith Primeau. The injury occurred near the Red Wings player's bench. Yzerman was seen crawling off the ice to the Detroit bench. It was not thought to be as severe as his last knee injury that required surgery.

The good news was that the knee injury to Yzerman had nothing to do with the injury he suffered in 1987-88. It was believed that he had strained his knee trying to skate around one of the Sharks. The Red Wings were concerned about entering the next round, the Conference Finals, without Yzerman.

The Detroit Red Wings knew it would be difficult to win the next round without their captain. Steve Yzerman has been devoted to the Wings quest of winning the Stanley Cup for 12 years up till 1995. He has stood back and watched Wayne Gretzky and Mario Lemeiux skate around the ice with the covenant Cup filled with dents. He remained envious of the two champions.

It was a moment Steve Yzerman has thought about in his mind throughout his personal struggles and agony along the way in Detroit. Yzerman made a point of always trying to see the last game of the season and the glorious presentation of the Stanley Cup.

Steve Yzerman could only picture in his mind the fulfillment of a dream. He had not won the Stanley Cup up to this point in his career.

Following a knee injury in the San Jose series, Yzerman would likely miss two weeks of action and the entire Western Conference Finals. Tentatively, Yzerman was scheduled to be out a maximum of two weeks.

With Steve Yzerman out, someone would have to step up and provide the leadership that would be missed with the captain out for the Red Wings.

Without Yzerman, the chances of winning were questionable, but it would not be impossible to beat Chicago without him. Scotty Bowman felt that without Yzerman, the Red Wings were the underdogs in the series against the Black Hawks.

This would be the second consecutive post season Steve Yzerman would miss due to a knee injury. Perhaps the team would learn to overcome the absence of Yzerman in 1995 because of the experience they had gone through together in the 1994 Stanley Cup playoffs.

The Detroit Red Wings would have a chance to introduce their new medical toy, the hyperbaric chamber. The new high-dose oxygen chamber sped up recovery for injuries such as damaged ligaments and cartilage, charley horses, and aided players worn out from the playoff banging. Thanks to the new oxygen chamber, Yzerman could return earlier than expected.

The Detroit Red Wings opened the Western Conference Finals at home, unlike their last trip to the Finals against the powerful Edmonton Oilers. This time, the Wings were expected to win over the Chicago Black Hawks; unfortunately, Steve Yzerman hurt his knee in the second round against the San Jose Sharks. Without Yzerman, Chicago went into the series confident that they could upset the Red Wings.

Game one was an indication of how close the two teams were. It was hard-hitting and low-scoring as expected with Mike Vernon and Eddie Belfour in goal for their respective teams. The first game of the series went to the Detroit Red Wings by a 2-1 score, which was an important victory for the Wings. They were able to win one without Yzerman in the game. Yzerman was most likely in the training room, relaxing or munching on pizza when Nicklas Lidstrom scored the overtime winning goal.

It was important for the Red Wings to take a two game lead heading into Chicago for game three of the series. It was another tight checking contest. Once again with the captain Yzerman watching from behind the scenes, the Detroit Red Wings came out hungry and won another close one by a 3-2 count. The series returned to Chicago, and the Red Wings knew with a victory in game three they would be in the driver's seat, it was indeed a pivotal game in the series.

In game three Detroit knew they would see Chicago's best effort of the series. The Red Wings knew they would have to be patient and wait for the scoring chances.

Steve Yzerman's status for game three was still on hold, but the possibility lingered that he would return soon. With Detroit up 2-0 in the series, there was no urgency to rush Yzerman back into the lineup. The Red Wings knew that they would need his leadership in the Stanley Cup Finals if they could eliminate the Black Hawks. Yzerman expressed that he would not be ready for game three prior to the start of the game.

Game three was tied at the end of regulation time, and the Red Wings knew that in overtime they would have to hold off the Hawk's best effort of the season. They also knew they needed to put the Hawks away to try and gain a 3-0 advantage in the best of seven series. After the first overtime, the score remained deadlocked. Both teams gave everything they had and fatigue was evident on both sides.

During the second overtime, it was the Red Wings who put one behind Chicago goalie Ed Belfour. Game three belonged to the Red Wings 4-3 in double overtime. The Black Hawks were one game away from elimination. Detroit was ready to move on to the Stanley Cup Finals to try to win their first Stanley Cup championship since 1955.

Going into game four, it was doubtful that Steve Yzerman would return to the lineup. Yzerman worked hard to rehabilitate his injured knee. He was not needed for game four with his team ahead 3-0 in the series.

A four-game sweep would be difficult to accomplish in the visitor's building, but the Red Wings were ready to face the challenge ahead of them in Chicago. The Red Wings knew Chicago would play with emotion to prolong their season; the Black Hawks would try to pull off a miraculous upset at the hands of the team with the longest Stanley Cup drought – the Detroit Red Wings.

Chicago was not about to lose at home and be swept by the Detroit Red Wings. The Wings played with emotion as well with the return of their captain and leader, Steve Yzerman. Yzerman proved his devotion to his team. Once again he gave his heart and soul to return in a series that was all but over.

Game four in Chicago saw the ice tilted in favor of the home team. The Black Hawks were able to avoid a sweep by the Red Wings. The Black Hawks won 5-2 rather easily.

Joe Louis Arena was packed to the rafters for game five of the Red Wings/Black Hawks series. Detroit was one victory away from returning to the Stanley Cup Finals. Many fans believed that the Red Wings would put the Black Hawks away in game five, but some people still wondered if this Red Wings team would let them down again.

Game five of the Western Conference Finals was filled with excitement and electricity. If the Red Wings could win game five, they would be headed to the Stanley Cup Finals to play against the New Jersey Devils. They expected another close game, knowing the Black Hawks were not going to give up easily.

Game five ended after three periods of play, just as two previous games in the series. Both teams were even on the scoreboard after regulation play. The score was tied 1-1; this game would be settled in overtime.

After the first period, Chicago had a 1-0 lead. Denis Savard scored first for the Black Hawks. During the first period the Red Wings captain, Yzerman, twisted his tender right knee. He left the game briefly, giving the fans and his team a scare. Before the first period ended, he returned to action. Detroit came back to even the score in the second period.

Not only did Yzerman return in the second period, he tied the game for the Red Wings with his first goal of the series. Steve is not the type to showboat or celebrate after a goal, but when this one slid past Belfour, Yzerman showed emotion by leaping in the air and pumping his fist. His teammate, Paul Coffey, was glad to see him get the goal because he has been with Detroit the longest.

The third period was scoreless and for the third time in the series, another game would be settled in overtime. Overtime games end so suddenly, either players leave the building overwhelmed with joy or they scratch their head wondering why a great effort was in vain? This particular overtime between Detroit and Chicago decided whether the Black Hawks ended their season or the Red Wings continued to chase their 40-year-old illusive dream.

During the second overtime, Slava Kozlov skated toward Ed Belfour, hoping to make the perfect shot. Kozlov indicated that he missed beating Belfour to the stick side. He did not put the puck where he intended, but fortunately he put it behind Belfour. After another overtime victory against the Hawks, the Red Wings were headed to the Stanley Cup Finals for the first time since 1965. At last it was time for the Red Wings to celebrate!

Incredible! They were only four victories away from their quest, one that had not been resolved in forty years.

Steve Yzerman began his career with the Red Wings in 1983, and 12 years later, he was on his way to the Stanley Cup Finals. Yzerman had to pay a dear price to get to the final dance. He played injured, fought off criticism from the media and coaches, and dodged trade rumors to hang around long enough to take the team he began with to the ultimate finale. Following the Western Conference Championship, the wounded Yzerman skated around the ice hoisting the Clarence Campbell Trophy, a trophy that he was proud of, but not the one the team hoped to capture in two more weeks.

Paul Coffey, a former Stanley Cup winner, knew that the Campbell Conference championship was relatively meaningless. Captain Steve Yzerman was elated with emotion after winning the Conference Finals. He had thought about the moment for a long time. Steve was happy to be headed to the Stanley Cup Finals.

While the Red Wings celebrated on the ice, it was the coach who had led them to success. In his second year as coach, Scotty Bowman was not going to let his players dictate the fate of this team. During his first season in Detroit, Bowman relied upon the veteran players to provide leadership. When the team failed, he insured them in 94-95 that he would run the show. Bowman knew the only thing that counted in the NHL is to win.

Bowman realized that much of the credit went to Yzerman for the success of Red Wings. During his first season, Bowman was not afraid to offer an earful to Yzerman in front of his teammates. Yzerman came to camp in September with something to prove as he was again amidst the trade rumor talk.

Steve Yzerman had waited a long time to get his chance at winning the Stanley Cup...a chance to carry the Cup around the rink with much of the world watching. This is what every NHL player lives for, but when the opportunity comes it may only happen once in a career. Steve Yzerman knew he had better make the best of this opportunity.

From the moment Steve Yzerman was drafted, he was the future for the Detroit Red Wings. As the team became better, Yzerman's statistics have been on the decline. These declining numbers do not bother Yzerman as long as the team is winning.

While the team was adjusting to assistant coach Barry Smith's defensive tactics, no one has had to sacrifice more than Steve Yzerman did. He did not complain though, he just went out and did his job. Since coming to Detroit, Yzerman heard it all from the media. Everything from being too fragile, selfish, and one-dimensional as a player.

Through all the criticism Yzerman still remained as dedicated as he was when he came to Detroit at the age of 18. He still worked hard at practice, on the bicycle, in the weight room, and he was still the last one to leave the dressing room. It was his team that changed. They became so reliable upon the captain in the playoffs earlier in his career. He had more help now to carry the Red Wings toward their ultimate goal – The Stanley Cup.

The Red Wings were long overdue to win the Stanley Cup. It had been 40 years since they last hoisted the prized trophy. Going into the Stanley Cup Finals, the Wings were confident they could beat the New Jersey Devils. They had not seen the Devils at all during the abbreviated regular season. The Red Wings knew they had to have their offense clicking to win the series, because like Detroit, New Jersey was a defensive-oriented team. This series came down to who had the most patience to hold the defensive scheme.

Game one of the Stanley Cup Finals belonged to the department of defense. It was low scoring and tight checking. This style of hockey was not favorable for the Red Wings' high-powered offense. New Jersey was used to cutting off the opponent's neutral zone; they were a patient team that would capitalize on mistakes when given the opportunity.

Game one was low scoring as was expected by many of the experts. New Jersey was able to get two goals past Mike Vernon, but Detroit could only manage to sneak one goal by Martin Brodeur. As a result, game one went to the Devils 2-1. The Red Wings were not about to panic heading into game two.

Game two was another lesson in discipline for the Wings. New Jersey was playing at home and expected to hold the home ice advantage after game two ended. Detroit was looking to steal one on the road. This was not a must win for the Wings, but it was sure to improve their chances in the series. The Red Wings fought hard in game two, but once again it was discipline and turnovers that cost Detroit another close game by a 4-2 count.

The Red Wings were returning home, confident they could win the next game and put the pressure back on the Devils. The Red Wings had to figure out a way to solve the defensive puzzle the Devils threw at them in the first two games. Detroit only had 35 shots in the first two games combined, and most of those were not good scoring chances.

Steve Yzerman remained the leader of the Detroit Red Wings in terms of providing motivation and incentive. Yzerman realized that the Wings were not facing an impossible situation, and indicated the team had to keep the pressure on the New Jersey Devils. Detroit had to remain patient and not expect to win by a large margin. It was Yzerman's job to instill in his teammates that the Red Wings could come back and win the series against New Jersey.

The way the Red Wings were beaten in game two was back-breaking for the high flying Detroit Red Wings. The Wings took a 2-1 lead into the third period but the Devils came back to score three unanswered goals in the third period. The Red Wings were returning home with confidence for game three.

Steve Yzerman was not about to count the Wings out in the Stanley Cup Finals. He believed that if the team stayed determined and focused they could win against the Devils in the series.

It may have been an omen, but the last time the Detroit Red Wings appeared in the Stanley Cup Finals in 1966, the road team won the first two games. The road team in the 1966 series was the Detroit Red Wings, but the Montreal Canadiens came back to win four in a row to win the series in six games. With the Red Wings returning home, game three became a critical game for Detroit.

The crowd was ready and excited. But were the Wings ready to challenge the stubborn Devils? If the Devils were able to contain Detroit with their defense, the series would be over. Detroit had to find a way to break loose its explosive offensive weapons.

The Devils bottled up the middle of the ice, forcing Detroit to shoot from the outside. Defense was the secret for head coach Jacques LeMaire and his New Jersey Devils. The Devils were able to shut down Detroit at center ice, and were even accused of providing a boring game for the fans to watch. Game three was not boring for the New Jersey Devils; they were the ones who provided the offense in a 5-2 victory.

New Jersey now had Detroit of the brink of elimination. Could New Jersey eliminate the Wings on their home ice? Detroit pledged that they would not go down without a fight. Coming back to win four straight was not impossible, but Detroit had to change their game plan to generate some offense against the New Jersey Devils.

Following game three, Scotty Bowman felt as though his team just did not compete. The Red Wings had to contend in game four to avoid another playoff embarrassment, a sweep in the Stanley Cup Finals. Following game four, the result remained the same as it was in game three. The New Jersey Devils completed a sweep over the favored Red Wings in the Stanley Cup Finals.

The loss to New Jersey became another lesson for Yzerman and the Red Wings. Steve Yzerman's long awaited dream had ended again in disappointment. Isiah Thomas led the Detroit Pistons in a similar fashion before he finally won a championship.

After the humiliating loss to the Devils, it was Yzerman who came out to face the media. Once again showing his class and leadership for the Red Wings, Yzerman answered the questions.

What went wrong?

Steve Yzerman realized that the year had been exciting for the Wings and their fans. He also knew coming up short again in the playoffs spoiled the atmosphere. The goal was to win the Stanley Cup and the Red Wings had failed again. Losing the Stanley Cup would keep the drive burning for Yzerman to come back and try to win the Cup in 1995-96. Sometimes it takes losing a championship to come back and win one. The experience of being on the losing team made him even hungrier. The Detroit Red Wings had a great opportunity of climbing their way back to the Stanley Cup Finals with all of the talent they had during the 1990's.

The Detroit Red Wings came into the 95-96 season confident that they had what it took to win the Stanley Cup. They came so close in 94-95, only to be swept by the New Jersey Devils. The Red Wings added some talent to the 95-96 team they believed would take them to Lord Stanley's prized trophy.

CHAPTER THIRTEEN

LIFE IS NOT EASY AT THE TOP OF THE MOUNTAIN

My father once said, "life is like a roller coaster...enjoy the ride to the top, because it won't be as nice on the way down." The Detroit Red Wings enjoyed the ride to the top of the NHL by making it to the Stanley Cup Finals, but they came to a crashing halt in four games, leaving some fans wondering what they had really missed over the past 30 years.

During the 95-96 season, the Red Wings added four new players that had an impact upon the success of the team down the road. The Red Wings added a new young goalie named Kevin ("Ticker") Hodson. They brought up a promising defenseman in Anders Eriksson, a product of Sweden. Detroit also acquired the services of Kirk Maltby (from the

Edmonton Oilers), who proved to be crucial to the team's success. The last of the foursome added to the Red Wings provided an offensive punch matched by none in the NHL. The Red Wings traded away Ray Sheppard for the services of Igor Larionov. With the acquisition of Larionov, Detroit now had a line they called "The Russian Five."

In 1985 the Vancouver Canucks drafted Igor Larionov. With the addition of Larionov, Scotty Bowman had five former Central Red Army teammates in the Red Wing jersey. Larionov was in his sixth season in the NHL, and was happy to be coming to Detroit.

No NHL team had ever placed five Russian players on the ice at one time. That changed on October 27, 1995, in Calgary, Alberta. In a game against the Calgary Flames, the master at tinkering with lines made a historic line change. Early in the first period of their game against the Flames, Scotty Bowman instructed the five Russian players to take the ice together.

There they were jumping over the boards as teammates for the Detroit Red Wings. The defensive pairing was Slava Fetisov and Vladimir Konstantinov. Up front was center Igor Larionov, right wing Sergei Federov, and left wing Vyacheslav Kozlov. The Russian Five scored on their second shift of the game when Kozlov put a rebound past Trevor Kidd. The Red Wings went on to beat Calgary 3-0 and the rest is history.

In 1995-96, The Russian Five made a significant offensive impact during the regular season en-route to a record setting season for the high-powered Red Wings. Sergei Federov led the way with 39 goals and 68 assists for a total of 107 points. Slava Kozlov was fourth on the team in scoring behind Steve Yzerman and Paul Coffey. Kozlov was only one point behind Coffey, who totaled 74 points for the Red Wings.

Igor Larionov, who played 69 of his 73 games in a Red Wing uniform, ended up dead even with Kozlov in total points during the regular season. Igor had 22 goals and 51 assists for a total of 73 points, and is one of the best playmakers to wear a Red Wing uniform since Adam Oates. Larionov seemed to have magic when it came to delivering a perfect pass that would result in a goal for his teammate. In terms of leadership, not many had what Larionov brought with him from his years of leading the Central Red Army team in Russia.

As was expected, the last two Russian players to have an impact on the success of the Red Wings were defensemen. Slava Fetisov, the senior member of The Russian Five, finished tenth on the Wings in scoring with

42 points in 69 games. More importantly, he had an excellent defensive style of play that brought aggressiveness back to Hockey Town.

Slava Fetisov's defensive partner, Vladimir Konstantinov was not afraid to take on anyone in the NHL. He was one tough guy who employed a very rugged style of play. When players crossed the Detroit blue line, they knew Konstantinov would be waiting to greet them with a hard hit of some sort; Konstantinov was tough and knew how to avoid taking penalties.

The Detroit Red Wings' offensive output was well-balanced during the 95-96 regular season. Two players stood above the rest of the team in scoring: Sergei Federov led the team with 107 points, and the team captain Steve Yzerman followed Federov in scoring with 95 points. All of the offensive punch was nice, but it was winning that was most important. Anything short of winning the Stanley Cup would not be acceptable to Steve Yzerman, Scotty Bowman, and the fans in Hockey Town.

The Red Wings knew that goal tending was the one weakness they needed to improve upon to win the Stanley Cup. Chris Osgood and Mike Vernon shared time in goal during the regular season. Osgood had a record of 39-6-5 between the pipes, and MikeVernon had a 21-7-2 record. The two allowed the fewest goals in the league, and as a result, Osgood and Vernon shared the Jennings Trophy for the season.

The Red Wings had apparently learned from being swept in the Stanley Cup Finals in 1995. The team compiled a NHL single season record for victories by a team. The Red Wings broke the record of the 1976-77 Montreal Canadiens who compiled 60 wins during the regular season. Incidentally, the legendary Scotty Bowman coached that Canadien team. The Red Wings rang up 62 victories during the 95-96 regular season. It was not the regular season that would bring Lord Stanley's Cup back to Hockey Town.

The season was filled with highlights for the Detroit Red Wings, but one moment was frozen in time in Red Wing history. On January 17, 1996 the Red Wings were playing at home against the Colorado Avalanche. As usual Joe Louis Arena was sold out. Many of the fans wondered if this would be the night that their beloved captain would score his 500th career NHL goal.

Yzerman wanted his milestone goal to come in a team victory. During the second period, with Detroit leading 1-0, the Red Wings went on the power play. At about the 7:45 mark of the second period, Sergei

Federov passed to Greg Johnson who found Steve Yzerman in the slot. Yzerman reeled in and fired a shot at Patrick Roy. The initial shot was blocked, and Steve Yzerman gathered in the rebound and let go a backhand shot that found the back of the net at 7:52 of the second period.

Just like that, the fans at Joe Louis Arena stood and applauded their hero of 13 years in Detroit. At last, all the criticism Yzerman had taken over the years came to a standstill for a moment. Ironically, the goal was number 19 of the season for Yzerman, the same as the number he had worn so proudly on his winged jersey for 13 seasons.

With the utmost class, Steve Yzerman shared his special moment with the fans. He appreciated the fact that he had been with the same team for 13 years. For all the fans that had been so loyal to Steve Yzerman and Detroit Red Wings, he felt as though they shared the heroic moment of goal number 500 against the Colorado Avalanche.

It was special that Yzerman got number 500 in a victory. It was also unique that he scored it against a future Hall of Fame goalie, Patrick Roy. His teammates acknowledged and thanked him on the ice. The fans at Joe Louis Arena showed their appreciation by giving him a two-minute standing ovation. When Yzerman finally reached the bench, head coach Scotty Bowman gave him a pat on the back and a congratulation handshake. When the moment was over, the captain sat on the bench with an uncharacteristic smile upon his face. At last Steve Yzerman was having fun. The fun continued during this historic season for the Detroit Red Wings, but would it last through out the playoffs?

Going into the playoffs, the Detroit Red Wings had the numbers on their side to cruise to the evasive moment they had waited for...to bring the Stanley Cup back to Detroit. The Red Wings led the league in penalty killing and were third best on the power play during the regular season. Detroit was the best team in the NHL in protecting a lead after two periods, which was important heading into the Stanley Cup playoffs.

The playoffs in the NHL are a total different game from the regular season. The Red Wings had to play one team in a seven game series, and were quite familiar with how difficult it was to play at a high tempo against one team in a series. The first round opponent for the Red Wings was the Winnipeg Jets, seeded eighth. Detroit was heavily favored to advance to the second round, and most fans were counting on a sweep from the Wings.

Heading into game one at the packed Joe Louis Arena, the Winnipeg Jets knew they had nothing to lose in this series. They were hoping that

105

maybe their goalie could steal the series from the Detroit Red Wings. Detroit was the team that had all the pressure on them; the Red Wings had a lot to lose.

Everyone in Hockey Town was sure that this would be the year. The popular slogan around town was "We Want Stanley!" It became so popular that a CD was made echoing the sentiments of the Red Wings fans' most popular words, "We Want Stanley."

During the 1996 Stanley Cup playoff run, the issue of concern for the Red Wings was in goal. Who would it be the veteran Mike Vernon or the goalie of the future Chris Osgood? The Detroit Red Wings failed in the Finals the previous year with Vernon between the pipes. Scotty Bowman had a tough decision to make, but based upon the regular season, he chose Osgood as his starter.

The Winnipeg Jets were not faced with a goalie controversy going into the playoffs. The Jets went with their sensational goalie from Russia, Nikolai Khabibulan. Winnipeg knew that if they could get strong goal tending from Khabibulan, they could upset the Red Wings in the first round.

Going into game one at home, the Red Wings were focused. They had been the victims of first round elimination in the past. This season, they knew they had to win one game at a time.

The Red Wings came out and played hard in game one. Winnipeg took too many penalties for the overpowering Red Wings. Detroit made them pay with a lopsided 4-1 victory to open the series. The win was just what the Red Wings needed to get off to a good start, but they knew that game two would be another crucial game at home.

In game two the Winnipeg Jets played without discipline again. They took many penalties that they could have avoided. The result was the same for the Detroit Red Wings. After two games, it looked as though the Red Wings, who were getting excellent goal tending from Chris Osgood, were in for a short series.

Game three saw a twist of fate for the Winnipeg Jets. They returned to home ice, and Mike Vernon took the place of the injured Chris Osgood in net for the Red Wings. In game three, the Jets played more disciplined hockey and Khabibulan was remarkable between the goal post.

Winnipeg made it clear with a 4-1 win that they were not going to hand the series to the Red Wings. If the Jets could win game four in Winnipeg they would be in good shape heading back to Detroit for game five. The Red Wings knew that they had to put the Jets away as soon as they could. Detroit had to make a statement in game four.

It was just what the Red Wings had hoped for to get back on track in their quest for the Stanley Cup. The Detroit Red Wings used all of their weapons in game four to show their dominance against the underdog Winnipeg Jets. Detroit skated to a 6-1 victory, and now had a great opportunity to return to Joe Louis Arena to wrap up the series in five games.

Game five returned to the bank along the Detroit River in the friendly building known as Joe Louis Arena. With one more victory, the Detroit Red Wings would move on to the second round in the Stanley Cup playoffs. The crowd was ready for the elimination of the Winnipeg Jets.

The Jets would not only face elimination from the playoffs; they would also play their final game in the NHL as the Winnipeg Jets if they lost. The next season, the team would move to Phoenix, however, the Jets under the brilliant goal tending of Khabibulan escaped Detroit with a 3-1 victory. The Jets would give their fans at least one more game to enjoy before they left for Arizona.

Game six was an emotional game for the Winnipeg Jets. If they did not win, it would be their last game in front of their loyal fans. Detroit had to remain focused upon their objective and not get caught up in the emotional aspect of the game. The Red Wings did not want to go back home to play a game seven, and many believed that the series should not have ever gone as far as it had already.

Game six had started the way the Red Wings had hoped. After the first period, Slava Kozlov netted two goals and Steve Yzerman added one goal to give Detroit a 3-0 lead. Neither team scored in the second period, leaving Detroit just 20 minutes away from moving on to the second round of the Stanley Cup playoffs. During the third period, Detroit and Winnipeg exchanged goals to make the final score 4-1 in favor of the Red Wings. The final chapter was written on the Winnipeg Jets. Next year they became the Phoenix Coyotes.

Round two matched Detroit against the St. Louis Blues, a team loaded with talent. St. Louis had Grant Fuhr in goal, with Brett Hull and Wayne Gretzky up front. Detroit was the overwhelming favorite to win the series, but anything was possible in the Stanley Cup playoffs.

Game one was played at Joe Louis Arena, and following game one Detroit knew they were in for a tough series. The Detroit Red Wings played well defensively, which proved to be key in this series. Detroit came out on the winning side in a close game by a 3-2 count.

Game two was another must-win for the Red Wings, but Detroit had been through this situation several times over the past few years. They knew how important it was to get off to a good start by winning the first two games at home. If Detroit could place the Blues in a hole by putting them behind two games to none in the series, it would be very difficult for St. Louis to come back.

Detroit came out smoking in game two and never let up. They gave up three goals to St. Louis in game two. However, the offense for Detroit went on a terror, scoring eight times in game two, making the final score 8-3. Detroit had St. Louis right where they wanted them by winning the first two games of the series. Very rarely did a team get down 2-0 in a seven game series and come back to win.

Game three was played in the Keil Center, home of the St. Louis Blues. The Blues were hoping that the friendly hometown fans would help them beat the Red Wings to get back into the series. Game three was another high scoring affair that ended in a 4-4 tie after regulation time had expired. The Red Wings felt confident that they would win in overtime. Even if they did not come out on top, they would have had a 2-1 lead in the series. The Blues scored in overtime to record a 5-4 victory, the Blues' first win of the series over the Red Wings. Going into game four, both teams knew that they had to improve defensively.

Just three games into the series between Detroit and St. Louis and the Red Wings had scored 15 goals, but they also allowed 10 to the Blues. Both teams concentrated on defense in game four. As a result, the team who scored first in game four would win. In a 1-0 defensive battle, the Blues did what they wanted by winning two games at home and evening up the series at two games apiece. Game five became a pivotal game for the Detroit Red Wings.

Game five returned to the friendly atmosphere of Joe Louis Arena for the Red Wings. The Wings were hoping to get back on track against the pesky St. Louis Blues. It was another low scoring contest that was decided by one goal. Not often had a team been down 2-0 in a series and come back to win the series. After a 3-2 victory in game five, the Blues were headed back home for game six. The Blues were now just one win shy of eliminating the favored Red Wings.

Following the loss in game five, the third straight by the Red Wings, Steve Yzerman stood in the locker room and felt confident that his team was going to win game six. He ignored the criticism and urged his teammates that it was time to take care of business. The usually quiet Yzerman had something to say and when he did, it was time for his teammates to listen.

Game six returned to St. Louis, and the Blues were confident that they could wrap up the series at home. They did not want to return to Detroit for a game seven. The Blues had the Red Wings right where they wanted them, down but not out.

True to Steve Yzerman's word, the Red Wings took care of business in a professional manner. The Wings beat the Blues in game six, 4-2, and game seven was to be played in Detroit. The team with the best record in the NHL was still alive due to the performance of their beloved captain.

The goal for the Detroit Red Wings was to eliminate the Blues and move one step closer to the Stanley Cup championship. The Blues simply wanted to stay close in the game and try to leave Joe Louis Arena with a victory. The goal for both teams was to play well defensively. Neither team wanted to get involved in a shoot out. Both teams were aware that anything was possible in a game seven; it was a great series that neither team deserved to lose.

During Steve Yzerman's brilliant career as a Red Wing, he had been involved in five previous game seven playoff thrillers. The first was in 1987 when the Wings defeated the Toronto Maple Leafs to advance to the Conference Finals against Edmonton. In 1991, Detroit faced St. Louis the last time they met in the playoffs. The Blues won that series in seven games to eliminate the Red Wings. In 1992, the Red Wings fared better by beating the Minnesota North Stars in seven games. The following year, the Red Wings fell victim to the Toronto Maple Leafs, who eliminated Detroit in the first round. The last seven game series was a major disappointment in 1994 when Detroit was embarrassed in the first round by the expansion San Jose Sharks in a seven game series.

Game seven in 1996 between the Blues and Red Wings promised to be a thriller. The series was long, physical, and exhausting. Both sides had stars on the ice for game seven. St. Louis had Brett Hull and Wayne Gretzky, and Detroit had Steve Yzerman and Paul Coffey. However, only one man would decide the fate of this double overtime NHL classic. Game seven proved to be the battle of the goalies.

It all began with tension for both teams. Neither team wanted to make the first mistake.

Throughout the first period, both teams played well defensively in a real tight checking game. After one intense period of hockey, the game was scoreless. The feeling-out process was behind the two teams, and some believed the second period would open things up more.

In game seven it was the objective of the underdog to stay close, to have an opportunity to win the game with one goal, especially when the underdog was playing in the opposing team's building. St. Louis had Detroit on the brink of elimination for the second time in the series.

The goalie that played the best usually decided a game seven in the decisive game of the series. Going into the second period of game seven both goalies were spectacular. Chris Osgood was expected to be good in net, but Jon Casey carried the Blues on his back after replacing the injured starting goalie Grant Fuhr. During the second period, it was expected that the action and scoring chances would increase. The tempo of the game remained the same as the first period with defense dominating the contest.

Game seven of this series was being played mostly in the neutral zone. As the third period approached, the tension mounted for both teams. It appeared as though one goal would decide the game. After two periods in game seven, the scoreboard above the ice at Joe Louis Arena read, 'Detroit Red Wings 0, St. Louis Blues 0.'

Following the second intermission, the fans were sitting on the edge of their seats waiting for one of the Red Wings to sneak one by Jon Casey, but it did not happen in the third period. Game seven between Detroit and St. Louis was heading into overtime. Indeed one goal would be the difference in this game.

Overtime was referred to as sudden death for one team, but sudden life for the other team who won the game. The pressure was on the heavily favored Red Wings at this stage of the game. This game seven seemed different from many others, as the Red Wings seemed focused, patient and poised. The crowd almost sensed something special would occur at Joe Louis Arena for the home team.

Any sense of urgency was not evident for the Red Wings as they headed into overtime. The players on the Red Wings came out relaxed and confident that they would win. Perhaps all of the past playoff experience would at last pay off for Detroit.

After the first overtime ended, the pressure mounted at Joe Louis Arena. After four periods of hockey, game seven remained scoreless. Both goalies were simply outstanding! Neither team wanted to lose, but only one would survive while the loser would be forgotten. Someone would be a hero when this game ended.

Early in the second overtime, it appeared as though this great game would end. Steve Yzerman fed a pass to Sergei Federov, who stood alone in front of Casey. Federov let an excellent wrist shot go that was on its way to the back of the net. The players on the Red Wings' bench jumped to their feet in anticipation, but they quickly sat back down in disbelief as Casey came up with yet another miraculous save. Federov was stoned on a golden scoring opportunity, and Jon Casey had given his team another chance to steal one from the Red Wings.

It seemed as though the team that failed to score on a great chance came out on the losing end of the final score. The anticipation in the second overtime had everyone who was watching this classic hockey game holding his/her breath. This game was becoming difficult to watch because it would be over within a matter of a second with one miscue by the goalie. One team would experience overwhelming joy, while the losing team would express shock and depression.

At about 1:45 of the second overtime, Vladimir Konstantinov fed a routine pass up ice to Steve Yzerman. The pass was almost interrupted by Wayne Gretzky. Yzerman skated with the puck up the right side of the ice.

The Blues had a defenseman shadowing Yzerman who approached the St. Louis blue-line. Just before Yzerman reached the blue-line, he ran out of options. The only thing that Yzerman could do was to use the defenseman as a screen. Yzerman let go a rising slap shot backed with velocity from the impact of the shot.

The wicked shot was headed toward Jon Casey. As the puck whistled past Casey's right shoulder, the question was whether it would be above the cross bar or would find the upper right hand corner of the twine piecing the net together.

Would the captain who suffered from criticism, injuries and humiliation finally prove his worth as leader of the Detroit Red Wings? Would luck finally be on the side of Steve Yzerman? Would this be the moment fans had dreamed about? Would Steve Yzerman be the hero in this long exhaustive game?

Steve Yzerman waited anxiously as the puck sailed over the right shoulder of Jon Casey. This time, Steve Yzerman had found the magic that would help to erase the past disappointments of his previous playoff exits. Some of the cruel critics of Yzerman forgot, at least for the moment, that this captain could not provide the leadership necessary to carry his team to the championship. It was as though a burden had finally been lifted off of Yzerman.

As Yzerman skated around the right side of the St. Louis goal, a smile emerged and the captain left his feet in celebration. He jumped through the air pumping his fist, in what had to be the finest moment of his hockey career. His teammates joined Yzerman behind the St. Louis net to celebrate. The team mobbed their captain in a mass of piled-up bodies. Even Scotty Bowman came out from the bench to join his team for the on ice festivities.

When Yzerman left the ice, he was filled with excitement after scoring what was one of the biggest goals he had recorded as a Detroit Red Wing. The captain was surprised that the shot went into the net. He believed that his team would win the game. The Detroit Red Wings had gained confidence heading into the next round. When Yzerman was asked about the next round opponent the celebration ended and the captain became seriously focused on the next challenge - the Colorado Avalanche.

It was as though reality was setting in, and Yzerman assured fans that the celebration would be short-lived. He mentioned two names that the Red Wings would have to deal with in the next round, Peter Forsberg and Joe Sakic. He referred to them as two of the best in hockey. The stage was set for the Western Conference Finals.

The next match-up for the Detroit Red Wings was against the Colorado Avalanche. A physically exhausted Detroit team had to try and find a way to stop a great team. The Avalanche were well rested and ready for the Red Wings. They were graced with players like Peter Forsberg, Joe Sakic and Patrick Roy. The Red Wings knew they would have to play better than they had against St. Louis in order to return to the Stanley Cup Finals.

Game one of the Western Conference Finals took place in Detroit. The fans in Detroit were still buzzing over the overtime victory against the St. Louis Blues. The first game was filled with playoff intensity right from the start. The teams seemed to be evenly matched, and the series promised to be a dandy.

Detroit opened the scoring in the first period on a power play. Dino Ciccarelli was battling in front of the Avalanche net when Steve Yzerman fed a pass to Paul Coffey. Coffey whistled a slap shot through traffic and found the back of the net behind Patrick Roy. Six minutes into the game and things were looking good for Detroit, but the goal that Detroit scored was no easy task. These were the kind of goals Detroit would need to beat the Avalanche. The first period ended with Detroit ahead 1-0, thanks to Coffey, Yzerman and Ciccarelli.

It was not long into the second period when Coffey put in his second goal, with Detroit on another power play. Stephane Yelle skated past the Red Wing net and sent a centering pass in front of the Red Wing goal. Paul Coffey was standing alone in the crease and accidentally deflected the puck past Chris Osgood. The score was now tied 1-1, but this was a goal not to be forgotten by Red Wing supporters. This may have marked the end for Paul Coffey as a Red Wing.

The third period began with bad news before the action resumed. As the Detroit players returned to the bench, one key ingredient was mysteriously missing for the Detroit Red Wings. Steve Yzerman remained in the locker room, with a reported groin injury. The Red Wing players had to resume the critical third period without their inspirational leader for the 1996 Stanley Cup playoff season.

Less than two minutes into the third period, Adam Deadmarsh tallied a disputed goal that gave the Avs a 2-1 lead. About four minutes later, the Red Wings answered the call. Once again it was Paul Coffey who redeemed himself by scoring a short-handed goal. The game remained tied at the end of regulation time.

The Red Wings were headed for their second straight overtime game. However, this time the hero of game seven against St. Louis, Steve Yzerman, could only watch. The Red Wings needed a new hero to emerge if they wanted to hold home ice advantage in this series against Colorado.

This game was a physical battle that made its mark on the Red Wings. Colorado banged up veteran defenseman Paul Coffey during game one. Red Wing captain Steve Yzerman spent much of his time in the oxygen chamber and did not return to be the hero in this overtime affair.

Late into the first overtime, the game came to an abrupt end. The hero in this game was an unlikely choice. With less than three minutes remaining in overtime, Mike Ricchi sent a pass to line-mate Mike Keane. Keane fired a wrist shot at Osgood, and found a hole between Osgood's pads. Colorado set the tone for the series with a punishing physical style of play. Game one was a big win for the visitors who now had the home ice advantage in the series.

The good news going into game two was that the Red Wings were playing at home. The bad news was that Detroit had to play without the services of Steve Yzerman. He was unable to play because of the groin injury he aggravated in game one. Detroit had several good scoring chances in the first period but could not capitalize, due to the excellent play of Patrick Roy in goal for Colorado.

The Avalanche opened the scoring mid-way through the first period. Joe Sakic scored on Mike Ricchi's rebound, and the first period ended 1-0 in favor of the visiting Colorado Avalanche.

Early in the second period, the physical play picked up again. This time it was Paul Coffey and Claude Lemeiux who were entangled in a scuffle. Chris Osgood did not like what he saw between Coffey and Lemeiux. Osgood and Lemeiux continued to rough up one another, and as a result both teams were dealt double minor penalties for roughing.

With almost six minutes gone in the second period, Warren Rychel stood in front of the Detroit net and took a pass from Stephane Yelle that he whacked in over the sprawling Chris Osgood. The Colorado Avalanche were now in control with a 2-0 lead.

About two minutes later, Colorado added to the lead on a goal scored by Sandis Ozolinsh. The second period ended with the Avalanche in complete control with a 3-0 lead. Nothing seemed to be going right for the Detroit Red Wings.

When the third period began, Detroit was without the services of two key players; Steve Yzerman was sidelined with his groin injury, and Paul Coffey was unable to return because of back spasms. At the end of the third period, Detroit had out shot Colorado 35 to 20, but on the scoreboard the Avalanche ended up on top by a 3-0 count.

With the series shifting back to Colorado, the Avalanche felt triumphant to be ahead in the series two games to none. Meanwhile, Detroit was happy to be on the road where the pressure of winning was lessened. The Red Wings felt confident knowing that their captain would be returning to action for game three.

The Red Wings knew that this game was a vital situation in order to have any chance of winning the series. The Wings responded as they broke out of their scoring slump to post a 6-4 victory over the Avalanche. Detroit had two goals from Nicklas Lidstrom and four assists from Sergei Federov.

Game four was another critical game for the visiting Red Wings. With the return of Steve Yzerman, things seemed to be going in favor of Detroit. The Wings were playing without the services of star defenseman, Paul Coffey, but Colorado was playing without Claude

Lemeiux, their 'hustle and go-to' guy. Lemeiux was suspended for sucker-punching Slava Kozlov in game three.

During the first 15 minutes of game four, both teams were held scoreless. With about three and a half minutes left in the first period, the scoring began. Joe Sakic, with his great speed, created a two on one situation. Sakic found Adam Deadmarsh, who slipped one past Chris Osgood, to open the scoring; however, the goal by Deadmarsh was the only scoring in the first period. The fans in Colorado seemed to be witnessing another great game between two excellent hockey teams.

The second period was a little less than five minutes old when Detroit evened the score. Yzerman spotted teammate Sergei Federov and fed him a pass. Federov let go with a slap shot that was tipped between the legs of Patrick Roy by Dino Ciccarelli, who was in his familiar position - parked in front of the goalie. Creating traffic in front of Roy seemed to be the answer for the Red Wings to generate offense.

Colorado took the lead 2-1 on a goal by Joe Sakic, and the second period ended with the Red Wings down by a goal. It was important that Detroit score the next goal, because if they failed to win this game, they would face elimination in the next game.

Early in the third period, Colorado went on the power play, one that was not successful against Detroit in the regular season. Alexei Gusarov was setting up the play at the left point. He sent a pass to Uwe Krupp, who let go with a wrist shot to beat Chris Osgood. The fate of the Red Wings was all but doomed in this game. Later in the third period, Peter Forsberg added an empty net goal that lifted Colorado to a 3-1 lead in the series. Game five was going to Detroit, where the Red Wings faced elimination once again in the Stanley Cup playoffs.

The best team in the NHL during the regular season needed a miracle to pull off this series, but with 62 regular season victories, this Red Wing team was capable of winning three in a row. First, they had to win game five. It would be the third time that Detroit faced elimination in the Stanley Cup playoffs in 1996, and it definitely was good news that Paul Coffey would be ready to play in game five.

The Detroit Red Wings had to get off to a good start in game five especially since they were playing at home. About half way through the first period, it looked as though the crowd was down the road at Tiger Stadium. As Doug Brown unleashed a shot at Patrick Roy, the puck deflected into the air and Slava Kozlov took his best baseball swing at the round object (puck). He connected, and as Detroit Tiger broadcaster

Ernie Harwell would say it was "long gone." Kozlov's limited baseball skills put the Red Wings ahead on a very important goal that set the tone for game five.

Red Wing captain Steve Yzerman guaranteed the team would win game five. To win game five, the Red Wings needed help from the famed Russian Five members. About one minute following the goal by Slava Kozlov, Steve Yzerman skated with the puck behind the Colorado net. He sent a blind pass in front of the Colorado goal where Vladimir Konstantinov was waiting. Vladdy fired a shot wide of Patrick Roy, but the puck rebounded to the right side of the net; Igor Larionov banged a back hander into the empty section of the goal.

Detroit now had a 2-0 lead, and three of The Russian Five had contributed on the score sheet. The Red Wings were dominating just like they did during the regular season. The first period ended with Detroit leading 2-0 over Colorado in game five.

The second period was crucial for the Detroit Red Wings. If they could hold the lead going into the third period, it would be difficult for Colorado to come back in the final twenty minutes. The Avalanche began their comeback with a little more than two minutes gone in the second period. Mike Ricchi blasted a rebound past a sprawling Chris Osgood. Suddenly, Colorado had cut the Red Wing lead to 2-1.

About two minutes later in the second period, the Russian-born superstar, Sergei Federov, found his scoring touch for the Red Wings. Federov won a face off in the Colorado zone. He drew the puck back to Paul Coffey who let a soft shot go toward Patrick Roy. Federov deflected the puck past Roy and Detroit was in command once again with a 3-1 lead.

Mike Ricchi countered with a goal to cut the deficit to one goal. Ricchi took a pass from Sandis Ozolinsh and buried it past Chris Osgood to cut the Detroit lead to 3-2. Colorado would not go away and Detroit knew they had to prevent the Avalanche from hanging on; otherwise, their season could end in yet another losing cause.

Detroit responded well to the pressure by expanding their lead against Colorado. The Red Wings regained their two-goal lead when Doug Brown scored with less than eight minutes remaining in the second period. With less than a minute remaining, Greg Johnson beat Patrick Roy on a rebound to widen Detroit's lead to 5-2.

Game five ended with the Red Wings holding off elimination again in the 1996 Stanley Cup playoffs. The Wings felt that if they could win game six and bring the seventh and deciding game back to Joe Louis Arena, they would stand a good chance of winning the series. This team was confident for a good reason; they were the all-time single season record holder for wins during the regular season.

Colorado knew it would be important to score the first goal against the talented Detroit Red Wings. The Avalanche opened the scoring in the first period when captain Joe Sakic beat Chris Osgood. About six minutes later, Detroit's fate was sealed when Claude Lemeuix hit Red Wing Kris Draper from behind. The blow left Draper with a serious injury to his face that required surgery during the off season.

The cheap shot to Draper seemed to take the life out of the Red Wing team. Lemeuix received a five-minute penalty and was ejected from the game. Scotty Bowman felt that the injury to Draper was the turning point of the game.

With a five-minute power play, the Red Wings knew it was crucial to score with the man advantage. Paul Coffey flipped a shot off the skate of Avalanche defenseman, Sylvain Lefebvre, which redirected past the sprawling Patrick Roy. With a little luck and a good bounce, the Red Wings were alive again for a brief moment.

The remainder of the game belonged to Colorado. The Avalanche tallied the next three goals. The loss in game six for the Red Wings ended a great season that went down as another failure for the Detroit Red Wings. The Detroit fans grew impatient and anything short of winning the Stanley Cup became unacceptable.

Any loyal Red Wing follower or true fan knew it was a matter of time before changes would be made that would bring the elusive Stanley Cup back to Hockey Town. The chemistry on the team needed to be adjusted. The problem was who to boot and who to replace them?

One Red Wing remained on the roster for the next season: Steve Yzerman. After a disappointing ending to a phenomenal regular season, Mike Illitch complimented the play and dedication of his team captain. Yzerman had established himself as the leader of the Detroit Red Wings on the ice.

Exactly whose status was on the ropes after the crushing loss to the Colorado Avalanche? Perhaps it would be Sergei Federov, since many fans had questioned his heart and desire during the playoffs. Maybe it would be Keith Primeau, who had not yet lived up to his expectations; it might be Paul Coffey, who was plagued by injuries throughout the Stanley Cup playoffs. The coaches and management realized they were close to winning the Cup, and with the proper mixture of players, the next season might bring Lord Stanley's prize back to Detroit.

The 1996-97 season brought several changes to the Red Wings roster. Paul Coffey and Keith Primeau went to the Hartford Whalers in exchange for Brendan Shanahan. Tomas Sandstrom came from Pittsburgh to replace Greg Johnson. The Wings stole veteran defenseman Larry Murphy from the Toronto Maple Leafs. Kirk Maltby resulted in a trade between Detroit and the Edmonton Oilers. Detroit rescued Joey Kocur from the local beer leagues to provide toughness and leadership. Scotty Bowman was assembling a team that was stacked with role players who were committed to winning.

One Red Wing did not pack his bags, as he remained a fixed figure with Detroit. Steve Yzerman had finally earned his worth with the Detroit fans and media. His dedication to win was comparable to that of ex-Red Wing legend, Gordie Howe. Yzerman had passed the test that Scotty Bowman set for him...he had changed his potent offensive game. Yzerman was one of the best defensive-minded centers in the game. With maturity, Steve learned how to become a complete player in the NHL.

Those who questioned his leadership after each early playoff departure would do so no more. He came to a team that perhaps could not have earned a playoff spot in the minor leagues in 1983. Yzerman immediately accepted his role as captain and leader, and he handled the media with amazing grace. The young boy who arrived in 1983 had at last grown into a man. Steve accepted responsibility at a young age, and when the Red Wings bowed out to the Colorado Avalanche, the finger pointed in a different direction.

Following Steve Yzerman's overtime goal against St. Louis in game seven, no one could legitimately question the character of the captain as the team leader. Win or lose, this captain could stay with the Red Wings as long as he wanted.

In the 1996-97 season, Yzerman had to lead a team that included many new faces. His longtime friend, Bob Errey, was gone; his old teammate, Joey Kocur, was back with a Stanley Cup ring that he had earned while playing with the New York Rangers. Three new rookies would join the Red Wings and Yzerman in their quest to win the Stanley Cup.

The new additions to the Detroit Red Wings blended well with the crafty veterans. The team chemistry for the 1996-97 team was strong, appearing relaxed and focused going into the new season. With last years record breaking regular season in victories, the Wings realized that the President's Trophy for the best record during the regular season meant nothing. It was the Stanley Cup that Steve Yzerman and Scotty Bowman set their goals for in the 96-97 campaign.

The newcomers added depth to the Detroit Red Wings' roster. Young Matheiu Dandenault played 65 games during the regular season for the Wings. Dandenault was a fast skater who scored three goals and added nine assists during his initial season with the Red Wings.

Another newcomer was the young Swede named Tomas Holmstrom. He did not live up to the Swedish reputation of being a non-physical player in the NHL; Holmstrom was tough. He threw his weight around and was not afraid to stand in front of the opposing goalie. He played 47 games for the Red Wings, and showed great promise by scoring six goals and adding three assists.

University of Michigan graduate, Mike Knuble, came up at the end of the 1996-97 season. Mike played only nine games with the Red Wings, but in those nine games, he was able to score his first NHL goal.

As a team, the Red Wings finished third overall in the Western Conference and took the pressure off going into the Stanley Cup playoffs. The expectations were not as high because the Wings were not the favorite going into the Stanley Cup playoffs. These Detroit Red Wings had learned a lesson and carried a business-like attitude with them into the playoffs. The business agenda would include taking care of unfinished business. The goal was not based upon the regular season record for this Red Wing team; these Wings, had one thing on their minds: to win 16 games and bring the Stanley Cup back where it belonged, in Detroit, Michigan - Hockey Town, USA.

The Detroit Red Wings were focused heading into the Stanley Cup playoffs. The regular season was forgotten and now it was time to get serious for this new group of Red Wings.

Detroit had a balanced scoring attack during the regular season. Brendan Shanahan led the team in scoring with 47 goals and 41 assists, for a total of 88 points. Steve Yzerman finished second in scoring with 85 points, but he led the team in assists with 63.

As a team, the Red Wings compiled a 38-26-18 record during the regular season in 1996-97, which wasn't even close to the last season when they set a NHL record for victories in a single season with 62. Detroit did not win the President's Trophy, but managed to finish third overall behind the Dallas Stars and the Colorado Avalanche. This team had a different demeanor heading into the playoffs; they were confident and focused.

Who would play in goal was questionable heading into the first round of the Stanley Cup playoffs for the Red Wings. Chris Osgood was clearly the starter during the regular season and had a far better record than his backup Mike Vernon. Scotty Bowman postponed the decision until the end of the regular season.

Mike Vernon was better down the stretch, and Detroit wanted him for playoff experience. Mike had previously won the Stanley Cup with the Calgary Flames. Both goalies had failed in the last two successive playoff runs for the Red Wings in their quest to capture the Cup. Scotty Bowman was faced with a tough decision.

Bowman played a hunch and decided on his starter for the 96-97 playoffs. At last the goalie controversy in Detroit was over. Scotty Bowman had spoken. The Detroit Red Wings would ride out the playoff season with Mike Vernon between the pipes.

The first opponent for the Detroit Red Wings promised to keep the guys sharp if they made it to the second round. The Red Wings opened against the St. Louis Blues, a team they had beaten in recent playoff runs, but not with ease. The Blues wanted nothing more than to eliminate the powerful Red Wings in the first round.

Game one of the Stanley Cup chase for the Wings took place in the friendly confines of Joe Louis Arena. While the fans were confident, the expectations were not as high as they had been in the previous season, allowing Detroit to relax and focus going into game one.

During the regular season, these two teams were as close as two teams could get on paper. Each team won a game, and they tied the other three games. Detroit had the offensive advantage, but many felt that St. Louis had the upper hand in net with the veteran Grant Fuhr in goal.

Joe Louis Arena was packed and enthusiastic as usual for the start of game one. During the first period, the Blues silenced the home crowd by opening the scoring in the series. At 12:44 of the first period, Geoff Courtnall scored for the visiting Blues. About seven minutes later, the Blues leader in scoring, Pierre Turgeon, added a power play goal that had the Blues ahead 2-0 on the scoreboard.

The Red Wings had to regroup before the start of the second period. During the second period, the Detroit Red Wings were outshot 15 to eight, but neither team scored, thanks to the excellent play of the goalies.

St. Louis was a superb defensive team and Detroit had to strategize in the third period to gain back home ice advantage in the series.

It was playoff time again in Hockey Town. The pressure was back on the Red Wings. Game one went to the underdog visitors from St. Louis. If Detroit lost the next game, the latest edition of a Stanley Cup champion impostor would possibly face elimination against the St. Louis Blues in the first round.

Game two was a must-win situation for the Red Wings. If St. Louis won this game, they would return home for game three with the heavily-favored Red Wings scrambling for their playoff lives. Just under five minutes into the game, St. Louis defenseman, Marc Bergevin, slipped one by Detroit goalie, Mike Vernon to give the Blues a 1-0 lead. The first period ended with the Blues up 1-0 after twenty minutes.

Both goalies were playing well. If the Wings were to get past the first round, they had to find a way to beat Grant Fuhr. The Red Wings outshot the Blues in the second period 19-14, but they still were unable to put one past Fuhr. After 40 minutes, the first round series for the revamped Red Wings seemed to be slipping away fast. With twenty minutes remaining in regulation time, it was critical for the Red Wings to score the next goal.

Four minutes were gone in the third period, and the Red Wings were killing a power play. An unlikely hero emerged in this penalty-killing role. One of Scotty Bowman's key role players, Kris Draper, finally found a way to beat Grant Fuhr. The Red Wings had life once again with about 16 minutes remaining in regulation time. Just three minutes later, the final goal of the game was scored. Another unlikely hero emerged in the person of Larry Murphy who fired one by Fuhr.

The rejuvenated and newly-assembled Red Wings responded to adversity to win a big playoff game. Most importantly, Detroit showed great patience against a hot goalie named Grant Fuhr. This group of Wings exemplified character that had never been present before. Detroit still had the leadership from Captain Steve Yzerman, but now it was the role players who were contributing. Mike Vernon was also sizzling hot between the pipes in the first two games against St. Louis.

With the series returning to St. Louis, it was important for the Red Wings to win at home. The Wings wanted to regain home ice advantage in St. Louis by winning one of the two games.

The first period of game three opened with a quick goal less than three minutes into the game. Kris Draper and the famous Grind Line put the Wings up 1-0 early in game three. With three minutes remaining in the first period, Brett Hull evened the score with an unassisted goal.

The Red Wings opened the second period on the power play. Less than one minute into the second period, Brendan Shanahan beat Grant Fuhr to put Detroit ahead 2-1. Six minutes later, the Blues evened the score on a goal by former Detroit Red Wing, Joe Murphy. Then with a little less than five minutes remaining in the second period the Wings went on the power play again.

This power play opportunity would mark the turning point of the game if the Wings could cash in with a goal. It was critical in this defensive struggle. At 15:22 into the second period, the Red Wing captain came to the rescue with a key power play goal. This was all the Wings needed to build their confidence heading into the third period. After two periods, the scoreboard read Detroit 3, St. Louis 2.

In the third period, Detroit had relied heavily upon Mike Vernon. Not only did Vernon save the puck; he literally saved the game. St. Louis fired 15 shots at Vernon during the third period, and he stopped all 15 third period shots to preserve the 3-2 victory. Meanwhile, the Red Wings managed only six shots against Grant Fuhr.

Detroit won game three to take a 2-1 lead in the series, but they were not dominating the Blues as expected. This series was up for either team to win. The Blues were not about to hand Detroit an easy win in game four at the Kiel Center.

The series created a reversal for the Blues, who now had to work extra-hard to have any hope of winning the series against Detroit. Game four began just as the home team and fans had wished. The Blues had two goals in the first period and things seemed to be going their way in the contest.

In the second period, both teams had ten shots on goal, but neither team could put one in the back of the net. Grant Fuhr was in the zone in the first two periods, and he stopped all 19 shots that the Red Wings fired at him.

The Red Wings knew that they had to come out and get a quick goal to have a chance of winning this defensive struggle. The first goal of the third period was scored on a power play. Geoff Courtnall added his second goal of the game about one minute into the third period. The scoreboard now read 3-0 in favor of the Blues. The Blues added one more goal late in the third period to skate away with a 4-0 victory in game four. Momentum shifted again in this series, but now the teams were heading back to Joe Louis Arena. Once again, this was a crucial game for the Wings to win. With just three games left in the series, home ice became essential. The stage was set for the new look Red Wings; would they answer the critics, or would they be exploited to further criticism with another early playoff exit at the hands of a lesser opponent in the first round?

The Red Wings needed someone to step forward and provide leadership in game five. Soon into the first period of game five, the Red Wings got the leadership they were searching for on a nifty goal from Steve Yzerman. Yzerman had the Red Wings ahead on the scoreboard 1-0.

St. Louis scored their first goal on the power play. Al MacInnis let go of one of his wicked slap shots, and it found the back of the twine. Although the Red Wings out shot the Blues 11 to three, the tennis match-type series continued. At the end of one period, the advantage went to the Blues.

In the second period, the Red Wing fans witnessed an offensive explosion in a series that had been a defensive struggle. Four goals were scored in the second period of game five. The first was a power play goal scored by Slava Kozlov of the Red Wings. If the Wings could score the next goal they would be in a good position to put this one away.

Almost eight minutes into the second period, a Red Wing favorite, Darren McCarty, scored his first goal of the series. The Red Wings now had a commanding 3-1 lead. Joe Louis Arena was rocking as the fans responded to the new look Red Wings determination to come from behind.

St. Louis was now under pressure to score the next goal. If St. Louis could not score the next goal this game would be over. Suddenly, the Blues responded with an unlikely hero. Jim Campbell scored his first goal of the series to close the Detroit lead to 3-2.

Seconds later, the Red Wings scored another big goal. This time, newcomer Brendan Shanahan beat Grant Fuhr to widen Detroit's lead to 4-2. Going into the third period, the Red Wings looked as though they had finally figured out the pesky Blues.

In the third period, the Red Wings were back on the power play. Steve Yzerman fed a pass to Brendan Shanahan, who in return, passed to Larry Murphy who beat Grant Fuhr. The Red Wings were in command with a three-goal lead, a lead they would hold on to for the rest of the game. Detroit needed one more victory at St. Louis in game six to eliminate the determined Blues.

St. Louis knew it was important to get an early lead in game six against the powerful Red Wings. With almost two minutes gone in the game, the Blues superstar, Brett Hull, beat Mike Vernon to give the Blues a 1-0 lead. Afterwards, Detroit would go on the power play and it was important that they cash in on a golden opportunity.

Scotty Bowman sent out the famous Russian Five Line in hopes that they would produce offensively. On a beautiful goal by Slava Kozlov, assisted by Igor Larionov and Sergei Federov, the Red Wings tied the score at one goal apiece. After the first period, Detroit had the upper hand in the series and the game.

The Red Wings were on the power play early in the second period, and if they could cash in on the opportunity, they would have the Blues in a strangle hold. Brendan Shanahan cashed in on the power play with his third goal of the series. The Red Wings confidence was building as the game wore on. After two periods, Detroit was in command, but the Wings knew they could not sit on the lead. They would have to come out as the aggressors in the third period.

Detroit scored the final goal of the game and awaited their opponent for the second round. The final goal typified how the playoffs were going for the Red Wings when a key role player, Kirk Maltby, scored his first goal of the playoffs. The next opponent for the Red Wings was the up-and-coming expansion team, the Anaheim Mighty Ducks.

The Red Wings had just experienced a tough six game series against the St. Louis Blues, but their opponent in round two had even a tougher road to get to round number two. The Mighty Ducks fought back from a 3-2 deficit to win their first round series against the Phoenix Coyotes in seven games.

The Anaheim Mighty Ducks were an explosive team with superstar Paul Kariya and teammate Teemu Selanne. This duo was one of the best pair to play together in the NHL; however, they lacked experience in the Stanley Cup playoffs, something the Red Wings were quite trained for.

Game one opened at Joe Louis Arena in Detroit. During the first period, neither team could score a goal. The Wings looked to Mike Vernon for another stellar performance in the series opener, but Vernon was not really tested in the first period.

The second period was another defensive struggle between the Red Wings and the Mighty Ducks. With one minute remaining in the second period, the Mighty Ducks were on the power play. Paul Kariya opened the scoring in the series with his sixth goal of the playoffs. The Red Wings found themselves in a familiar situation. They were behind at home in game one of another series.

The Red Wings still had one period remaining to erase the one goal deficit.

The Red Wings scored the only goal in the third period to force sudden death overtime. A little better than 11 minutes into the third period, Sergei Federov scored his first and most important goal of the 96-97 playoffs. The question now was who would be the hero in overtime.

It ended quickly in game one of the second round of the Stanley Cup playoffs. An unlikely hero emerged during the first minute of overtime; Martin LaPointe scored his first playoff goal and put the Red Wings ahead in the series 1-0. Even with a one game lead, the Red Wings were not taking the Mighty Ducks lightly in this series.

Going into the series, some people thought that it would be dominated by offense. After game one, the goalies demonstrated dominance. Game two would be played at home for the Red Wings.

The first period of game two was another defensive struggle. The Mighty Ducks had outshot the Red Wings 10-8. It did not take long, as the Wings scored less than five minutes into the second period.

Steve Yzerman rose to the occasion again by scoring a key goal early in the second period. His goal gave the Red Wings the advantage heading into the third period of game two. The third period witnessed a scoring assault as the offense for both teams took charge.

The third period gave way to the most productive offensive output of the series. Anaheim opened the scoring at the 4:18 mark of the third period. Veteran defenseman and former Stanley Cup champion, Jari Kurri, tied the score at 1-1. In turn, Detroit responded with the go ahead goal by Doug Brown. With less than five minutes remaining, many Red Wing fans thought the Wings had won this game to go up 2-0 in the best of seven series.

The Mighty Ducks responded when high-scoring forward Teemu Selanne scored his sixth goal of the playoffs to even the score at 2-2. If the Red Wings thought that the Ducks were going to roll over and play dead, they had underestimated this determined group of athletes.

Following the first overtime, everything remained even in this hockey game: the score, the shots on goal (13 for each team in the first overtime), the intensity, and the momentum. Which team would wear down in the second overtime?

During the second overtime, the Red Wings outplayed the Mighty Ducks, but the scoreboard still read Detroit 2, Anaheim 2. After 100 minutes of exhaustive playoff hockey, the tired warriors on both teams had to try to settle game two in a third overtime session.

Detroit went on an early power play. Scotty Bowman sent out his famous Russian Five unit, hoping their quickness and team chemistry could end this battle with the stubborn Mighty Ducks. Joe Louis Arena came to life and the fans were awakened when Slava Kozlov fired a shot past his countryman, Mikhail Stalenkov, in net for Anaheim.

Then the Red Wings took their tired bodies out to the West Coast and continued the war on ice with the Anaheim Mighty Ducks. This series was evolving into a true test of strength, determination, and resilience. It reminded some of a prizefight, the type of bout where the most determined team survived.

It was expected that both teams would come out a bit weary in game three. The Mighty Ducks had a slight advantage by being at home; game three was crucial for Anaheim. Detroit could relax a little, but would they?

The Wings' record against the expansion Mighty Ducks during the regular season was 0-3-1, far short from spectacular and convincing. However, this was the Stanley Cup playoffs and the second season.

Experience was the key in the Stanley Cup playoffs. The more experience a team had the more likely they were to succeed. Going into game three the Red Wings' playoff experience was far ahead of the Mighty Ducks'.

Game three at the Pond was a defensive struggle ten minutes into the first period. During the next ten minutes, three goals were scored. Anaheim opened the scoring on a power play when Paul Kariya put his seventh goal of the Stanley Cup playoffs past Detroit netminder Mike Vernon. To answer the first goal, power forward, Teemu Selanne, scored his seventh goal of the playoffs, putting Anaheim in control in game two with a 2-0 lead.

With the hometown fans behind them, the Mighty Ducks made it look as if the Red Wings were in for a long evening. Detroit went on the power play with about five minutes remaining in the period, a golden opportunity for them to get back into the game.

Sergei Federov fed Slava Kozlov a pass in the Mighty Ducks zone, and Kozlov fired a shot past Stalenkov. Suddenly, Detroit was back in the game trailing by just one goal. The first twenty minutes ended with Anaheim up 2-1. The Red Wings knew they had to pick up the intensity in the second period if they wanted to put the Ducks within one game of extinction in the 96-97 campaign.

The Mighty Ducks owned the first half of the second period during game three. Ted Drury scored his first ever playoff goal in the second period. Anaheim now led in game three, 3-1 over the Red Wings. With half of game three completed, the Wings found themselves in a hole.

Teams that won the Stanley Cup found a way to overcome diversity. They were able to remain focused until they won 16 playoff games and hoisted the prized Cup for all to see. This was a time to see if the Red Wings finally had what it took to rise above and rebound to overcome a two-goal deficit. Could these Wings come back? Could they respond?

Thirteen minutes into the second period, the Red Wings went on another power play. Scotty Bowman played a hunch by relying upon The Russian Five unit to produce. The Russians came through again for the Detroit Red Wings; Igor Larionov scored a critical goal that was assisted by Slava Kozlov and Vladimir Konstantinov.

Minutes later, the Red Wings evened the score at 3-3. This time the hero was a role player; Doug Brown scored his second goal of the playoffs. Suddenly, Detroit was back in the game, and with one period remaining in regulation time, the game was theirs for the taking.

Two goals were scored in a wild third period. Was overtime in the cards again, or would the Wings put Anaheim on the brink of elimination? Detroit seemed re-energized with the scoring of the last two goals in the second period.

During the third period, the scoring barrage began. Sergei Federov took a pass from veteran journeyman, Larry Murphy. Federov beat Stalenkov, and the Wings had their first lead of the game. With Detroit ahead 4-3, Red Wing fans were waiting and hoping that the Wings would finally nail this game down.

Would all the years of playoff experience pay off for the Red Wings? Had they finally learned how to put a team away? Confidence was the key in the Stanley Cup playoffs for winning. With every comeback, the new look Red Wings were gaining confidence like they never had before. The team esteem reached a peak in game three when Slava Kozlov scored his fifth goal of the playoffs.

This latest group of Red Wings was confident, and it was getting contributions from everyone. The Wings had a different look than past Red Wing playoff teams, who stumbled around in the Stanley Cup playoffs. This team had the makings of a champion.

The tasks that remained for Anaheim were almost insurmountable. They had no previous playoff experience and found themselves in the position of trying to knock off one of the best and most experienced teams of 1990's. Anaheim scored first when Joe Sacco beat Mike Vernon to put the Ducks ahead 1-0 in game four. The Red Wings evened the score when Doug Brown scored with less than two minutes remaining in the first period. The Wings were right where they wanted to be after the first twenty minutes.

The second period was fifteen minutes old before the only goal was scored in the period. Brian Bellows scored on the power play at the 15:23 mark, and the Mighty Ducks were now up 2-1 going into the third period. If they could hold the lead, the series would return to Detroit for game five.

Only one goal was scored in the third period. Detroit had 18 shots on goal while Anaheim managed just four shots against Mike Vernon. Nick Lidstrom scored the only goal of the period to force overtime in game four. Momentum was key going into any overtime period, advantage Detroit.

After the first 20-minute overtime, neither team scored, but during the second overtime a winner emerged. Again, the Detroit Red Wings outshot the Ducks in the second overtime. The victorious Red Wings left Anaheim and moved on to face the Colorado Avalanche again.

CHAPTER FOURTEEN

REMATCH, RESPECT, AND REMEMBER

The road to the Stanley Cup came through the Colorado Avalanche. The Red Wings won two tough series in the 96-97 Stanley Cup playoffs, but the real test was about to come. The Wings had to linger with the memory of the defeat the previous year by the Avalanche and the crushing blow inflicted upon Kris Draper.

The record during the regular season was relatively meaningless. The Wings had proved that a successful regular season was relatively meaningless come playoff time. The Avalanche won the regular season series with Detroit. The Wings won the physical dominance on the ice and sent a message to Colorado that they would not be pushed around this playoff season. Darren McCarty had taken care of Claude Lemeuix. He assured Mr. Lemeuix that he would not take a run at another player wearing a jersey with a Red Wing on it.

The final contest of the regular season between Detroit and Colorado was at Joe Louis Arena. It was a war of supremacy in the NHL, and would set the tone for the rematch between these two great hockey teams. Colorado handled Detroit in the first three meetings by beating the Wings in all three games.

The fourth game was at home for Detroit, and the Red Wings were out to send a message in this game. The two teams fought, including the goalies, but the reality was the Wings had to find a way to win on the scoreboard. The Red Wings were ahead in the third period and let their lead slip away to force overtime. Winning the fights was nice, but when it came to the playoffs, Colorado knew that they may not be able to win the physical war on the ice, but they could win on the scoreboard.

In the overtime session, the Red Wings had their cake and ate it too. Not only did Darren McCarty manhandle Claude Lemeuix earlier in the game, but also he scored the winning goal that sent another message to Colorado. Detroit could now claim that they could beat Colorado physically, and that they could beat the Avalanche on the scoreboard. The Avalanche were not looking forward to their next round opponent, a team that was searching for revenge and respect.

Game one was played in Colorado and now the pressure was on the Avalanche to win at home. The first period was very entertaining defensively. After twenty minutes, the first period ended scoreless.

The second period was another great show by the goalies. Patrick Roy stopped every shot he faced for the Avalanche. Mike Vernon equaled his counterpart by stopping every puck that came his way for the Detroit Red Wings.

The scoring in the third period began early. Just over one minute into the third period, Brendan Shanahan scored to put the Red Wings on top 1-0. Less than one minute later, the Avalanche captain Joe Sakic equaled the score with his fifth goal of the playoffs. The next goal decided the outcome of game one of the Western Conference Finals.

With less than fourteen minutes left in the game, Colorado sniper Mike Ricchi scored on a pass from Red Wing nemesis, Claude Lemeuix. Game one went to the Colorado Avalanche, placing the Red Wings in a must win situation for game two.

In order to win the series, the Red Wings could not afford to get down two games to none to the defending Stanley Cup champions. The stage was set for game two. The first goal would be important; whoever could set the pace early should have had the upper hand in this pivotal game.

Colorado scored first, late in the first period on a power play goal by Scott Young. The Red Wings found themselves down by a goal early in this contest. They had to prove resilience and bounce back in the second period, or they would be in serious trouble in this best of seven series with the Avalanche.

A little better than half way through the second period, the Avalanche added a little salt to the Red Wings' wound. The second goal of game two belonged to the Colorado Avalanche. It was scored by Claude Lemeuix, which added further insult to a fading Red Wing team. The Wings now found themselves down 1-0 in games, and 2-0 on the scoreboard.

It was during the second period of game two against the Colorado Avalanche that some Red Wing faithful began to wonder if this team would ever win the Stanley Cup again. Maybe they were cursed or someone put a spell on them. They seemed to have it together in the first two rounds, but against Colorado they seemed to be falling apart again.

With about three minutes left, the Red Wings mounted a comeback. The Wings were on a late power play in the second period when Igor Larionov beat Patrick Roy. Maybe, just maybe, this latest addition of Red Wings led by Steve Yzerman would come from behind to win a big game.

Early in the third period, the Detroit Red Wings went on the power play. Steve Yzerman fed line mate Sergei Federov a pass, and Federov did the rest. Federov beat Patrick Roy to even the score at 2-2. The next goal would be crucial for both teams.

Detroit needed a big goal to complete their comeback and steal a game on the road. With four minutes left in the third period, Steve Yzerman skated in alone on Patrick Roy. Yzerman buried the puck in the back of the net to complete the comeback against the Colorado Avalanche. The Avalanche pulled their goalie, hoping to tie the score.

Darren McCarty added an empty net goal to assure the Red Wings of a much-needed victory on the road. The Red Wings did what they could not do in the past playoff years: they came from behind to win a critical playoff game. With the series tied 1-1, the Red Wings were coming home to Hockey Town for game three.

The difference between this Red Wing team and previous playoff teams of recent years was they were getting contributions from everybody. They had proven leadership in their 14-year veteran, Steve Yzerman. They had adjusted to the system of Scotty Bowman. The time was right for the Wings to capture what had been missing in Hockey Town for 42 years: the Stanley Cup. They would have to win game three against the Colorado Avalanche, the team who possessed the prized Cup.

Game three was played before an enthusiastic crowd at the sold-out Joe Louis Arena. This game was crucial for both teams to win to gain the upper edge in the series. A little better than one minute into the game, the Red Wings set the tone when Slava Kozlov scored an early goal to put Detroit ahead 1-0. The period ended with one goal scored. The home fans in Detroit were feeling good about the Red Wings in this playoff year. The excitement could be felt inside the Joe Louis Arena between the first and second period.

The only goal in the second period was scored on a power play. Both teams had two power play opportunities during the second period; the Red Wings were unable to convert on their two attempts, but Colorado faired a bit better. With about five minutes left in the second period, the Avalanche relied upon their captain, Joe Sakic, to even the score after 40 minutes in game three.

Game three was decided in the final 20 minutes. If Detroit could win this game, they would have the upper hand for game four. At the 8:20 mark of the third period, Detroit took the lead on an excellent goal by Slava Kozlov, his second of the game.

The Red Wings knew that if they could hold off the Avalanche, the Wings would be right where they wanted to be going into game four. Thanks to the superior goal tending of Mike Vernon, the Wings held on to defeat the Avalanche by a 2-1 margin. The Red Wings now led the series two games to one. If they could win game four at home, they would be one game away from another Stanley Cup Final round.

The Detroit Red Wings came out with a lot of jump in game four in the first period. This was a very aggressive and hungry Red Wing team. Some fans could sense that this team would not fail. Detroit out shot Colorado 14 to two in the first period. The Red Wings scored two goals by Igor Larionov that seemed to deflate the defending Stanley Cup champions. The Russian Five unit was responding in the 96-97 Stanley Cup playoffs.

The second period was played defensively for the first 10 minutes, but the remaining of the period was an offensive assault. Slava Kozlov scored the third goal for the Wings, making the score 3-0. Detroit went on a power play with about four minutes left in the second period when another Russian, Sergei Federov, scored to put the Wings ahead 4-0. The Red Wings went on to score one more goal by Kirk Maltby to end the second period with the Wings up by a 5-0 count.

The third period brought about the look of frustration and humility to the defending Stanley Cup champions – The Colorado Avalanche. Kirk Maltby added his second goal of the game to ice game four for the Red Wings. The final score read Detroit 6, Colorado 0. Advantage Red Wings! Heading back to Colorado the Red Wings were relaxed. The Avalanche knew they had to play a perfect game to beat this group of Red Wings. The Detroit fans felt confident that the Wings could wrap up the series in game five.

With the Colorado Avalanche on the brink of elimination, game five was a must-win situation for the 1996 Stanley Cup champs. If the Red Wings thought that the game four shellacking they inflicted upon the Avalanche would carry over, they were mistaken. Colorado came out aggressive and ready to take on the rejuvenated Red Wings. The Avalanche were reluctant to hand over the Stanley Cup they had worked so hard for the previous season.

The first period was proof of how determined the Avalanche were to play game six back at Joe Louis Arena. Claude Lemeuix was going to make a statement of his own, and he did by scoring two goals in less than five minutes. Joe Sakic added a third goal, and the first period ended with Colorado up 3-0 even though the Wings out shot Colorado 11-9. The Wings were hopeful they would mount a comeback and wrap-up the series on the road.

The second period belonged to the home team again. Colorado scored their fourth goal early in the second period when Stephane Yelle beat a stunned Mike Vernon. Joe Sakic and Scott Young each added another goal, and after 40 minutes, Detroit was behind 6-0.

In the third period, Detroit simply wanted to set the tone for game six back at Joe Louis Arena. The Red Wings did not hang their heads. Instead, they put together a solid effort in the third period. Detroit out shot Colorado 13-4. More importantly, they sent a message that they would not quit even when behind 6-0. Detroit still led the series 3-2, and knew they would play much better at home for game six.

The Detroit Red Wings came out focused upon their goal: to win game six at home and eliminate their toughest opponent in the playoffs. They did not want to return to Colorado for a game seven.

Some fans at Joe Louis Arena were wondering if the Wings could put the 6-0 defeat in game five behind them. After one period of scoreless hockey, many fans knew these Wings meant business. Detroit out shot Colorado 14-3, and if not for Patrick Roy the Red Wings would have been ahead on the scoreboard. After one period of play, advantage Red Wings!

The Red Wings dominated play in the second period. They fired 16 shots at Roy, and Colorado managed only five shots on Mike Vernon. Martin LaPointe scored the lone goal of the second period. Suddenly, Avalanche fans could sense their run for a back-to-back championship was in jeopardy at the hands of the Detroit Red Wings.

Sergei Federov put Detroit ahead 2-0 with his fifth goal of the playoffs. Colorado was running out of time and had to score twice just to stave off elimination. With a little better than five minutes remaining, Scott Young scored to cut the Detroit lead to one goal. The problem for the Avalanche was that time was running out.

Detroit was playing their best defensive hockey of the season in this round of the playoffs. They just seemed to get better and better with each game. At last the Red Wings were dominating their opponents in the Stanley Cup playoffs.

Colorado pulled their goalie in a last ditch effort to force overtime, but Brendan Shanahan took a pass from Igor Larionov and fired it between the pipes. With thirty seconds remaining in game six, the Red Wings had won respect and the right to represent the Western Conference in the Stanley Cup Finals. This time, the underdog Red Wings had spoiled Colorado's bid for a repeat championship.

The Detroit Red Wings were moving on for another opportunity to capture what had eluded them for 42 years, the Stanley Cup. Would this be the year of celebration and joy for the much deserving captain Steve Yzerman? Would all of the past playoff failures finally be laid to rest and forgotten?

If Detroit were to win the Cup, they would have to play flawless hockey against the Philadelphia Flyers. They had just beaten the defending Stanley Cup champions in the Avalanche, but beating the offensively-talented Flyers would be no easy task. The Flyers were loaded with offensive talent, and the Wings had to try to put behind them what had happened in the 1995 Stanley Cup Finals against the New Jersey Devils.

The Detroit Red Wings' previous trip to the Stanley Cup Finals ended in disappointment with a four game sweep by the New Jersey Devils. The opponent for the 1997 Finals was the Philadelphia Flyers. This was the first time ever that these two great hockey franchises had met in the Stanley Cup Finals.

Game one of the Finals was played before a hostile Flyers crowd in Philadelphia. Detroit knew it would be important to win at least one game on the road. They felt as though winning one game in Philadelphia would give them momentum when they returned to Joe Louis Arena.

The Red Wings opened the scoring on a beautiful short-handed goal by Kirk Maltby. Detroit was hoping that the goal by Maltby would set the tone for game one. On the Flyers next power play, the result was not as fortunate for the visiting Red Wings.

The Flyers had a potent power play with the likes of Eric Lindros, John LeClair, and Rob Brind'Amour on the front line. True to form, Brind'Amour continued his scoring assault in the Stanley Cup playoffs when he scored for the eleventh time during the playoffs to even the score at 1-1. As the first period was winding down, the Red Wings were led by another old friend who scored the go ahead goal that put Detroit ahead going into the second period.

Joey Kocur was a Red Wing favorite ever since he became a Red Wing. Kocur was traded away to the New York Rangers where he won a Stanley Cup championship. His former team the Detroit Red Wings, who picked him up from the local beer leagues, reinstated him in the NHL. Most Red Wing fans welcomed the return of Kocur.

He was popular in Hockey Town because he was a bully who knew how to protect his valued superstar teammates. It was quite comforting, if not surprising, when Kocur scored his first goal of the playoffs during the first period of game one to put the Red Wings ahead 2-1 after the first twenty minutes of play.

The second period witnessed two goals that made the game interesting heading into the third period. The fans in Philadelphia were treated to a very entertaining opening game of the Stanley Cup Finals. The Red Wings opened the scoring in the second period to widen their lead to two goals. However, the Flyers' power forward, John LeClair, scored late in the second period to make the game entertaining heading into the third period. With the score 3-2, in favor of the Red Wings, it was almost certain that the game would be decided in the next twenty minutes of play, barring overtime.

Less than one minute into the third period, the game ended with one flick of the wrist. The Red Wings' ageless leader, Steve Yzerman, scored to put the Wings ahead to stay. As a result of Yzerman's goal, the Wings accomplished what they wanted, a victory on the road. Heading into game two this round of the Stanley Cup Finals was already looking more promising than the last trip in 1995.

Going into game two in Philadelphia, the Red Wings were looking for the kill if they could pull off another victory on the hostile ice. The Flyers made the first mistake of replacing veteran goalie, Ron Hextall, with their young inexperienced back-up, Garth Snow. Did the Flyers forget that Hextall had previously won the Conn-Smythe Trophy as the most valuable player in a prior Stanley Cup playoffs?

Less than two minutes into game two, Red Wing forward, Brendan Shanahan, skated in all alone on Snow. Shanahan flipped the puck past him and Detroit was up early 1-0. Perhaps Flyers coach Terry Murray had made an error by starting his young goalie?

Just before the halfway point in the first period, the Red Wings went on the power play. Detroit passed the puck around until they seized the opportunity to go up 2-0 early in game two. Once again, it was Steve Yzerman leading the way on the power play. He was just waiting for the right moment to cash in with a goal. Steve scored his sixth goal of the playoffs, and the Red Wings were off and running in game two.

The Flyers went on the power play with about three minutes left in the first period. Once again, the Flyers looked to Rob Brind'Amour. Brind'Amour beat Mike Vernon for his twelfth goal of the playoffs. About one minute later, Brind'Amour scored his second power play goal of the game to even the score heading into the first intermission.

The famous Grind Line of the Red Wings struck early in the second period to put the visiting Red Wings back on top 3-2. Joey Kocur fed a pass to Kirk Maltby, who scored his second goal in as many games. After two periods in an exciting hockey game, the Red Wings were on the verge of a two-game advantage for their return to Hockey Town.

With 20 minutes left in regulation time, the Red Wings simply had to hold their one goal lead to be two victories away from their illusive prize. Detroit tried to protect their lead in the third period. The Wings were out shot 8-5 in the last twenty minutes. With almost 10 minutes remaining in the game, Brendan Shanahan, scored his second goal of the game to wrap up a 4-2 victory for the Red Wings.

The Wings were returning home to Joe Louis Arena for game three. If Detroit could win, they would be one game away from a long awaited championship. The Red Wings were home in Hockey Town, and the fans were anxious to see their team in action for game three. Hockey Town was buzzing with memories from the good old days, but no one was counting the Flyers out just yet. With the Wings' previous playoff blunders of late, some fans realized that nothing was a guarantee until it was over.

Seven minutes into game three, it was the Flyers who scored. John LeClair scored on the power play to temporarily silence the hometown fans in Detroit. The Flyers had gotten the attention of the fans and had them waiting in anticipation for the next goal.

Exactly two minutes after the Flyers took an early lead, the Red Wings responded with a scoring barrage of their own. A string of consecutive goals by the Red Wings began with Steve Yzerman leading the way. Yzerman scored a power play goal that tied the score at 1-1. Two minutes later in the first period, the Red Wings struck again.

Detroit took a 2-1 advantage in game three when Sergei Federov streaked in alone to beat Ron Hextall. Federov's goal had the hometown fans in Hockey Town believing that the Cup would be presented again in Detroit. One minute before the first period ended, the Red Wings increased their lead.

At the 19:00 minute mark of the first period Martin LaPointe scored his third goal of the playoffs to add to the scoring depth of the well-balanced Red Wings'offensive machine. The Flyers were relying upon John LeClair and Rob Brind'Amour to carry the goal-scoring on their backs. Up to this point of the series, LeClair and Brind'Amour had accounted for all of the goals scored by the Flyers in the Finals.

Detroit scored three goals in the first period by three different players. This Red Wing team was getting contributions from the whole team. Going into the second period, the Flyers had to have a more balanced attack to survive against the Red Wings in the Stanley Cup Finals.

Early in the second period, Detroit widened the gap in game three. Sergei Federov scored his second goal in as many periods. With Federov's power play goal, Detroit found themselves ahead on the scoreboard 4-1. With one period remaining, the Flyers could feel their season slipping away.

Early in the third period, Detroit scored another power play goal to put game three out of reach. Marty LaPointe scored his second goal of the game, and all that remained in game three was the final buzzer. Would game four result in a sweep for the Detroit Red Wings?

What a difference a couple of years could make. Just two years before, the Red Wings were the team scrambling to stay alive in the Stanley Cup Finals. In 1997, the Wings found themselves up in the series 3-0 over the Flyers.

The Detroit Red Wings looked a golden opportunity in the face heading into game four at Joe Louis Arena. Red Wing fans had waited patiently for 42 years to see their hockey team recapture the Stanley Cup. There were good times and bad times, victories and defeats, but there was never a more deserving Red Wing than Steve Yzerman to hoist the Cup.

Yzerman could not sleep well before game four in anticipation of winning his lifelong dream. Yzerman came to the Red Wings when they were at the bottom of the NHL, and some questioned whether he could lead them to the Stanley Cup championship. Red Wing faithful saw him mature and grow into a successful leader and community icon. Yzerman was hoping that on a beautiful June evening at Joe Louis Arena, he would humbly have the opportunity to silence his critics.

The fans had waited a long time to claim the Stanley Cup, but it was Steve Yzerman who paid the ultimate price and was waiting for his moment in the sun. Yzerman took a lot of undeserving criticism that he brushed off as part of the job. He kept his mouth shut, and did his job to the best of his ability. There was no doubt in Hockey Town that Yzerman earned the right to hoist the Stanley Cup above his head. All fans were rooting for him to hoist the Cup after game four.

When it comes to winning a championship, there was no place like home!

Joe Louis Arena was packed for game four, and Red Wing fans nationwide could not wait for this game to begin. Gordie Howe (Mr. Hockey) was present for the game. Howe was one of the last Red Wings who was fortunate enough to win the Stanley Cup 42 years earlier.

The Detroit Red Wings knew they had one more game to win, and they wanted nothing more than to win the championship at home. The fans had waited a long time to have the Stanley Cup hoisted in Hockey Town. The pre-game activities were exciting and the players were eager to get started on both sides.

The game opened with both teams playing good defensive hockey in the first period. With almost thirty seconds left in the first period, Nick Lidstrom found the back of the net to give Detroit a 1-0 lead. The Flyers knew they had to have the next goal in order to have a chance of silencing the fans at Joe Louis Arena.

Philadelphia out shot Detroit in the second period, but Mike Vernon kept the Flyers scoreless. Vernon was outstanding in goal throughout the Stanley Cup playoffs; he was the big reason that the Wings were in the position to win. In the latter half of the second period, Darren McCarty put on some flashy moves that had Ron Hextall sprawling to retrieve the puck that McCarty had deposited into the open net. Going into the third period, the excitement was escalating at Joe Louis Arena. The Red Wings were possibly minutes away from parading the Stanley Cup around a festive Joe Louis Arena.

The third period was a defensive masterpiece. The Flyers had seven shots on goal, and Detroit had seven on Hextall. Detroit was determined to protect the two-goal lead.

The public address announcer made the traditional statement that it was "the last minute of play in the third period." The fans jumped to their feet, sensing that the time had finally come. The Wings could not blow a 2-0 lead in the last minute of play, or could they?

With fifteen seconds remaining, the Flyers cut the lead in half and held on to a slim hope of surviving for a return trip to Philadelphia for a game five. Their captain, Eric Lindros, scored the Flyers' first goal of the game. As the long awaited countdown began, the Flyers managed to dump the puck into the Red Wing zone, but this time Mike Vernon grasped much more than a puck when time expired.

The final buzzer sounded and the celebration began at Joe Louis Arena. Mike Vernon could not leave his crease before an elated Steve Yzerman leaped into his waiting arms. Finally, Yzerman had what he deserved, and what some fans believed he would never bring to Detroit, the Stanley Cup. Any previous bad memories as a Red Wing for Yzerman were erased.

Forty-two years of frustration for the Red Wings organization at long last had been forgotten. Gordie Howe was on hand to witness the new Stanley Cup champions. Even Mr. Hockey had nothing but kind words to compliment the latest captain of the Red Wings. Once again, there was joy in Hockey Town.

After the Wings' mini on ice celebration, they had to line up to shake hands with the Philadelphia Flyers. The Wings felt bad for the Flyers, because just two years ago many of these same Red Wings were on the losing end of the greeting line. Once the Flyers left the ice, the real celebration began.

Gary Bettman, President of the NHL, was at center ice to present the Stanley Cup to the world champions. Bettman introduced Steve Yzerman and handed the cherished Cup over to the captain. Finally, the party was on at Joe Louis Arena.

Life as the captain of the Detroit Red Wings was good, but it was not always that way for Steve Yzerman. He spent many of his last games during the season in disappointment trying to figure out what went wrong. Yzerman often stood by his locker and answered questions for reporters about how the Red Wings failed again. He faced humiliation, and was labeled as a captain who could not lead his team to capture the Stanley Cup. On this special night, Yzerman left the past behind.

Yzerman spoke of watching others in the Stanley Cup Finals and of the winners raising the Cup for the world to see. Finally, in his fourteenth season with the Detroit Red Wings, his time had come. Yzerman immediately wanted to share this trophy with his teammates, but they knew that this was his moment to take the long stroll around the ice surface in front of the hometown fans. Some of the same fans that sold Yzerman out in his early years were watching and celebrating with the new hero of Hockey Town.

Steve Yzerman came to Detroit as a kid, and as he grew, he took the blame for early playoff exits. On June 9, 1997 it was time to watch the Red Wing leader capture what he truly deserved. It was one of the most touching moments in Detroit sports history. It was better than any of the highlights that Yzerman had provided fans with in the past fourteen years as a Detroit Red Wing. When Steve Yzerman skated away with the Stanley Cup it symbolized how this man mirrored his community.

Detroit was a city that was made up of people who worked hard at their jobs and took pride in what they did. The people of Detroit enjoyed watching a good hockey game, but in the end it was always the Red Wings who were number one in the fans' hearts. Detroit was a special place to play hockey in the NHL. They were one of the original six teams in the NHL. The city of Detroit has established a long lasting love affair with the Red Wings.

When Steve Yzerman skated around Joe Louis Arena with the Stanley Cup above his head, he became an instant icon. Some fans had followed Yzerman since the beginning, and some believed that his hard work ethic on and off the ice would one day pay dividends. In the world of sports, things did not always work out as everyone wanted them to be. The same was true in life, but when you gave as much of yourself to others as Yzerman had, there was always a dividend coming somewhere down the road.

All the fans that watched Yzerman grow up in Detroit shared in this special moment with their beloved captain and favorite Red Wing. Many tears of joy came from the celebration, tears that were shed by grown men and women, not because the Red Wings had won the Stanley Cup after 42 years, but because the man who took so much abuse to get them there never gave up.

The tears were for Yzerman, a great leader who inspired many Detroit fans. Yzerman was the man who gave up so much of his time to help others in the community. It was only fitting that his teammates, who gave the utmost respect to him, stood back and let him enjoy his moment of glory.

Steve Yzerman had been with the team the longest, and Red Wing fans abroad knew that this was his team. He solidified his commitment that he had promised the fans so long ago. Steve Yzerman for a few short moments owned the Stanley Cup all to himself. All the fans who waited to see the Cup let him embellish in his special moment. They all felt good, they cheered, but mostly they stood back and watched a real modern day hero reap his long awaited reward.

He came to Detroit as the Renaissance kid who was going to bring respect back to Hockey Town. He was going to restore the tradition in Detroit. At the age of 18, the responsibility and pressure was insurmountable in building the foundation and future for the Detroit Red Wings. The front office had high hopes for the young rookie prospect. They believed that the future success of the Detroit Red Wings centered around the youngest NHL captain in history ever selected by a team.

Joe Louis Arena was filled with joy and celebration. Steve Yzerman took a few strides before he shared the prized Cup with owner Mike Illitch and his family. He skated with the trophy around the ice and held it over his head. Yzerman enjoyed his moment and relished upon who would be next on the Wings to carry the ultimate prize in the NHL.

Steve Yzerman paid the ultimate price to earn the right to carry the Stanley Cup around a festive Joe Louis Arena. He had tried year after year only to fail time and time again, but he never gave up on the Red Wings. He accepted the blame, yet he remained humble with his soft-spoken demeanor. He sacrificed his offensive skills to some degree for the good of the team. He learned how to be a leader and he did it his way. Yzerman also had a lot of help from his friends within the Red Wings organization.

Steve Yzerman knew he was not the only player to sacrifice to win the long lost Stanley Cup in Hockey Town. The two men he selected next to carry the Cup around the Joe Louis Arena had labored tremendously to win the grand prize in hockey. They played together for the Russian Red Army team, they were beaten in 1980 by the United States in the Olympics' famous "Miracle on Ice Game." Now they were teammates of Steve Yzerman, and Yzerman knew the meaning of sacrifice and defeat. He decided that Igor Larionov and Slava Fetisov would carry the Cup next for the Red Wings.

Yzerman knew that these two Russian heroes had given up their homeland and much of their family lives for a short period of time to play in the NHL. Steve knew that they paid a great price to come to Detroit and play for the Red Wings. Yzerman recognized that these two legends might not get another opportunity to hoist the Cup. He admired their bravery and determination. Following the melee on the ice, the party continued in the Red Wing locker room. The players spoke about how great they felt. Scotty Bowman hinted at how successful his plan was, and how grateful he was that the organization let him have his way with the team. Mike Vernon won the Conn-Smythe Trophy and redeemed himself in Hockey Town after his previous playoff failure against the New Jersey Devils in the '95 Finals.

The price that the players paid and the friendships that developed on the team were priceless, and it was evident in the locker room interviews. It was good to see the friendship among the Russian players, and the friendship between Darren McCarty and Kris Draper.

The togetherness of goalies Mike Vernon, and his backup, Chris Osgood, showed that it took more than one good goalie to win a championship. This team built a championship by giving a total effort where all members played a role. However, the core of this unit remained constant for 14 years.

Some of the reporters that hounded Yzerman defeat after defeat in the playoff finale from the past years were on hand to corner him once again in his priceless moment of triumph. He stood next to his locker, just as he always had, his hair matted, and his body exhausted. One thing was missing: the disappointment.

After winning the Stanley Cup, it was much easier for Yzerman to respond to the media. He was relieved, relaxed, and exhausted. The cost that Steve Yzerman had to pay to obtain his goal was much heavier than the physical strain he endured on this glorious night in June.

The shining silver trophy that Yzerman had longed to capture for 14 years was physically heavy, but the long burden and personal sacrifice he had endured was also painfully heavy. After all, 14 years of questioning were answered in an instant when NHL Commissioner Gary Bettman handed over the Stanley Cup for Yzerman to raise above his head. He responded to his critics and now he was a superstar.

The celebration continued well into the next morning inside Joe Louis Arena. Many other Red Wing supporters celebrated peacefully outside Joe Louis Arena. This championship was great for the city of Detroit.

It all began with Steve Yzerman receiving the Stanley Cup at center ice. At three in the morning, Yzerman left Joe Louis Arena with the prized trophy. He loaded the Stanley Cup into his Porsche and headed for the house. The Stanley Cup would not be seen again publicly until it was displayed in a mass celebration that took place on the streets of downtown Detroit.

Forty-two years was a long time for a proud hockey town to wait to reclaim the Stanley Cup. It was not surprising that downtown Detroit streets were lined with people waiting to see the Red Wings victory parade. The summer of '97 would be endless in Detroit.

On June 10, 1997, over one million fans lined the streets of downtown Detroit to join in on the Detroit Red Wings' Stanley Cup parade. The weather was extremely hot, but the fans overcame the heat to get a last glimpse at their newly-crowned world champions. They also came to see the Stanley Cup that had been missing from Hockey Town for 42 years.

Detroit Red Wing fans also came to witness Steve Yzerman enjoy his moment in the hot sun. He held the Cup high above his head while traveling through the streets of downtown Detroit. His wife, Lisa, and their daughter, Isabella, accompanied him. Yzerman felt especially good on this day knowing that so many people were behind him and the Red Wings. When he reached the podium to speak at Hart Plaza, after being driven through a maze of people, the captain was happy to share the moment with the fans that had supported the Red Wings so faithfully. He assured the fans that he would never forget the support they had shown for the team on that hot summer day in June. It was a beautiful parade that Yzerman and the Wings would never forget.

The players enjoyed the Stanley Cup, but tragedy struck that would cast a dark shadow on the celebration. The Red Wings had attended a golf outing and had a good time together as the newly crowned Stanley Cup champions. After the outing had ended, Slava Fetisov, Vladimir Konstantinov, and team masseuse Sergei Mnatsakanov were headed home in a limousine. The driver made an error and the limousine crashed into a tree. All of a sudden, the Stanley Cup was not as important to the Red Wings as their teammates and friends were. Slava Fetisov was injured and would eventually fully recover, but Konstantinov and Mnatsakanov would never return to the sport they loved. Konstantinov and Mnatsakanov suffered severe head injuries and were in critical condition in a nearby suburban Detroit hospital.

The Red Wings' endless summer dream had turned into a nightmare overnight. The team came to visit their teammates and friends in the hospital, but the two could not recognize the love and time that the Red Wings offered.

Konstantinov and Mnatsakanov were both in a coma, and their lives were in danger of ending. Slava Fetisov was injured and released from the hospital, but he still spent much of his time visiting his friends in the hospital, as did many of the Red Wings. Some of the fans and players throughout the NHL offered their prayers and support for the recovery of these two members of the Detroit Red Wings. The hospital received letters from fans voicing their concern and support for Vladimir Konstantinov and Sergei Mnatsakanov. It was the Detroit fans that showed the most interest by placing the concern of these men's lives above the 42 year disappearance of the Stanley Cup.

The best the Red Wings could hope for following the tragic accident was that Konstantinov and Mnatsakanov would come out alive. The team knew they had lost the services of two valuable teammates, both on and off the ice. Going into next season, the Red Wings' incentive to repeat as Stanley Cup champions was focused around Konstantinov and Mnatsakanov.

There was good news and bad news concerning the Detroit Red Wings heading into the 1997-98 season. The good news was that

Konstantinov and Mnatsakanov were slowly recovering and they were never forgotten in Detroit. The bad news was that their careers in hockey were over. The fans poured out love and support, and the players dedicated the upcoming season to there teammates.

The slogan was 'BELIEVE' for the Detroit Red Wings during the 97-98 season. In the vacant locker of injured teammate, Vladimir Konstantinov, the Wings placed a rock with the word 'believe' written on it. The Red Wings believed they could repeat as Stanley Cup champions in spite of the adversity of losing a valuable defenseman.

Some of the so-called hockey experts believed that Detroit could not repeat without the intimidating physical presence of the Vladiator (Vladimir Konstantinov). The Red Wings were eager to get started and had plenty to prove in the upcoming season. Steve Yzerman and the Detroit Red Wings would never forget the two men they had lost as teammates. They made special arrangements to include Konstantinov and Mnatsakanov in their quest to win a second consecutive Stanley Cup championship.

CHAPTER FIFTEEN

AN UN"BELIEVE" ABLE SEASON

After winning the Stanley Cup in 1997 the Red Wings theme for the 1997-98 season was simply BELIEVE. The season was dedicated to two team members who were severely injured in an automobile accident in June of 1997. It was very difficult to win back to back championships in the NHL, but if ever a team could repeat, it was the Red Wings.

The Detroit Red Wings began the 1997-98 season with most of the same players on the roster. A few valuable members were missing and some new faces were added to the roster since the last season. The most notable loss for the Wings was goalie, Mike Vernon, who was sent to San Jose due to his high price tag. Three Russians were missing from behind the Red Wing bench when the season began; it was expected that Vladimir Konstantinov and Sergei Mnatsakanov would not return, but when Sergei Federov did not report to camp, worry began to set in for some fans in Hockey Town.

Without Konstantinov, Vernon, and Federov, the chances of repeating as champs looked dim unless the Red Wings could make some additions that would help them fulfill their promise to repeat for Konstantinov and Mnatsakanov. Many believed that Konstantinov could not be replaced on the blue line for Detroit.

Detroit picked up free agent, Brent Gilchrist, from the Dallas Stars. Gilchrist played an aggressive style of hockey and fit in well with the grinders. Two more late additions were made in an attempt to solidify the defensive core for the Wings. Demitri Mironov came over from Anaheim in exchange for Jamie Pushor, and Jamie Macoun was picked up on waivers from the Toronto Maple Leafs. Kevin Hodson, or 'Ticker' as he was known, played back up to Chris Osgood. As the season began, there were many twists and turns that took place along the way for the defending Stanley Cup champions.

The Wings had to overcome many obstacles in order to repeat and keep the Stanley Cup in Detroit for another year. The Red Wings lost some key players, but one player they did not lose was their leader. Steve Yzerman believed in his teammates and their commitment to win the Stanley Cup for their missing teammates.

The Winter Olympics interrupted the season in February, 1998. The Wings sent several players to the Olympic Games. Team Canada selected Brendan Shanahan and Steve Yzerman from the Wings in an attempt to win the gold medal. The Canadian team was one of the favorites to win the gold medal.

The Canadians lost to the Czech Republic in a shoot out eliminating them from entering the gold medal round. Dominic Hasek stopped all five breakaway shots by the Canadians in the shoot-out. Detroit Red Wing Brendan Shanahan was selected as one of the five shooters. Oddly enough, the coach, Mark Crawford, and other Canadian members of the hockey team did not select either Wayne Gretzky or Steve Yzerman in the shoot-out.

Team Canada lost in the bronze medal game and left the Olympics in Nagano, Japan, finishing with a disappointing fourth place finish. The gold medal went to the Czech Republic, the team that they came so close to beating.

Following the Olympics, Steve Yzerman was rejuvenated and returned to the Red Wings with a new source of energy. The captain played some of the best hockey of his career after the Olympic break. Yzerman put the Olympic disappointment behind him and concentrated on his ultimate goal, keeping the Stanley Cup in Hockey Town for his fallen teammates.

Sergei Federov was offered an outrageous multi-million dollar contract by the Carolina Hurricanes. The Red Wings agreed to match the offer in order to keep Federov in a Red Wing uniform.

Detroit finished the regular season with a 44-23-15 record. Once again Detroit finished behind Colorado and Dallas in third position in the Western Conference. Leading the way in scoring with a blazing second half of the season was Steve Yzerman. He played 75 games, seven short of the 82 scheduled games for the Red Wings.

Yzerman led the team in scoring, primarily because he turned up his scoring touch after the Olympics ended. He had 24 goals and 45 assists for a total of 69 points. He was 10 points ahead of Nicklas Lidstrom, who played five more games than the captain.

Detroit was looking good heading into the first round of the playoffs against the Phoenix Coyotes. The team was relatively healthy at the conclusion of the regular season. The Red Wings opened at home against Phoenix for game one.

Detroit began with a fast pace in the opening period of the first game. The Wings' quest to retain the prized Stanley Cup was off to a brilliant start. A little better than five and a half minutes into the first period, the Red Wings opened the scoring.

Steve Yzerman passed the puck back to Larry Murphy, who fed a pass to Nick Lidstrom, who fired a slap shot past Nikolai Khabibulin. Detroit was ahead early in game one. The Wings looked very good on the power play. If Phoenix hoped of upsetting the defending Stanley Cup champions, they had to avoid taking senseless penalties.

About five minutes later in the first period, the Wings were poised to strike again. This time, the scoring hero was an unlikely candidate to add to the 1-0 lead. Martin Lapointe fed a pass to line mate Joey Kocur, who slid one past Khabibulin. Detroit was off to a good start in defense of the Stanley Cup early in this series.

The eventful first period had two more goals added on to the scoreboard. The Coyotes cut the Wings' lead in half when Rick Tocchet scored the first goal of the series for the visitors. Only a minute later, Sergei Federov scored the final goal of the first period.

Three goals were scored in a wild second period of game one at Joe Louis Arena. The Detroit Red Wings added to their lead when Darren McCarty scored his first goal of the 98 playoffs. Martin Lapointe teamed up for the second time in the game when he fed a pass to Joey Kocur who scored his second goal of the game. Two goals in two periods was more than Scotty Bowman had expected from one of his role players, but Kocur contributed with his scoring skills in this game. With just 10 seconds remaining in the second period, the Wings extended their lead to 6-1 when Steve Yzerman found Kirk Maltby to finish the scoring in the second period.

After two periods, Detroit seemed to have the game in hand, but Phoenix had to make a statement for game two. The Coyotes needed to let Detroit know that they would be ready in game two and that they would not roll over and hand this series to the Red Wings without a fight. Cliff Ronning scored for Phoenix to cut the margin to 6-2. With nine minutes remaining, Phoenix scored on a goal by Bob Corkum, and suddenly the score was 6-3. The game ended with Detroit winning 6-3, but the Coyotes set the tone for game two in the third period. Going into game two, Detroit had everything in their favor. They were playing at home again and they had one win under their belt. Game two began just the way the Coyotes ended game one. A little better than two minutes into the game the Coyotes went on the power play. Mike Gartner scored to carry over the momentum Phoenix had gained in the third period of game one. With nine minutes left in the first period, the Coyotes extended their lead to 2-0 when Keith Tkachuk beat Chris Osgood. Suddenly, things looked gloomy for the defending Stanley Cup champions.

Thirteen seconds following the second goal by Phoenix, the Red Wings began to fight back. Igor Larionov scored to cut the Phoenix lead to 2-1. Heading into the second period the Red Wings knew they would have to pick up the tempo to go up 2-0 in the series.

Six goals were scored in the second period, but the bad news was that most of the goals belonged to the visitors. Rick Tocchet scored first for the Coyotes to widen the lead to 3-1. Phoenix added two short-handed goals, both scored by Jeremy Roenick. With seven minutes remaining in the second period, the Red Wings had fallen behind 5-1.

Eight seconds after Roenick scored, the Wings began a comeback, but they had a long way to go before they could win this game. Mathieu Dandenault scored a power play goal that gave the Wings slim hopes of mounting a comeback. With the score 5-2, it was crucial that Detroit score the next goal.

Nineteen seconds after Dandenault scored, it was Coyote captain, Keith Tkachuk, who netted his second goal of the playoffs to increase the Phoenix lead to 6-2. Detroit was not through just yet. Sergei Federov closed the wild second period when he scored to decrease the deficit to three goals heading into the third period.

Phoenix and Detroit exchanged goals in the final period. Phoenix scored early in the third on Keith Tkachuk's second goal of the game. The Red Wings found themselves behind in a shoot out. Detroit added the final goal when Sergei Federov scored to make the final score 7-4, advantage Coyotes.

The underdog, Phoenix Coyotes were heading home with the series knotted at 1-1. They felt confident after their shellacking of the defending Stanley Cup champions in game two. The Coyotes gleamed about their chances of winning game three against the Red Wings. The Coyotes just scored seven goals against one of the best defensive teams in the NHL, so they had every reason to believe they could win against Detroit in game three.

Detroit was off to a quick start in game three, and it appeared as though this game would belong to the visiting Red Wings. Sergei

Federov opened the scoring with his fourth goal of the playoffs. Federov scored just 30 seconds into the game. Seconds later it was Brendan Shanahan who scored to put Detroit ahead 2-0 early in game three. After one period of play, the Red Wings had the game under control.

Neither team scored during the second period, and it looked as though the Wings would win game three going into the third. Phoenix had 13 shots on goal and Detroit only had eight. The Coyotes were hoping that any momentum they had gained would carry over into the third period.

The Coyotes had the crowd on their side and were well aware that they could overcome a two-goal deficit. Rick Tocchet scored his fourth goal of the playoffs less than one minute into the third. Tocchet's goal cut the Wings' lead to one goal. Jeremy Roenick scored the next goal to tie the game at 2-2.

The next goal was key in this hockey game. The third period was a defensive battle, but the Wings managed to out shoot Phoenix. Detroit registered nine shots to the Coyotes six, but the outcome left Chris Osgood stunned in disbelief.

Jeremy Roenick scored his second goal of the period to complete the comeback against the defending world champions in game three. Detroit let a two-goal lead slip away in the third period. Now they found themselves behind in the series 2-1. Game four would be played in Phoenix, advantage Coyotes.

Game four began the way it ended for Phoenix in the first period. About halfway through, Rick Tocchet scored again. The goal by Tocchet was his fifth of the series. The Coyotes had an early lead in game four. If the Red Wings could not turn things around in the second period, they faced possible elimination upon their return home for game five.

The Red Wings showed resilience by scoring early and often in the second period. They came out with great jump and focus. Igor Larionov scored early to even the score at 1-1. Three minutes later, Vyacheslav Kozlov added to the Wings' lead with his first goal of the playoffs. The next goal proved to be the backbreaker for the Coyotes. With one second remaining in the second period, Red Wing defenseman, Jamie Macoun, beat Phoenix backup goalie, Jimmy Waite, to give Detroit a 3-1 lead.

The third period was evenly played between both teams. Detroit's Nicklas Lidstrom opened the scoring to increase their lead to 4-1. Phoenix scored late in the game when Shane Doan scored his first goal of the playoffs. The final score in game four was Detroit 4, Phoenix 2. The

Red Wings went home for game five with the series knotted at two games each, advantage Red Wings.

The Detroit Red Wings returned home to Joe Louis Arena eager to get started in game five. They felt they had the upper hand because Jimmy Waite had to replace the injured Khabibulan. Game five began exactly the way Detroit had hoped it would. Tomas Holmstrom (The Demolition Man) scored on a pass from Slava Kozlov to give Detroit a 1-0 lead. Phoenix answered later in the first period to tie the game after the first 20 minutes, giving Rick Tocchet his sixth goal of the playoffs. He was unstoppable in this series, keeping the Coyotes alive in the series. He was averaging better than one goal per game.

Detroit responded in the first period to the onslaught by Tocchet to take a 2-1 lead into the second period. Vyacheslav Kozlov scored his second goal to put Detroit ahead in game five. After one period of play, the Wings led 2-1.

Detroit knew that if they could score the next goal, they would be in good shape in game five. The Wings played flawless defense in the second period, and managed the only goal of the period. Sergei Federov scored his fifth goal to give Detroit a 3-1 lead. Federov was proving to be a thorn in the side for the Coyotes. While Detroit could not stop Tocchet, Phoenix could not figure out how to counter against Federov.

Both teams played evenly in the third period. Neither team managed to score and the series returned to Phoenix with Detroit up 3-2. Detroit wanted desperately to win game six and gain a little rest before facing their next opponent.

The Red Wings knew they had to play one of the finest games of the season to eliminate the Phoenix Coyotes. Detroit knew that Phoenix would be ready to play in front of their home crowd. The Coyotes came out focused, playing one shift at a time.

Less than halfway through the first period, the Coyotes drew first blood. Jeremy Roenick scored his fifth goal on the power play to give the Coyotes a 1-0 advantage. With about five minutes remaining in the period, the Red Wings had a power play opportunity.

Steve Yzerman provided the spark that the Red Wings needed with his first goal of the playoffs. Yzerman took a pass from Brendan Shanahan and buried his shot behind Jimmy Waite. The goal by Yzerman resulted in the first period ending in a 1-1 tie.

The second period began the way the Coyotes hoped that it would, with a scoring touch. Keith Tkachuk scored two minutes into the period, putting the Coyotes back on top, 2-1. The Red Wings had to play catch up in order to try to put away the pesky group from Phoenix.

Penalties marked the end of the season for the Coyotes against the defending Stanley Cup champions. Brendan Shanahan tied the score on a power play with his second goal of the series. He added one more power play goal in the second period to put Detroit up 3-2, deeming the next goal critical in this hockey game.

Sergei Federov could not be accused of not showing up for this series against Phoenix. Federov was criticized in the past Stanley Cup playoffs for his lack of production offensively for the Red Wings. With less than two minutes remaining in the second period, Federov cashed in on another power play opportunity for the Red Wings. The goal by Federov was his sixth of the playoffs, and after two periods, the scoreboard read Detroit 4, Phoenix 2.

Phoenix had to find a way to rally back and tie the score to extend their season. The Wings outshot Phoenix 18-4 in the second period. The Coyotes would need to score early and often in the third period.

The third period was a real defensive struggle for both teams. The Red Wings were the only team to score in the third. One of the Grind Line players, Brent Gilchrist, scored the final goal of the series. Following the victory against Phoenix, the Red Wings prepared for their next opponent, a familiar foe and formidable opponent, the St. Louis Blues.

The Red Wings opened the series on home ice against the Blues, who had improved defensively since they had met Detroit in the previous Stanley Cup playoffs. When two teams having good defense meet in the playoffs, the series is usually determined by the goalies. This series matched Chris Osgood against Grant Fuhr, a match-up that has been repeated over and over.

Game one at Joe Louis Arena began ironically with a defenseman scoring. St. Louis scored first when Todd Gill recorded his first goal of the playoffs. Less than four minutes into game one, the Blues led 1-0 over the defending Stanley Cup champions.

Scotty Bowman relied upon his role players to score, especially against a good defensive team like St. Louis. Martin Lapointe scored the only goal of the second period to even the score at 1-1.

The Blues opened the third period with a barrage of goals, lighting the scoreboard like a Christmas tree. Jim Campbell opened the scoring for the Blues when he scored just 18 seconds into the third period.

Brett Hull widened the Blues' lead when he beat Chris Osgood to give St. Louis a 3-1 advantage. Hull, the son of former NHL great, Bobby Hull, contributed in the Stanley Cup playoffs. The goal by Hull was his third of the playoffs. The Blues were not finished scoring in the third period.

Jim Campbell scored exactly seven minutes after Brett Hull to put the Blues ahead by a comfortable three-goal margin with less than 10 minutes remaining. The goal by Campbell was his second of the game and fifth of the playoffs. Suddenly, unexpected heroes were emerging for the Blues.

Late in the period, the Red Wings hoped to make a statement for game two. Tomas Holmstrom scored on the power play on a pass from Steve Yzerman. As the buzzer sounded to end the game, the Wings found themselves down 1-0 in the best of seven series.

Game two at Joe Louis Arena was a must-win for Detroit. They could not afford to get behind 2-0 against the Blues. Detroit had to take advantage of home ice before the series moved to St. Louis for game three.

Less than halfway through the first period, the Blues picked up where they had left off in game one. The Blues scored on a power play goal by Terry Yake.

Detroit went on the power play shortly before the first period expired. The Wings responded with the equalizer when Martin Lapointe scored his second goal of the playoffs. After one period of play the scoreboard read 1-1.

After the first period, it was the Red Wings who were trying to even the series at one game apiece.

Detroit had to respond in the second period if they hoped to put the Blues away in game two. Less than halfway through the second period, it was the Wings who scored first. Nick Lidstrom beat Grant Fuhr to record his third goal of the playoffs. Lidstrom's goal was crucial for Detroit; it seemed to set the tone for the remainder of the game.

The Red Wings increased their lead to two goals when Tomas Holmstrom beat Fuhr. Holmstrom notched his third goal of the playoffs with help from Sergei Federov. The goal scored by Holmstrom was not the last tally of the second period.

With less than two minutes remaining in the second period, it was Steve Yzerman who cashed in to cushion the Detroit lead heading into the third period. Yzerman put the Wings ahead by a 4-1 count, and Detroit was looking to add to their lead in the third period so that they could carry over the momentum when the series shifted to St. Louis for game three.

During the third period, Detroit secured a victory in game two with a couple of more goals to add to their 4-1 lead. Larry Murphy scored his first goal of the playoffs with less than two minutes left in the third period. Kirk Maltby finished the scoring for Detroit with only 20 seconds remaining in the game.

After two games, the series was tied one game each. The series continued back in St. Louis for game three and game four.

It was important for the Red Wings to get off to a good start in game three on the road. With three minutes gone in the first period, Darren McCarty beat Grant Fuhr to put Detroit up 1-0. Red Wing captain, Steve Yzerman, assisted on McCarty's goal.

Late in the first period, Al MacInnis fired one of his blistering slapshots past Chris Osgood for a power play goal. After 20 minutes of play, the Red Wings were in good shape with the score tied at 1-1 on the road. It was the goal of the visitors to try and take the home crowd out of the game early on. Going into the second period, Detroit hoped to take the lead to take away any momentum that St. Louis may have gained.

One goal was scored during the second period to the delight of the Red Wings. Tomas Holmstrom was known for his hard work ethic in front of the opposing goalies. Holmstrom scored his fourth goal of the playoffs with help from Kozlov and Federov. Holmstrom's lone goal in the second period put the Red Wings up 2-1 after 40 minutes of game three.

Al MacInnis scored the only goal of the third period with less than one minute remaining in the period. The goal by MacInnis tied the score at 2-2. Game three was decided in dramatic style in overtime.

Neither team scored in the first 20 minute overtime period. The longer Detroit could hang around on the road, the better their chances of winning were. During the second overtime, the game ended. Brendan Shanahan scored his fourth and most important goal of the playoffs. Detroit battled hard and won a key game in the best of seven series with the Blues.

The scoring in game four was well spread out for the Red Wings. In the first period, Brendan Shanahan picked up where he had left off in game three. Shanahan scored his fifth goal of the playoffs to put Detroit up 1-0 less than halfway through the first period of game four; it ended with just one goal scored by the visiting Detroit Red Wings.

It did not take long into the second period for the scoring to continue. Joey Kocur took a pass from Kris Draper and beat Grant Fuhr with a nifty move. Twenty-two seconds later, the scoring assault continued.

The Blues stayed in the game by scoring the next goal and cutting the Detroit lead to one goal. Jim Campbell, one of the Blues most consistent players in the series, scored the first goal of the game for his team. The goal by Campbell was his sixth of the playoffs. The Blues were now back in the game trailing by one goal with more than half of the game to be played.

The second period was all St. Louis, as the Blues tied the score with time running out in the period. Pierre Turgeon scored for the Blues with just seven seconds left. The Blues were hopeful that the momentum they had gained would carry over into the next 20 minutes. The Red Wings, who only generated four shots on goal, were confident that they could improve their performance in the third period.

It did not take the Red Wings long to respond. Slava Kozlov scored his third goal of the playoffs at the 1:12 mark. If Detroit could score the next goal, they would be in the driver's seat in game four.

St. Louis went on the power play with about 12 minutes remaining in the third period. Sergei Federov took off on a breakaway pass from Kris Draper toward the Blues goalie. Federov streaked down the ice and beat Grant Fuhr with a nice move to put Detroit up 4-2. The short-handed goal by Federov all but sealed the win for the visiting Red Wings.

The Blues pulled their goalie in desperation to score and get back into game four, but the move backfired. Sergei Federov scored his second goal of the period when he shot the puck into the empty net. The Red Wings won game four 5-2, and were now up in the series 3-1.

With the series returning to Detroit for game five, the Wings were in a good position. Detroit needed only one more victory to end the series against the Blues. The Detroit Red Wings were looking forward to game five with confidence.

The fans at Joe Louis Arena were eagerly awaiting the return of the Red Wings. They were hopeful that the Wings would win game five and eliminate the St. Louis Blues. The first period was very important for both teams to gain momentum in this important game.

The first period was a display of defensive talent. Fifteen total shots were directed toward the goalies. Both goalies were perfect, as neither team scored in the first 20 minutes.

All of the scoring in game five took place in the second period. The Blues opened the scoring when Geoff Courtnall scored less than two minutes into the period. One minute later, the Blues added to their lead when Mike Eastwood beat Chris Osgood.

Later in the second period, the Blues went on the power play. St. Louis scored their final goal of the game when Todd Gill found the back of the net with his shot. Less than half way through the game, St. Louis found themselves leading 3-0 at Joe Louis Arena.

St. Louis went on another power play two minutes after the goal by Gill. If the Blues scored, game five would have seemingly been over. Steve Yzerman fed a pass to a wide-open Martin Lapointe while playing short-handed. Lapointe did the rest as he cruised in on Grant Fuhr to score for Detroit. The second period ended with St. Louis on top 3-1 after 40 minutes of play.

The Red Wings came out with momentum in the third period and played excellent defense allowing just one shot on goal by the Blues throughout the entire third period. The problem for Detroit was they could not muster any scoring offense of their own. St. Louis won game five, and with the series returning to the Keil Center for game six, the Blues were feeling confident about their chances to force a game seven.

An onslaught of power play goals decided game six. The lack of discipline and penalties also determined the fate of the game. Detroit knew they would have to come out storming in the first period to take the crowd and the Blues out of the game.

Darren McCarty opened the scoring for Detroit on a nice pass from his line mate and friend, Kris Draper. About two minutes later, the Red Wings went on the power play. If they could score with the man advantage, they would have St. Louis backed into a corner in game six.

Doug Brown took a pass from Steve Yzerman and fired the puck past Grant Fuhr to put Detroit up 2-0. The first 20 minutes ended with the Wings leading by a two-goal margin. It was critical for the Blues to score the next goal in the hockey game.

Early in the second period, it was Detroit who scored to apparently put the series away. Martin Lapointe scored on a pass from Nick Lidstrom and the Red Wings were suddenly leading 3-1 in game six. The goal by Lapointe came on the power play, the second power play goal of the game for Detroit.

Nearly two minutes later at even strength, Martin Lapointe took a pass from Steve Yzerman and buried it behind Fuhr. Lapointe's second goal of the period extended the Wings' lead over the Blues to 4-1. The second period belonged to Marty Lapointe and his teammates. St. Louis was in a desperate do- or-die situation heading into the third.

The period belonged to Tomas Holmstrom and Steve Yzerman. The game, series, and match belonged to the defending Stanley Cup champs. Tomas Holmstrom took a pass from Steve Yzerman and beat Grant Fuhr who was pulled after Homer's goal. Tomas Holmstrom returned the favor to Yzerman with a pass that sent Yzerman cruising in on backup goalie, Jamie McLennan.

The captain skated in alone on McLennan and found nothing but the net to record his third goal of the playoffs. Steve Yzerman recorded four points in game six, the clincher for the Red Wings. The goal by Yzerman came on the power play. Detroit scored three power play goals in the game.

St. Louis hoped they could spoil the shutout bid by Chris Osgood in front of the hometown fans at the Keil Center. With the Blues on the power play late in the game, Jim Campbell netted his seventh goal of the playoffs. The game ended with Detroit winning by a 6-1 score, and four games to two in the best of seven series. With the Blues behind them, Detroit was off to Dallas to take on the Stars in the Western Conference Finals.

The Dallas Stars won the President's Trophy for the best record during the regular season. This honor won them home ice advantage throughout the playoffs. Detroit knew they were up against a tough opponent in the Western Conference Finals.

The series opener matched two excellent defenses, powerful offenses, and two of the best goalies in the NHL. Between the pipes for the Red Wings was Chris Osgood, who seemed poised to carry Detroit to a repeat Stanley Cup championship. In net for the Stars was Ed Belfour, who did not have a winning past history against the Red Wings in the playoffs. In this series, goaltending proved to be crucial for the winning team.

Defense dictated the first period of game one between the Stars and the Wings. Detroit managed only seven shots on goal, and Dallas had only six on Chris Osgood. Neither team scored in the first 20 minutes. Going into the second period, it appeared as though one goal might be enough to decide game one in Dallas.

The Red Wings were on the power play early in the second period and Dallas paid for the penalty. Vyacheslav Kozlov scored his fourth goal of the playoffs on the power play. Less than one minute into the second period, Detroit was ahead on the scoreboard. The shot total decreased in the second period from what it was in the first twenty minutes.

Detroit had just six shots on goal, and Dallas managed only four against the stubborn Red Wings defense. It was Detroit who made their shots count. Marty Lapointe scored the Wings' second goal of the period to give Detroit a 2-0 lead heading into the third period. If the Red Wings could continue to master the Stars defensively, Dallas would be in for a long final 20 minutes at Reunion Arena.

In the final 20 minutes, Detroit displayed another show of defensive brilliance against the home team. The Red Wings were not able to score any goals against Ed Belfour in the final period, and they only allowed Dallas four shots on goal in the third period. Chris Osgood stopped every shot he faced in game one. The final score was Detroit 2, Dallas 0. The Wings were beginning to BELIEVE that they could win the Stanley Cup for their long lost teammates, Konstantinov and Mnatsakanov.

The way Detroit was playing defense, it was clear that the loss of Konstantinov from the blue-line truly motivated his teammates. In game two, the Dallas Stars had to figure out a way to answer to the Red Wings' selfish defense. The Dallas Stars managed only six shots on goal in the first period of game two at Reunion Arena. The famous left wing lock defensive system that the Red Wing coaches implemented was working to perfection in the playoffs. The Wings were playing their defensive roles to perfection. They bought into the system from Yzerman, Federov, Shanahan, right on down to the defensemen.

During the first period, Detroit had only registered six shots on goal against Dallas. Once again, it looked as though one goal would be the difference in this game. This time, it was the Stars who drew first blood when Bob Bassen scored his first goal of the playoffs against Chris Osgood.

In the second period, the offense came to life, as two goals were scored by the two powerhouse teams. Greg Adams of the Stars scored at 11:12 to give Dallas a 2-0 lead in game two. Less than two minutes later, the Red Wings responded when Slava Kozlov beat Ed Belfour to cut the deficit to one goal. The Red Wings entered the third period of game two down by just one goal.

The third period was another defensive struggle. The Red Wings out shot Dallas 10-7, but only one goal was scored. Time was running out and the Wings pulled their goalie to try to tie the score with the Stars.

With just 12 seconds remaining, the move backfired for Detroit. Guy Carboneau placed a long shot accurately into the empty net and game two belonged to the Stars. The final score was Dallas 3, Detroit 1.

The series was heading back to Detroit with both teams winning one game in Dallas. Game three could be the pivotal game in the Western Conference Finals. The Red Wings needed a victory back in front of the hometown fans at Joe Louis Arena. They needed a quick start in the first period to set the tone for game three. Detroit was counting on their depth in the series against the Stars. Detroit was able to throw out three to four good lines that were stacked with key role players.

Brent Gilchrist, a former Dallas Star who was acquired to play a key role for Detroit in the playoffs, scored the first goal. Gilchrist took a pass from Steve Yzerman and beat Ed Belfour to give Detroit an early lead in game three. The crowd was rocking at Joe Louis Arena, just what the Wings had hoped for.

The next goal was scored on the power play. The Red Wings cashed in when Nicklas Lidstrom beat Belfour to give Detroit a 2-0 lead. Detroit was happy to escape with a 2-0 lead because they were out shot by the Stars 13-7 after the first 20 minutes.

Dallas was in a position that was not to their liking. They had to find a way to silence the crowd at Joe Louis Arena. The next goal was critical.

The first half of game three belonged to the Red Wings, but the Stars dominated the second half. The Wings opened the scoring in the second period when Nicklas Lidstrom whistled one past Belfour to put his team up 3-0 against Dallas, and everything seemed to be going well for the home team.

Role player, Jamie Macoun, who added his second goal of the playoffs, put Detroit up by a four-goal margin. Such a lead seemed impossible to overcome with these two defensive-minded teams. Dallas had to get the next goal if they had any hopes of mounting a comeback in game three against Detroit.

Jere Lehtinen scored with less than seven minutes left in the second period. The goal by Lehtinen gave his team hope that they could bounce back to even the score later. After 40 minutes of play, things were looking good for the Wings in game three of the Western Conference Finals against the Dallas Stars.

Three goals were scored in the third period when the Red Wings registered just five shots on goal. Lehtinen picked up the scoring where he had left off earlier; the goal by Lehtinen cut the Detroit lead to 4-2. If

Dallas could get another quick goal, they would be back in game three. Suddenly, it looked as if the Wings were beginning to let this one slip away.

Less than halfway through the third period, Mike Modano beat Chris Osgood to make a real game out of this contest. The goal by Modano gave the Stars a real chance as the scoreboard read Detroit 4, Dallas 3. With about 12 minutes to play, the next goal proved to be crucial.

With five minutes to play in regulation time, the Red Wings were not generating any offense. The Red Wings appeared to be hanging on for their lives in this game. Detroit was searching for a break that would end the game.

Dallas was shadowing every move made by the Wings, but one lucky break and Detroit could put an end to the battle. It was the sign of a champion to have resilience when they faced adversity, and the three unanswered goals by the Stars was an adverse situation Detroit had created. Detroit was in a situation where they had to produce in order to establish superiority for the remainder of the series with Dallas.

The Detroit Red Wings answered the call with a goal late in the third period. Marty Lapointe scored his seventh goal of the playoffs with help from Vyacheslav Kozlov. The Red Wings held on to win game three by a 5-3 score. With game three behind them, Detroit had a chance to widen the lead in the series while playing at home in game four.

Dallas went on the power play early in the first period of game four, but it was Detroit who responded with a short-handed goal. Kirk Maltby, a member of The Grind Line, skated in alone on Ed Belfour, where he deposited a nifty shot past the Stars goalie.

With about eight minutes remaining, Detroit went on the power play and added to their lead. This time, Steve Yzerman broke in alone on Ed Belfour. Yzerman beat Belfour for his fourth goal of the playoffs. The goal by Yzerman gave the Red Wings a 2-0 lead at the first intermission.

One goal was scored in the second period on another breakaway. The defense seemed to be breaking down in game four. The breakaway goal by Pat Verbeek for the Stars was the third penalty shot type goal scored in the game. The goal by Verbeek cut the Detroit lead to just one goal with 20 minutes remaining in regulation time.

Dallas opened the third period on the power play, giving them a golden opportunity to even the score with plenty of time left. Less than one minute into the third, Sergei Zubov scored to knot the game at two goals each. The next goal would prove to be the difference in game four.

The Red Wings knew they had to get the next goal in game four. Detroit broke out to an early two-goal advantage in game four and seemed to be cruising along in the first period. Dallas had the momentum in the third period after scoring two unanswered goals. The Stars knew that if they could get the next goal it would turn the series around.

With nine minutes and 30 seconds remaining in the game, it happened. Steve Yzerman assisted on Vyacheslav Kozlov's sixth and most important goal of the playoffs. The goal by Kozlov gave Detroit a 3-2 lead that they would not relinquish in game four. The Red Wings had a chance to wrap up the series in game five at Reunion Arena.

Dallas was one game away from elimination against the Stanley Cup champion Detroit Red Wings. Detroit learned from experience to take out an opponent when they had them on the ropes. The Stars had other plans for the Red Wings. Dallas hoped for a return match in Detroit in game six.

The scoring began with a goal by the former Colorado Avalanche thorn in the Red Wings side. The Dallas version of a grinder, Mike Keane, opened the scoring for the Stars in game five. Detroit was in need of a goal before the first period ended.

The Wings went on the power play late in the first period with a chance to even the score. Red Wing grinder, Tomas Holmstrom, scored with less than one minute remaining to tie the score at 1-1 after the first 20 minutes of play. Detroit was feeling confident that they would return to the Stanley Cup Finals on this June summer night.

One goal was scored in the second period. Igor Larionov scored for Detroit to give his team a 2-1 advantage heading into the third period. If the Red Wings could hold on to their slim lead for 20 more minutes, they would be guaranteed a return trip to defend their Stanley Cup championship.

Detroit knew that Dallas would come out reeling in the third period. The Stars had to turn up the offense or face elimination at home. Detroit had to be careful not to just lay back and protect their one goal lead.

Detroit surrendered 15 shots on goal to the Stars in the third period. The Wings were indeed trying to hold off the Stars. With two minutes remaining, the Red Wings looked as though they were headed to their second consecutive Stanley Cup Finals. It was getting close to the time that Dallas would have to pull their goalie to bring out an extra attacker.

With about one minute and 30 seconds remaining, veteran forward, Guy Carboneau, battled behind the Wings net to gain control of the puck in the Detroit zone. Five seconds later, Carboneau stationed himself in perfect position to fire one past Chris Osgood. The goal by Carboneau deadlocked the score at 2-2. Game five was headed for overtime in Dallas.

Less than one minute into overtime, game five ended. Jamie Langenbrunner took a long range slap shot toward Chris Osgood. The puck skipped off the flat ice surface and past Osgood into the net. Game five, in a come-from-behind fashion, Dallas won by a score of 3-2. Heading into game six, the Stars had gained momentum.

The good news for Detroit was that they were returning home for game six. The fans at Joe Louis Arena were eager for things to get started. Chris Osgood was the topic of adverse conversation in Hockey Town. He knew he had to come through in game six or face more criticism from the Detroit media. The first goal in game six was scored in unexpected fashion. Dallas went on the power play with about 14 minutes left in the first period. Veteran defenseman, Larry Murphy, beat Ed Belfour to give the Wings a shorthanded goal and a 1-0 lead.

At the first intermission, the Red Wings were ahead on the scoreboard and knew if they could score the next goal Dallas would be in big trouble. Less than two minutes into the second period, it was Larry Murphy who figured in the scoring again. Murphy spotted a streaking Sergei Federov and fed him a perfect pass. Federov broke in on Belfour and deposited his ninth goal of the playoffs past a sprawling Belfour. Detroit found themselves up 2-0 early in game six.

With a two-goal lead heading into the third period, the Red Wings had to be careful not to play too defensively and let this one slip away as they had done in game five. One significant difference in game six was that Osgood seemed to be focused and determined to silence his critics once and for all. He was enjoying the moment, and after two periods, he was perfect between the pipes for the defending Stanley Cup champions.

Both teams had good chances to score in the final 20 minutes. The defense was good on both sides, and when the final buzzer sounded, it was Chris Osgood who had the last laugh by recording a shutout to send him and his teammates on a return trip to the Stanley Cup Finals. With Dallas out of the way, the Red Wings could concentrate on their next opponent.

162

Detroit faced the Washington Capitals for the first time ever in the Stanley Cup Finals. Detroit enjoyed home ice advantage in the Finals best of seven series. The Red Wings were determined to win for their fallen comrades Mnastakanov and Konstantinov who were slowing progressing from their near fatal auto accident in June 1997. If Detroit was to repeat as Stanley Cup champs, they would have to solve the mystery of how to crack Olaf Kolzig, also known as Oly The Goalie.

CHAPTER SIXTEEN

THE CAPTAIN PULLS OFF A REAL "CONN" JOB...

The Conn-Smythe Trophy was awarded to the most valuable player of the Stanley Cup playoffs. In 1997, the recipient was Mike Vernon of the Detroit Red Wings. Vernon left Detroit during the off season. The Wings hoped to have a repeat representative win the Conn-Smythe Trophy in 1998, following the Stanley Cup Finals against the Washington Capitals.

The number one goal of the Detroit Red Wings was to win the Stanley Cup for a second consecutive year in 1998. If Detroit could repeat as champions, the Conn-Smythe Trophy would take care of itself. Individual goals were secondary for the defending Stanley Cup champions. The Wings were focused on winning for Konstantinov and Mnatsakanov, and keeping the Cup in Hockey Town.

Several of the Detroit Red Wings were in the running for the Conn-Smythe Trophy heading into the Finals. Sergei Federov was enjoying a good playoff season with nine goals going into the final round of the playoffs. Chris Osgood had a legitimate shot at winning the Conn-Smythe Trophy if he played outstanding in the Finals. Martin Lapointe and Tomas Holmstrom were playing well and had an outside shot at the award given to the best player during the Stanley Cup playoffs. Steve Yzerman was playing good hockey all around in the playoffs; he seemed to be doing well in all aspects of the game.

Steve Yzerman could not be overlooked for the Conn-Smythe Trophy if Detroit won the series against Washington. Yzerman was scoring, assisting, playing well defensively, blocking shots, providing leadership, killing penalties, and winning key face-offs time and time again in the playoffs. If Steve could have a good effort in the final round, he had a good chance of truly being the Red Wings' most valuable player in the 1998 playoff season. First, the Detroit Red Wings had to beat a formidable opponent in the best of seven series in order to accomplish anything in the 97-98 season. Second best meant nothing in the NHL. The only thing that mattered was who possessed the Cup, Lord Stanley's prized possession.

The Washington Capitals were well aware that they had to have a win at Joe Louis Arena in order to have any real chance of winning the series. The stage was set for game one in Hockey Town. The Red Wings faithful were anxiously awaiting the drop of the puck to begin game one in the Stanley Cup Finals.

The quest for the Cup ran through Hockey Town once again. The defending Stanley Cup champions were poised and ready to defend their title. Game one began where the NHL season had ended the previous year when the Red Wings defeated the Philadelphia Flyers in the Stanley Cup Finals.

It was a difficult task to repeat as champions in the National Hockey League. Few teams of late have won back to back championships. The season was so long and the playoffs are so draining physically and mentally on the players. The Detroit Red Wings in 1998 had a clear purpose and mission to drive them in their quest to keep the Cup in Hockey Town.

The theme was 'BELIEVE,' in respect to the two former teammates who were slowly recovering from a near fatal accident in June 1997. Vladimir Konstantinov's locker remained open in the Red Wing dressing room at Joe Louis Arena. Going into game one, the Wings had a clear objective in the upcoming series with the Capitals.

The Detroit Red Wings relied upon their role players to produce in the opening game of the Stanley Cup Finals. On paper, Detroit had much more depth than the Washington Capitals, but they had to prove themselves on the ice where statistics are meaningless. Some people questioned the defensive unit of the Red Wings with the absence of Konstantinov. Could Detroit win without his physical play?

Game one began as a defensive struggle halfway through the opening 20 minutes. With about six minutes remaining, the scoring began.

The Detroit Red Wings opened the scoring just the way they had hoped they would, by relying upon their depth and role players to wear down the opponent. Joey Kocur looked liked a scoring expert when he beat Olaf Kolzig with a flashy move to give Detroit a 1-0 lead in game one. Two minutes later, the Wings struck again.

The second goal scored by Detroit came from a more likely source. Steve Yzerman fed a slick pass to Nick Lidstrom, and the young Swedish defenseman did the rest. Lidstrom's sixth goal of the playoffs gave Detroit a 2-0 lead at the first intermission of game one of the Stanley Cup Finals.

The Red Wings played extremely strong defensively in the second period, and they only made one mistake. Richard Zednik recorded the first ever playoff goal for the Washington Capitals in the Stanley Cup Finals when he scored with about four minutes remaining. The Red Wings were unable to score. After 40 minutes of play, the Wings led 2-1, but Washington was in good shape after two periods in a hostile building.

The third period was another well-played defensive display by both teams. Detroit was unable to score in the final 20 minutes, but the Capitals could not beat Osgood. Game one went to Detroit. The home team led the best of seven series 1-0. Game two was played in Detroit, and the Capitals were suddenly engaged in a must win situation if they had any realistic chance of capturing the Cup from Hockey Town.

The crowd was enthusiastic at Joe Louis Arena for game two of the Stanley Cup Finals. Most fans and reporters were expecting another defensive struggle. With only one goal scored in the first period, it appeared as though the game would indeed be a low scoring event.

Detroit managed the only goal of the first period, but unlike game one, this goal came from a more suitable figure. The captain, Steve Yzerman, recorded his fifth goal of the playoffs to give Detroit a 1-0 advantage in the first period. After 20 minutes of play, Detroit held on to a one-goal lead, but an offensive outburst was yet to come.

The second period belonged to the Washington Capitals. Washington tied the score when Peter Bondra fired a shot that eluded Chris Osgood. Less than two minutes into the second period, the score was deadlocked at 1-1.

Chris Simon was known for throwing his weight around against the opposition. In game two in Detroit, Simon surprised many viewers when he beat Osgood to give his team a one-goal lead. Suddenly, the much-questioned Detroit defense was unraveling.

Former Red Wing, Adam Oates scored next for the visitors to give Washington a 3-1 advantage. The Red Wings found themselves behind by two goals going into the third period. Detroit would have to generate some offense in order to bounce back from a miserable second period.

The next goal came with Washington on the power play. Steve Yzerman rallied his team one more time when he scored a crucial shorthanded goal. The goal by Yzerman cut the Capitals lead to just one goal. Not only did Yzerman contribute in killing the power play, but he also scored a big goal to put his team back in the hunt in game two.

As it turned out, Washington saw two goals on the power play. The one by Steve Yzerman, and the other by Joe Juneau of the Capitals. The goal by Juneau gave Washington a two-goal advantage with about 13 minutes remaining in the third period. The Red Wings had to respond quickly if they hoped to have any chance of winning game two in Hockey Town.

Two more goals were scored in the third period. Martin Lapointe drew the Red Wings back to within one goal when he scored his eighth goal of the playoffs. With eight goals scored by Lapointe, nobody accused him of not being productive in the 1998 Stanley Cup playoffs.

The next goal was a big goal scored in game two. Another role player, Doug Brown of the Red Wings, cruised in all alone on Kolzig. Brown made his move and deposited the puck behind the sprawling Kolzig. The goal by Brown shifted the momentum as the game was headed into overtime. The Red Wings came from behind and were dead even at 4-4 after regulation time. The crowd came to life after the goal by Lapointe, but when Brown tied the score, the fans at Joe Louis went into a frenzy, bad news for the Capitals.

Detroit outshot Washington 12-3 in the overtime session. The Red Wings were buzzing in the Capitals zone through out the overtime period. It seemed as though it would only be a matter of time before Detroit would beat Kolzig to take a 2-0 advantage in the series.

Overtime hockey in the Stanley Cup Finals was exciting beyond belief. In an instant one team celebrated, while the other team tried to forget what went wrong. If the Red Wings scored, Joe Louis Arena would have rocked with a sudden thunderous ovation of joy from the fans in Hockey Town. However, if the Capitals scored silence and disbelief would have lingered in the house of the Red Wings.

With less than five minutes remaining in overtime, the game ended suddenly. In an instant, everything done previously had been forgotten. The one to score this goal was an unlikely hero in game two.

Scotty Bowman knew it had to be his role players to rise above in this Stanley Cup Final. He believed that the depth of his hockey team would prove to be the difference in this series. Kris Draper made Bowman look like a genius when he fired his first goal of the playoffs past Kolzig to give the Detroit Red Wings a 5-4 victory and a 2-0 advantage in the series.

The Detroit Red Wings were right where they wanted to be, heading into Washington with a two game advantage over the Capitals. The Wings knew they had to win at least one game on the road to keep the home ice advantage in the series. Detroit also believed that they could win for their fallen teammates of 1997, Konstantinov and Mnatsakanov.

Detroit went to Washington with confidence, but they knew that the series was far from over. Game three was the current task on hand for the Detroit Red Wings. The Wings knew it would be important to get off to a quick start on the road.

The crowd was excited at the MCI Center in the nation's capital. This was the fans first taste of the Stanley Cup Finals in Washington, DC. The Capitals were eager to put on a good showing at home in game three.

The Red Wings came out and silenced the crowd at the MCI Center as they totally dominated the first period. Detroit did just what they had to do, took the crowd out of the game. The Red Wings outshot the Capitals 13-1. This was one of the Wings best periods in the playoffs. If not for Olaf Kolzig the score would have been a lot worse than it was for Washington.

The Red Wings came out like gangbusters in the opening period. Detroit scored just 35 seconds into the hockey game when Steve Yzerman assisted on a goal scored by Tomas Holmstrom. The Detroit Red Wings had several other chances to increase their lead, but Kolzig kept his team in the game with his superb goaltending. After one period of play, the Wings were ahead 1-0. Washington had to feel good that it was only a one-goal margin that they had to make up.

The second period was dominated by the goalies. Kolzig enjoyed another stellar performance in the second 20 minutes. Chris Osgood stopped everything that came his way. The Detroit Red Wings were holding on to a narrow one goal lead in game three.

The Washington Capitals responded with a solid effort in the third period. About half way through, the Washington Capitals went on a power play. Brian Bellows scored for the Caps to even the score at 1-1. The next goal decided the outcome of game three.

With five minutes remaining, Doug Brown fed a perfect pass to Slava Kozlov. Kozlov found a wide-open Sergei Federov, and Federov did the rest. Sergei beat Kolzig to give Detroit a 2-1 lead.

Washington tried desperately to tie the score, but fell just short. Once again, Detroit was one game away from a sweep in the Stanley Cup Finals. It had been a long time since a team had won back-to-back championships. It had been even longer since the winner had consecutive four game sweeps over their opponents.

Detroit suspected that Washington would come out ready to play in game four. The Capitals were not about to give away the series, yet Detroit was eager to reclaim the Stanley Cup they had won in 1997. The suspense was building during the pre-game hype prior to game four in Washington DC.

The Detroit Red Wings were focused and ready to recapture the prized trophy. Detroit dominated play during the first period. The Wings fired 14 shots at Kolzig, but only one found the back of the net.

The lone goal scored by Detroit came from Doug Brown who was filling in well as another key role player for Bowman's Red Wings. Brown took a pass from Sergei Federov and slipped the puck past Kolzig. After one period of play the Wings were clinging to a one-goal lead over the Washington Capitals.

The second period was the true test of heart for the Capitals. If they let Detroit dictate the tempo during the next 20 minutes, any dreams Washington had of ousting the Cup from Detroit would be vanished. Three goals were scored in a somewhat wide-open style of play.

Martin Lapointe scored his ninth goal of the playoffs early in the second period to give his team a 2-0 lead. Lapointe was enjoying the best playoff season of his life. When Scotty Bowman pointed to his role players in this series, one of the first names mentioned was Marty Lapointe. The Red Wings were pleased with the play of Lapointe, who was a big factor in the Wings' quest for a back to back Stanley Cup celebration.

Washington had to answer the call quickly or their season was over. Less than half way through the second period, Brian Bellows beat Chris Osgood to cut the Wings lead to 2-1 with plenty of time remaining in the game. Suddenly, Washington was back in game four.

In the second half of period number two, the Red Wings went back on the power play. Larry Murphy fired a slap shot from the point that eluded Kolzig.

The period ended with Detroit leading 3-1. Time was running out for the Washington Capitals.

The final 20 minutes belonged to Detroit again, and so did the series and the Stanley Cup. Doug Brown scored his second goal of the game on the power play less than two minutes into the third period. The goal by Brown spelled the end for the Washington Capitals. All that remained in game four was the final buzzer and the victory celebration for the Detroit Red Wings.

169

Many of the Red Wings were vindicated in the 1998 Stanley Cup Finals. Chris Osgood proved at last that he was capable of leading the Wings to the top. Osgood struggled his way through the ups and downs of playoff goaltending. He proved his critics wrong; this time was not a repeat of the 1995 Finals against New Jersey when Osgood and the Wings bowed out in four straight defeats. He let in what appeared to be some soft goals, but he also handled the criticism and stood tall in the end.

Ozzie learned to concentrate on his game. Perhaps the captain, Steve Yzerman, was wearing off on him. He no longer had to listen to what others had to say about his inability to win the big one. At the end of the game in the MCI Center, it was Chris Osgood who threw his gloves and stick into the air with a sigh of relief.

Sergei Federov was another Red Wing whose heart and courage was in question by some fans and media. Federov held out for big money and many were beginning to wonder whether he was worth the huge price tag the Wings agreed to pay him. Some people believed that Federov had a tendency to let up during the playoffs. The media no longer questioned his desire and heart.

In the 1998 playoffs, Federov showed his true colors by leading the team in goals during the Stanley Cup run. He played for his friends Konstantinov and Mnatsakanov. Federov put his critics to rest with his excellent play during the Finals.

The role players for the Detroit Red Wings did their part in the Stanley Cup run with their hard work and contributions. Marty Lapointe scored nine goals and played a part in several others. Doug Brown had some timely goals for the Red Wings when they needed them most. Tomas Holmstrom was a pest for every goalie he faced in the playoffs. Holmstrom screened many goalies, and he chipped in with his choppy scoring touch. Joey Kocur showed a unique scoring touch in the Stanley Cup playoffs and provided toughness and leadership when he was called upon.

The Detroit Red Wings simply believed that they would win. They had a reason to return the Cup to Hockey Town, but the real reason was to win it for Konstantinov and Mnatsakanov. The Red Wings insisted upon having their lost, 'but not forgotten teammates' names inscribed on the latest version of Lord Stanley's Cup.

The Stanley Cup championship won by the Wings in 1998 truly was a solid team effort, but one player led the way above all others. Steve Yzerman came to Detroit in 1983 and the franchise was built around him.

He was named captain at an early age, but he handled the pressure in his own humble way. Yzerman battled back from injury after injury. The captain took criticism when things went wrong, but he still climbed the stairs one step at a time toward the ultimate prize, the Cup. His leadership was constantly being questioned. He changed his game to compliment his team and new coach when Scotty Bowman arrived in Hockey Town. Yzerman won the Stanley Cup championship in front of his loyal fans in Joe Louis Arena in 1997. He came up short in the Olympics for Team Canada in Nagano, Japan. Yzerman was runner up for rookie of the year honors to Tom Barasso in 1983. Individual honors eluded him all of his professional career with the Detroit Red Wings, but in Detroit he was respected, idolized, and loved for his caring attitude toward the community.

When NHL Commissioner Gary Bettman walked out to present the Conn-Smythe Trophy for the most valuable player of the of the Stanley Cup playoffs, Steve Yzerman's teammates and fans hoped that this would be his moment of recognition. Personally, Steve Yzerman was not interested in individual honors, but this one was somewhat different and special to him. Gary Bettman captured the moment when he complimented Yzerman for his great leadership qualities as a player. As Yzerman skated away with the Conn-Smythe Trophy, he was mobbed by his teammates who praised him with the utmost respect.

After receiving the most valuable player award, Steve Yzerman was thankful to have his name added to the prestigious trophy. He had come a long way since joining the Wings in 1983. He was not very well known when he was drafted, and his name was hard to pronounce. It was very gratifying for Yzerman to have his name amongst the other Conn-Smythe recipients.

The presentation of the Conn-Smythe Trophy and the Stanley Cup was very exciting for Steve Yzerman, but the series of events that followed were remarkably moving. NHL Commissioner, Gary Bettman handed the Stanley Cup over to Yzerman for a second consecutive year. The previous year, the captain took his spectacular skate around Joe Louis Arena where Red Wing fans joined in on the joyous festivities.

In 1997, the Red Wings and their fans had their long-awaited moment of celebration that included a parade that packed the downtown Detroit streets with over one million people. In 1998, the celebration took place on the opponent's ice in Washington DC, but it was just as meaningful as the Cup celebration in 1997 for the Detroit Red Wings.

While Steve Yzerman had to think about who would get the Cup next from his golden scoring hands in 1997, he had no doubt who the recipient would be in 1998. During the presentation of the Conn-Smythe Trophy and the Stanley Cup, a special guest was being transported from the stands onto the ice. His name was Vladimir Konstantinov.

Steve Yzerman did not take the ceremonial stroll around the ice with the Stanley Cup hoisted above his head. It was not his style to rub salt into the wound of the opposition fans. Ironically, he had an alternative to save the Capital fans from humiliation. The fans at the MCI Center were about to enjoy a tribute to a fallen athlete and human being. The Capital fans were in for a memorable moment in NHL history.

Steve Yzerman was a compassionate leader in the community during his long career with the Detroit Red Wings. He led by example, but did not seek recognition. On June 16, 1998 he and his teammates showed the world the love they had for their fallen teammate known as Vladdy.

The Detroit Red Wings went into the 1998 Stanley Cup playoffs knowing they had to win 16 games for number 16, Vladimir Konstantinov, and it just happened that on June 16, 1998 that was what happened. Steve Yzerman accepted the Stanley Cup from Commissioner Gary Bettman, but what he did next is what separated him from celebrity and hero. Yzerman lifted the Cup and skated toward Vladimir Konstantinov, who entered the ice in a wheelchair with help from his friends. Yzerman placed the Stanley Cup in the lap of Konstantinov, and as he did his teammates gathered around to take part in the joyous occasion.

Slava Fetisov felt redemption to see his friend back on the ice. Fetisov was involved in the auto accident, but he was not injured as severely as Konstantinov and Mnatsakanov. The Russian Five reunited once again as they huddled around Konstantinov to celebrate victory with their teammate, countryman, and friend. They even assisted him in giving the victory sign by holding up two fingers.

Konstantinov was all smiles as he paraded around the MCI Center with the Stanley Cup. Slava Fetisov explained the reason behind the repeat championship with Darren Pang (*ESPN*). Fetisov reminded people that Konstantinov was thought about often during the season.

On a June summer night in the United States Capital, it was a Russian who was being honored and recognized by his teammates. Kris Draper summed up the team's emotions best when he made reference to how close the team was and how the accident brought them even closer together as a unit. Oh, what a night!

After a long season, Steve Yzerman and the Detroit Red Wings were ready for a break. As Yzerman faced reporters in the locker room, he seemed relieved that the season had come to an end. He reflected back upon how long the season was with the Olympics interrupting the schedule. He realized that the season was over, and he was happy that he would finally have time to relax. Yzerman was delighted that the year had come to an end. He was also delighted with the outcome that had Detroit preparing for yet another victory parade.

The streets of downtown Detroit were crowded again with fans awaiting a glimpse of their favorite Red Wing. Chris Osgood carried the Cup in the 1998 parade. Meanwhile, Steve Yzerman displayed his Conn-Smythe Trophy with pride. The best spot to be was at Hart Plaza, where the parade concluded. Reminiscent of last June, the hockey players spoke one at a time. They thanked the fans for their support of the Detroit Red Wings.

Once the team reached Hart Plaza, it was time to bid the fans farewell for the summer of 1998. Before the Red Wings said goodbye, they wanted Hockey Town to know just how much they appreciated the support throughout the year and during the playoffs. Trainer John Wharton assured Red Wing fans that they did witness Vladimir Konstantinov walking across the stage.

The loyal Red Wing fans lined the streets to catch a glimpse of their favorites, but it was at Hart Plaza where fans would have one last chance to hear what the team had to say about Hockey Town and the championship. Scotty Bowman characterized his team as one that displayed good values. He gave credit to the players for believing in each other.

Chris Osgood has taken abuse from the media throughout his career, and those fans that were present appreciated his remarks. Osgood told the crowd at Hart Plaza what they meant to him during the playoffs. He complimented the fans by implying that the fans support for him during the playoffs was greatly appreciated. It made him feel good to hear the fans chant his name to the tune of, "OZZIE, OZZIE!"

The name 'Hockey Town' is in regards to the two-way love affair between the Detroit Red Wings and their fans. The fans in Detroit stood behind the Red Wings through good times and the bad. They were rewarded at Hart Plaza when Steve Yzerman paid them the ultimate compliment by recognizing the support the team received. Yzerman let the large crowd know that the support given to Red Wings by the fans was deeply appreciated. It is nice that Yzerman appreciated the support of the fans in Detroit. At last the time had come to give the credit to a man that was long overdue to be thanked for all of his contributions.

The Detroit Red Wings hoped that the summer of 1998 would not duplicate the tragedy of June 1997. Disaster seemed to follow the Wings after their recent Stanley Cup championships. That summer, it was Scotty Bowman who was dealt a cruel blow. His brother died of heart complications during the summer of 1998. To further complicate matters for Bowman, he was scheduled for surgery on his ailing knees. Bowman went in for a physical and the results were not promising for the Red Wing coach. His coaching future with the Detroit Red Wings was now in jeopardy.

Suddenly, the talk of a dynasty in Detroit for the Red Wings was fuzzy. If Bowman did not come back, who would replace him? What did the future hold for the Detroit Red Wings hope of a dynasty?

CHAPTER SEVENTEEN

WHERE DO WE GO FROM HERE?

Photograph by Bobby Lewis

After winning back-to-back Stanley Cup championships the talk circulating around Hockey Town was about a Red Wing dynasty. The team was headed into the 1998-99 season with the same cast of main characters that brought the Cup to Detroit for two consecutive years. However, one main ingredient was missing behind the bench – Scotty Bowman. The team was also without the services of veteran defenseman, Slava Fetisov, who retired.

The Detroit Red Wings had a legitimate chance to win the Stanley Cup in the 98-99 season. Steve Yzerman was having fun playing hockey after two Stanley Cup titles and 14 seasons with the Detroit Red Wings. He hinted that he wanted to play 20 years with the Red Wings. Twenty years with one team was unheard of in the modern day sports era. The NHL was a business and players normally went where they could cash in on the most money for their services.

Steve Yzerman had come a long way in his 14 seasons with the Detroit Red Wings. He helped to rebuild a team that had reached rock bottom in the standings in the NHL. He guided his team back to the playoffs. He was criticized for every early exit the team made in the playoffs. He never quit and kept playing hard every night. He took his team to the Stanley Cup Finals in 1995, but that was not good enough. He was rumored to be on the trading block several times during his career with the Red Wings. He took on the responsibility of being team captain at the age of 21.

His career turned the corner for the better in the 1996 playoffs when Yzerman scored the game-winning goal in game seven in double overtime against the St. Louis Blues. In 1997, he helped to return the Stanley Cup to Hockey Town after a 42-year absence. In 1998, he helped retain the Cup in Detroit, and he won the Conn-Smythe Trophy.

The NHL career of Steve Yzerman turned from sour to sweet in a span of two to three years. He was the present day icon of the Detroit Red Wings. He was the first to come along and fill the skates of Red Wing legend Gordie Howe. In June 1997, when the Wings won the Stanley Cup after a 42-year drought, Gordie Howe knew that it was a real special night for Steve Yzerman. He also realized that Steve Yzerman had become a complete player. Mr. Hockey himself had to be proud of what Mr. Yzerman had accomplished as a Detroit Red Wing.

When Steve Yzerman hangs up number 19 for the Detroit Red Wings, his jersey will be draped amongst the rafters with Gordie Howe, Alex Delvecchio, Terry Sawchuck, Ted Lindsay and others. He will be mentioned in Hockey Town conversations in the same breath as Gordie Howe. Number 19 for the Detroit Red Wings will never be forgotten.

It did not really matter to the fans and media of Hockey Town if the Wings won the Stanley Cup in 1999. They had proven themselves to be champions with back to back Stanley Cup championships. The captain, Steve Yzerman, had proven himself over the past two seasons. The heat was off of Steve Yzerman and would never be on him again. A burden was lifted when Stevie hoisted the hardware one by one over his head.

Yzerman looked forward to an enjoyable and successful season heading into 1998-99. The Red Wings made few changes to the roster at the start of the season. Some of the rookies moved up during the season to gain valuable experience with the parent club. The Detroit Red Wings took a glance at Philipe Audet, Darryl LaPlante, and Yan Goloubovsky. One of the up-and-coming players was Stacey Roest who impressed Scotty Bowman with his hard work ethic on the ice. Roest fit in well with the Grinders and enjoyed a successful season for the Red Wings.

The Red Wings added two names to the roster that were very familiar in the NHL. Detroit took a second look at Petr Klima, who was given a chance to play on a limited basis. The major signing for the Red Wings was when they acquired Uwe Krupp from the Colorado Avalanche.

Uwe Krupp was a welcome addition to the depleted Red Wing defensive unit. With the loss of Bob Rouse and Slava Fetisov, the Wings believed that Krupp would stabilize the defensive core for them. Defense was the shortcoming heading into the 1998-99 season. Larry Murphy and Jamie Macoun were older while Aaron Ward, Anders Eriksson, and Mathieu Dandenault were inexperienced and untested. Nicklas Lidstrom was solid and proven, but he needed some help. With the addition of Krupp, the Red Wings were confident that they had a good unit on the blue line.

The season began without Scotty Bowman behind the Red Wings bench. Assistant coaches Barry Smith and Dave Lewis shared the interim coaching duties for Detroit. Following his operation, Bowman made his appearance at Joe Louis Arena for the ceremonial raising of the Stanley Cup banner to the rafters. Bowman looked good following his surgery; he had lost weight and appeared healthy. The question was whether he felt well enough to endure another grueling season behind the bench.

Detroit jumped to a good start with Smith and Lewis behind the bench. When Scotty Bowman returned, the Red Wings began to fall into a slump. The chemistry they had the previous two years seemed to be fading away. Uwe Krupp was sidelined with a back injury and did not return. Suddenly, defense was a big problem for the Red Wings.

They were not playing the aggressive style of hockey that they had previously. The opposition outplayed Detroit on many nights during the regular season. The desire seemed to be missing, but the Wings believed that come playoff time, they would be ready to recapture their championship form.

The Detroit Red Wings made some blockbuster trades to make their run for their third consecutive Stanley Cup championship. The Red Wings gave up some youthful players in an attempt to solve the current woes they encountered in 1998-99. The Red Wing organization took a chance on their future, but they felt the only way to win immediately was by way of trading for proven veteran players.

The Red Wings acquired three defensemen before the playoffs began. Todd Gill came over from St. Louis and filled a void for much of the season for the depleted defensive core of the Detroit Red Wings. The Wings beefed up on defense when they acquired Ulf Samelsson. Ulf played a physical and punishing style of hockey on the blue line, but he suffered an injury that hampered his play late in the season. The third defenseman that Detroit acquired was by way of a blockbuster trade.

The Red Wings traded away Anders Eriksson and future draft picks to the Chicago Black Hawks. Anders Eriksson was a young Swedish defenseman who played well for the Red Wings, but the Wings wanted help for the immediate playoff run to three peat as Stanley Cup champions. Detroit received, in exchange for Eriksson, a future Hall of Fame defenseman in Chris Chelios.

It was hard to believe that Chicago would part with Chelios who had been with the Black Hawks for most of his career. Chelios was a proven veteran who logs a lot of minutes and plays a rugged defensive game. Detroit was very happy to have Chelios in a Red Wing sweater.

Chris Chelios continued to wear number 24, the same number he wore with the Black Hawks. While Chelios played in Chicago, he was known to get under the skin of his new teammates in Detroit, especially in his earlier years in some grinding playoff battles. Chris Chelios was another future Hall of Fame player to be added to the Detroit Red Wings roster.

During the last ten games of the regular season, the Detroit Red Wings looked like prohibitive favorites to win the Stanley Cup again. Newly-acquired Wendal Clark was scoring goals that added to the offensive equation for the Red Wings. Ulf Samuelson brought a physical presence to the blue line for the Wings, and Chris Chelios was playing his usual reliable defense with his new team. The Wings gambled by trading away draft picks and some younger players. The question was, whether the gamble would pay off with another Stanley Cup championship.

During the regular season, the Red Wings were unable to get on track. The team did not seem to have the same domination that they had displayed the previous two seasons as Stanley Cup champs. Perhaps the other teams around the NHL were figuring out how to dethrone the champions. At the trade deadline, the Red Wings made some moves in attempt to improve their chances of winning a third consecutive Stanley Cup championship. The newcomers appeared to be peaking just as the playoffs began. The Red Wings ended the season with a strong chance to repeat as champions. Things were looking promising in Hockey Town again.

During the regular season, Yzerman led the Wings in scoring. Steve Yzerman led the way just as he has done since he arrived with the Red Wings in 1983. Yzerman was prepared to make another run for the Cup in the playoffs. He restructured his game when Scotty Bowman arrived, but he led the team in scoring in 1998-99. Even though his offensive output has dropped off, he has become a more complete player since Scotty Bowman arrived in 1993. He scored 29 goals and added 45 assists. Yzerman was one of the few consistent players who the Wings could depend on during the regular season. He had 74 points during the regular season, finishing 11 points ahead of Federov and Larionov.

The regular season was over and the Red Wing fans were confident that their new-look team was poised to win yet another Stanley Cup. It was playoff time and the Detroit Red Wings were looking like the favorites to repeat for a third straight Stanley Cup title.

The Red Wings opened the first round of the 1999 Stanley Cup playoffs at home in Hockey Town. The opponent was the expansion Anaheim Mighty Ducks. Detroit was favored, but the Ducks posed a threat with the likes of Paul Kariya and Teemu Selanne.

The teams scored eight goals in game one at Joe Louis Arena. The Mighty Ducks scored first on the power play. Marty McInnis scored to give the visitors a brief 1-0 lead.

It did not take Steve Yzerman long to pick up where he had left off in his previous Stanley Cup performance when he won the Conn-Smythe Trophy. Yzerman tied the game with Red Wings' first goal of the playoff season. The Red Wings took a 2-1 advantage into the locker room after the first 20 minutes of play.

Wendal Clark scored late in the first period to give Detroit a one-goal advantage. The Wings acquired Clark to give them some offensive thrust in the playoffs; Clark had a hot hand going into the playoffs, and the

Wings were hoping he would accelerate his play the further the team went into the playoffs. The next goal scored in game one was a crucial goal in the contest.

Less than one minute into the second period, the Red Wings added a power play goal to widen their lead to 3-1. Steve Yzerman continued his hot hand by scoring his second goal of the game early.

Anaheim found themselves behind 3-1. The Mighty Ducks knew they had to score next if they stood any chance of mounting a comeback in game one on the road. The Mighty Ducks big name player, Paul Kariya, beat Chris Osgood to cut the deficit to 3-2.

The final goal of the period may have been the backbreaker for the Mighty Ducks. Doug Brown took a pass from his newly-acquired linemate Wendal Clark and he put the puck past back up goalie Tom Askey. After 40 minutes of play, the Red Wings were ahead 4-2. The Mighty Ducks found themselves in a position that was not pleasant.

Anaheim knew they had to strike next to have any chance at beating the Red Wings. The Mighty Ducks responded when Teemu Selanne beat Chris Osgood to cut the margin down to just one goal with plenty of time remaining in the third. The next goal would be a must for Anaheim to force overtime in game one.

Any thought of such came crashing to an end when the Red Wings scored late in the third period to wrap up game one. Just when the Wings needed it most, Steve Yzerman broke in alone on Askey to record a hat trick in game one of the first round of the Stanley Cup playoffs. It was rare when a player scored three goals in one game but Yzerman did just that in the first game. He scored once in the first, second, and third period to complete the hat trick.

Yzerman was on his way to repeating as a back-to-back Conn-Smythe recipient. His play was dazzling in game one against Anaheim. He showed the hockey world that he was indeed the "go-to guy" on the Detroit Red Wings. He was at last the unquestionable leader of the team from Hockey Town. Any doubts that lingered from the past had been long forgotten since his heart-stopping goal in game seven of the 1996 playoffs against the St. Louis Blues in double overtime. The image was played over and over as a reminder to Red Wing fans that there never was, any doubt of whom the leader was for the Detroit Red Wings.

The goal that Yzerman remembered as one of his biggest during his career erased any doubt that he could not be the leader he was christened to become when Jacques Demers appointed him as captain in 1986.

Heading into game two at Joe Louis Arena, one thing was for certain, Steve Yzerman was the leader of the two time defending Stanley Cup champions. Being recognized as the leader had a nice ring to it for a guy who was questioned for more than a decade during his career as to his leadership qualities with the Detroit Red Wings.

Detroit knew that if they could win convincingly in game two they would have the series right where they wanted - they would be in control again. During the first period, the Wings appeared to be unstoppable as they unleashed four goals against Guy Herbert and the Mighty Ducks. The Red Wings looked serious again just in time for the second season.

It took Detroit one minute to open the scoring in game two. Brendan Shanahan scored his first goal of the playoffs with help from Sergei Federov and Steve Yzerman. Almost nine minutes later, Shanahan scored again on the power play for Detroit. The Wings were not finished scoring in the first 20 minutes, and the Mighty Ducks were becoming frustrated.

The next two goals came from two of the role players that Scotty Bowman was counting upon to deliver in the playoffs. Tomas Holmstrom gave Detroit a 3-0 lead in game two when he beat Herbert. In the last minute of the first period it was Doug Brown who joined in on the Detroit massacre to give his team a 4-0 lead at the first intermission. Anaheim was outplayed in the first 20 minutes. They had to rebound in the second period or else their playing days would be numbered in the 1999 Stanley Cup playoffs. It was critical that Anaheim play disciplined in the second period.

Almost half way through the second period the Mighty Ducks took yet another costly penalty against Detroit. The Red Wings took advantage on the power play. Steve Yzerman cashed in for his fourth goal of the playoffs to give Detroit a 5-0 lead. The Wings were in command in this game against Anaheim.

Teemu Selanne of the Mighty Ducks scored only one goal in the third period; he ruined the shutout bid for Chris Osgood. Detroit made the best of the mistakes the Ducks had made during the game. Anaheim gave the Red Wings nine power play opportunities in game two. The Wings converted on three of the nine chances. The Mighty Ducks had to regroup as they headed into game three back home at the Pond.

In sunny California, the crowd was excited to be attending a Stanley Cup playoff game. The Detroit Red Wings knew they would have to come out storming to take the hometown crowd out of the game.

It took the Red Wings less than two minutes to score in game three. Sergei Federov scored his first goal of the series to put his team up 1-0. The remaining time in the first period saw Detroit making mistakes they would pay for later.

Anaheim converted on two power plays to give them their first lead of the series following 20 minutes of play in game three. Marty McInnis scored on the power play to even the score at 1-1. Jason Marshall scored his first playoff goal to give the Mighty Ducks a one-goal lead. After the first period, the Red Wings knew that they had to take the play to the troublesome Mighty Ducks.

The scoring in the second period occurred as a direct result of penalties; Anaheim took four in the second period. The Mighty Ducks opened the period in good shape with a one-goal lead on home ice. Early in the second period, they began to self-destruct with useless penalties.

Less than one minute into the second, the Red Wings went on the power play, causing Detroit to tie the score with Tomas Holmstrom deflecting the puck past Guy Herbert. The goal by Holmstrom deadlocked the score at 2-2.

The next penalty by the Mighty Ducks proved to be costly. The final goal gave Detroit a one-goal advantage after 40 minutes of play in game three. Steve Yzerman scored his fifth goal in less than three complete games. Once again Yzerman was leading the way for his team. The goal by Yzerman gave Detroit a 3-2 lead after two periods of play. Now the Red Wings were right where they wanted to be heading into the third period on the road.

Detroit knew if they could come out storming at the start of the third period, they would have a good chance to put game three beyond reach of the Mighty Ducks. It took Detroit less than two minutes to seal the victory. Slava Kozlov scored his first goal of the playoffs to put the Red Wings ahead for good. As the final buzzer sounded, the scoreboard at the Pond read Detroit 4, Anaheim 2. With the Wings up 3-0 in the best of seven series, the faithful fans in Hockey Town sensed a sweep was inevitable in the opening round of the 1999 Stanley Cup playoffs.

Game four was a must-win situation for the Mighty Ducks. Suddenly, it seemed as though the Red Wings rekindled for the second season. Detroit was one game short of consecutive Stanley Cup playoff sweeps in another seven game series. The previous season, Detroit ended by sweeping the Washington Capitals in the Stanley Cup Finals to retain the prized Cup.

The Red Wings knew that the Ducks would come out full throttle from the drop of the puck. During the first period, Detroit was out shot by Anaheim 16 to 14, but Chris Osgood came up big when he had to. After 20 minutes, the teams were scoreless. (The Detroit Red Wings were right where they wanted to be). They had held back the all out effort by the Mighty Ducks in the opening period of game four.

With five minutes remaining, the Detroit Red Wings cashed in on the power play. Tomas Holmstrom redirected a Nicklas Lidstrom slap shot. The goal by Homer gave Detroit a 1-0 lead that held up till the end of the period. Heading into the third period, the Red Wings were up 1-0 with 20 minutes to play in regulation time.

In the third, it was Detroit who came out storming on offense. Detroit outshot Anaheim 17 to six in the final 20 minutes. The Wings played flawlessly in the third period. Whatever went wrong during the regular season seemed to be corrected during the playoffs. The "three-peat" was looking promising for the re-energized Red Wings.

The Red Wings scored twice in the final 20 minutes. Brendan Shanahan scored his third goal of the series to put Detroit in front 2-0 with about eight minutes remaining in the game. Three minutes later, Slava Kozlov scored to wrap up the best of seven series. Detroit completed a four game sweep in the first round of the 1999 Stanley Cup playoffs.

The way Detroit was playing defensively, it appeared as though it would be a cinch to win the Cup again in 1999. Chris Osgood was on top of his game in goal. The Red Wings seemed to put their miserable regular season behind them. The next opponent was their archrivals, the Colorado Avalanche.

There was certainly no love lost between the Red Wings and the Avalanche. During the regular season, the two teams split the season series with both teams winning two games. The series opened on the road for Detroit in game one. Chris Osgood was sidelined with an injury, and back-up goalie, Bill Ranford, had to step between the pipes for the injured Ozzie.

The Detroit Red Wings scored first on the power play in game one at the Pepsi Center in Colorado. The Red Wings jumped out to a quick start when Steve Yzerman beat Patrick Roy to give his team a 1-0 lead. The goal by Yzerman was his sixth of the playoffs. The 1998 Conn-Smythe recipient was closing in on a possible repeat as the most valuable player of the Stanley Cup playoffs in 1999.

Colorado made Detroit pay when Chris Chelios went to the penalty box for holding the puck with his glove hand. Avalanche newcomer, Theon Fleury, scored to even game at one goal apiece. The Avalanche were not finished scoring yet in the opening 20 minutes of game one.

Colorado added one more goal before the buzzer sounded. Adam Deadmarsh scored to give Colorado a 2-1 lead after the first 20 minutes of game one. The Red Wings had to score the next goal on the road to have any realistic chance of winning the opening game.

Dale Hunter took a meaningless high-sticking penalty that proved to be costly for the Colorado Avalanche. The Red Wings cashed in on the power play when Slava Kozlov scored to tie the score at 2-2. The goal by Kozlov was the only one scored in the second period. Once again, the Detroit Red Wings were in command in the opposing teams' building.

When playing on the road, any team was happy to be tied heading into the third period of a playoff game. Detroit knew that this would not be an easy series against Colorado. They also knew whoever scored the next goal would most likely be the winner in game one.

Detroit escaped the period without any damage being done, and game one had to be decided in overtime. The Red Wings had two penalties in the third period and Colorado had none. The Wings were able to kill the two penalties and force overtime.

Game one was settled quickly in the first overtime session. With Patrick Roy in net for the Avalanche, and Bill Ranford filling in for the injured Chris Osgood, Detroit knew they would have to strike quickly to win game one.

It took less than five minutes into the first overtime to end game one at the Pepsi Center. The Red Wings' Grind Line was not producing in the playoffs, but they came through in the first game of this series against Colorado. Kirk Maltby scored his first goal and most important one of the playoffs. The goal by Maltby gave Detroit a 1-0 lead in the series. The win was huge for Detroit because they were on the road.

Colorado was struggling at home, which was good news for the Wings because the Avalanche had home ice advantage in the seven game series. Colorado was unbeaten on the road, but Detroit would have been more than happy to take a 2-0 advantage back to Joe Louis Arena for game three. First, Detroit had to win game two with Bill Ranford in net for the ailing Chris Osgood.

The first period of game two was a defensive struggle for both hockey teams. The Red Wings scored the only goal of the period when their captain netted his seventh goal of the playoffs. Yzerman was leading the way again for the Detroit Red Wings. He had seven goals in just six games in the playoffs. After 20 minutes, Yzerman had his team right where they wanted to be, ahead on the scoreboard.

The offense opened up a bit in the second period, but the goalies stole the show. Only one goal managed to be scored during the second period. Who scored the second goal of the game?

Steve Yzerman seemed to be like a fine wine. He just kept getting better with age. Yzerman had eight goals and was on pace for a repeat Conn-Smythe Trophy if his team could three-peat as Stanley Cup champions. Colorado would have to somehow regroup for the third period if they had any hope of winning in game two.

Colorado unraveled as they took five penalties in the final twenty minutes. The Wings cashed in on two of their power play opportunities in the third period. Nick Lidstrom scored an unassisted goal to give Detroit a 3-0 lead. Wendal Clarke finished the scoring on a power play to seal the fate of Colorado in game two. The Red Wings were happy to be heading home with a 2-0 advantage in the series; the Colorado Avalanche were happy to be going on the road where they were undefeated in the 1999 Stanley Cup playoffs.

Game three was a critical game for the Colorado Avalanche. They had their backs up against the wall and did not want to let the two-time defending Stanley Cup champions go up 3-0 in the series. Bill Ranford hoped to repeat his performance of the first two games in Colorado.

The first period started out in the Red Wings' favor. Captain Steve Yzerman scored his ninth goal of the playoffs. He tied his personal best in goals that was accomplished in the 1995 Stanley Cup playoffs when Detroit lost to New Jersey in the Finals. It was good that Yzerman contributed for the Red Wings, but he needed some help from some of the other guys on the team who were in a slump. Detroit was off and running in game three at Joe Louis Arena.

About halfway through the first, Aaron Ward took a roughing penalty that proved to be costly for the Wings. Red Wings nemesis Claude Lemeiux scored a power play goal to even the score at 1-1. Colorado seemed to be gaining confidence following the goal by Lemeiux.

Theo Fleury added to the Avalanche lead when he beat Bill Ranford to give the road warriors from Colorado a 2-1 lead. The Avalanche were building momentum heading into the second period at Joe Louis Arena.

Colorado knew if they scored the first goal, they would have the Wings right where they wanted them, on the ropes.

Four goals were scored in a wild second period. Unfortunately, Colorado scored three of the four goals. It took Colorado five minutes to jump out to a 5-1 lead in game three. The crowd at Joe Louis Arena was silent and stunned.

Colorado scored often, Dale Hunter tallied first for the Avalanche in the second period. Chris Drury who scored his first ever playoff goal as a rookie, followed the goal by Hunter. Aaron Miller added his first goal of the playoffs to wrap up the trifecta for the Avalanche in Hockey Town.

The Red Wings gained a little momentum heading into the third period. Brendan Shanahan fed a pass to Tomas Holmstrom, who beat Patrick Roy. The second period ended with the visitors from Colorado ahead by a 5-2 count.

Detroit knew that if they did not catch the Avalanche on the scoreboard they had to gain momentum for the next game. The Red Wings did just that. They were unable to tie Colorado, but they did score the only goal in the third period. Slava Kozlov scored an unassisted power play goal. Game three went to the visitors again. Up to this point in the series home ice held no advantage for either team.

The home team in this best of seven game series was 0 for 3 after the first three games. The Detroit Red Wings hoped to change this statistic in game four at Joe Louis Arena. Colorado had other plans; they hoped to even up the series in game four on the Detroit riverfront.

One goal was scored in an evenly matched first period. Chris Drury scored his second goal in as many games less than two minutes into the first period. Colorado seemed to figure out the left wing lock system of the Detroit Red Wings. The Avalanche hoped to come out gunning in the second period of game number four.

Two goals were scored in the second period, and none of them belonged to the team from Detroit. Colorado extended their margin when Adam Deadmarsh beat Bill Ranford. Milan Hejduk added to the Avalanche lead when he scored against Detroit. The goal by Hejduk marked the end for back up goalie Bill Ranford as a Detroit Red Wing.

The Red Wings rested their hopes for the remainder of the game on third string goalie, Norm Miracle. With Chris Osgood still recovering, Miracle was now in the Stanley Cup playoffs for the defending Stanley Cup champions. With the score 3-0 in favor of Colorado, Detroit was running out of time in game four to mount a comeback.

Colorado continued the onslaught in the third period of play. Peter Forsbeg recorded his first goal of the game to give the Avalanche a 4-0 lead. The fans at Joe Louis Arena were in disbelief watching there home team Red Wings unravel before their very eyes. Valarie Kamensky scored next on the power play for Colorado to give his team a comfortable 5-0 lead against the Detroit Red Wings.

Detroit went on the power play late in the third period, hoping they could cash in to avoid the shut out by Patrick Roy. Slava Kozlov scored for the Red Wings to give the fans something to cheer about in game four. The Wings found themselves behind 5-1 late in the third period.

Adam Deadmarsh added another goal for the visitors from Colorado. The Red Wings were in jeopardy of letting the series slip away with this one-sided loss to the Avalanche. Detroit had to respond to gain back momentum they had lost in this game.

Slava Kozlov tallied again to close the scoring in a disappointing 6-2 loss in game four. Game five returned to Colorado. The Red Wings hoped to continue the trend of victories for the visiting team in the series.

The Detroit Red Wings placed the injured Chris Osgood back between the pipes. The Red Wings wanted, if nothing else, a less-than-100-percent Osgood to lift the morale of the team. Detroit was a two-time defending championship team that was losing confidence quickly. Colorado opened the scoring in game five with the only goal recorded in the first period. Jeff Odgers knocked in his first goal of the playoffs. Detroit knew they had to come out in the second period and reverse the trend to regain momentum in game five.

Two goals were scored in the second period. Adam Deadmarsh tallied first to give Colorado a 2-0 lead in the pivotal game five. The next goal came on the power play. Peter Forsberg beat a courageous Chris Osgood to give the Avalanche a commanding 3-0 lead after 40 minutes of play.

Detroit found themselves in a desperate situation heading into the third period. The Red Wings out shot Colorado 14-6 in the third period. The result, however, went by the wayside as Patrick Roy stopped all the rubber thrown his way. Roy recorded a shutout, and Colorado was one game away from eliminating the two-time defending Stanley Cup champions – the Detroit Red Wings.

Not too many people in Hockey Town believed that the Red Wings could be swept in four straight games by any team in the NHL. Detroit was coming into the game with some key players injured; Igor Larionov and Chris Osgood were wounded, but the show went on with or without them.

Colorado opened the scoring in the first period when Peter Forsberg tallied with less than four minutes remaining in the period. The injured Osgood looked good in goal, and that was encouraging for Detroit. The owners of the Stanley Cup had to find a way to get back into the game; time was running out for the Red Wings' season.

Five goals were scored in the second period to decide the outcome of game six. Milan Hejduk opened the scoring to give the visitors from Colorado a 2-0 lead. Chris Drury tallied next for Colorado, and suddenly the Wings found themselves behind 3-0 in a must win situation.

Being in the position of elimination was not one that the Red Wings were familiar with. They had not faced elimination in the previous two years. The last time that Detroit faced elimination, Steve Yzerman rescued them with a double overtime game-winning goal against St. Louis.

Number 19 scored the next goal as Detroit was on the power play. The captain came through for the Avalanche. That's correct, number 19 for the Avalanche. Joe Sakic recorded a short-handed goal to extend the Colorado lead. The Avalanche had scored five unanswered goals in game six in Hockey Town.

With two and a half minutes remaining, Detroit began their comeback. The Red Wings were on the power play when Nick Lidstrom took a pass from Steve Yzerman and let go a wicked slapshot that beat Patrick Roy. Twenty-nine seconds later, Darren McCarty scored the final goal of the season for the Wings.

The late game scoring charge simply gave the fans at Joe Louis Arena something to build on for next season. The two-year reign as Stanley Cup champions was over.

The fans during the final game of the 1999 season did not forget the back-to-back Stanley Cup championships. The Red Wings received a standing ovation by the fans at Joe Louis Arena late in the third period before they left the ice in defeat.

Unlike previous playoff exits, these Red Wings were shown appreciation for the hard work that they had done. The fans or the media had not singled out one player for the collapse against the Colorado Avalanche. Injuries hurt Detroit in the 1999 playoffs against Colorado.

The talk of a dynasty still lingered in Hockey Town, but many faces of the main characters were questionable heading into the 1999-2000 season.

It was uncertain if Scotty Bowman would return, and more importantly, if Nick Lidstrom would stay with the Wings or return to his native homeland in Sweden.

One player was certain to return in the Red Wing uniform just as he had done for the past 15 seasons; Steve Yzerman would return as the captain. Yzerman was the reason that Detroit remained as one of top contenders to win the Stanley Cup. No one questioned the leadership of Yzerman any more since Detroit won consecutive Stanley Cup championships.

With the retirement of Wayne Gretzky, Steve Yzerman received more recognition for his accomplishments. Entering the 1999-2000 season, Steve Yzerman closed in on goal number 600. Steve did not enter the season with personal accomplishments on his mind. He had a taste of winning the Cup, and he wanted to bring the Stanley Cup back to Hockey Town.

CHAPTER EIGHTEEN

CAPTAIN 2000
REACHES ANOTHER MILESTONE

The Detroit Red Wings were the best team during the 1990's. They won two Stanley Cup championships and finished as the runner up in 1995. The Red Wings compiled the best record during the decade of the 90's. Even though they finished the decade by bowing out to the Colorado Avalanche, they were still considered one of the favorites to win the Cup heading into the new millennium. That is, as long as captain Steve Yzerman was leading the way.

The Detroit Red Wings were a strong contender to win the Stanley Cup again in 1999-2000. Losing to the Colorado Avalanche in the playoffs was a humbling experience for Yzerman and his teammates. He expected his team to come back and make another run at the Stanley Cup. Yzerman believed that the Red Wings should be a legitimate contender for the Cup for several years to come. As long as Steve Yzerman was the captain of the Detroit Red Wings, winning the Stanley Cup will always be a realistic goal.

The Red Wings entered the 1999-2000 season optimistic. Scotty Bowman returned and Nick Lidstrom also rejoined the Wings. Without Lidstrom, the Red Wings would have been in serious trouble. Many of the faces were the same, but some newcomers were a welcomed addition for the Detroit Red Wings.

Detroit tried to solidify their defense and return to be one of the best defensive teams in the NHL. The Red Wings were solid on defense with Larry Murphy, Nick Lidstrom, Chris Chelios, Aaron Ward and Mathieu Dandenault returning. During the off season, Detroit picked up veteran defenseman, Steve Duschene, and promoted 19 year old Jiri Fischer from the farm club. With this core of defense for the Red Wings, they had every right to be considered as one of the favorites to the win the Cup again in 1999-2000.

The goaltending improved with the signing of veteran back up goalie, Ken Wregget. The Red Wings also acquired Manny Legace just in case anything should happen to Chris Osgood or Wregget. Osgood knew going into the new season that he would be the number one goalie for the former Stanley Cup champions.

Offensively, the Detroit Red Wings were deep with talent, but some of the familiar faces were questionable as the season progressed. Brent Gilchrist was still recovering from a lower abdominal injury that occurred during the Western Conference Finals in 1998. The fate of Gilchrist was still unknown, but some believed that his career was over in the NHL. Joey Kocur was battling a similar injury that put his hockey career on a hold. Kirk Maltby started in the Red Wings lineup in 1999, but he suffered an abdominal injury that took him out of the lineup for several months during the regular season.

Darren McCarty was a hold-out at the start of the season due to contract negotiations. With McCarty's return uncertain, the Red Wings called up Yuri Butsayev, Darryl Laplante and B.J. Young who were very impressive in the pre-season games for Detroit.

The Detroit Red Wings signed a late addition free agent that added much needed depth to the already talented offensive unit. Detroit signed Pat Verbeek, who is known to get under the skin of the enemy. Verbeek, who has scored more than 500 NHL goals, has made his living in front of the opposing goalies. He fit in real well on a line with Brendan Shanahan and Steve Yzerman.

The Red Wings began the season healthy and established themselves as the number one team in the NHL early in the 1999-2000 season. The defense was ranked number one in the NHL, and Chris Osgood was enjoying one of his best seasons between the pipes for the Wings. The offense was ranked number one in the NHL, but that was not a surprise. A few injuries tested the depth of the Detroit Red Wings during the regular season.

Some of the famous role players for Scotty Bowman played a key role in the success of the Detroit Red Wings in the 1999-2000 regular season. The Wings had to rely upon their rookies to step up while some of the role players were injured in mid-season. The Red Wings were already playing without the services of Joey Kocur and Brent Gilchrist when the season began.

Detroit lost several forwards and had to rely upon the youngsters to fill in the void. Doug Brown went down with a foot injury. Darren McCarty and Kirk Maltby were out with the dreaded abdominal injury that had sidelined Kocur and Gilchrist. Sergei Federov was lost due to a concussion, and other nagging injuries. Kris Draper was out with an injury to his hand. The injury that really tested the resilience of the Red Wings was when Chris Osgood was sidelined with a hand injury. It was time for the backups and role players to earn some respect in the NHL and Hockey Town.

Fortunately, the defensive core for the Wings was able to stay relatively healthy, until they lost Aaron Ward with a shoulder injury. The injury to Ward forced the Red Wings to make a move at the trade deadline to bolster the defensive unit. Detroit reclaimed the services of defenseman, Todd Gill, who played the previous season with the Wings.

With many of the forwards out of action, the Wings had to rely upon not only their regulars, but also the contribution of the newcomers. As was expected, Steve Yzerman, Brendan Shanahan and Pat Verbeek stepped up their play and helped to hold the team together until some of their fallen teammates could return to the lineup.

The surprise of the season came from the play of Stacy Roest, who was teamed up on a line with two rookies. The effort from Darryl Laplante and Yuri Butsayev was most pleasing for the coaches. The line played a key role in holding the season together for the Detroit Red Wings in a critical part of the season.

With Chris Osgood out, the Red Wings had to rely upon Ken Wregget. Wregget deserves credit for keeping the Red Wings in the chase for the best record in the NHL during the regular season. The play of Wregget was steady and he proved that he would be a capable backup come playoff time. The defense in front of Wregget had a mid-season lapse, but they, too, returned to top form as the regular season concluded.

When Chris Osgood returned, many people believed that Detroit would return as the top team in the league. Osgood suffered a broken hand on a slap shot by Al MacInnis of the St. Louis Blues. Osgood struggled in net for a few weeks until he regained his confidence that he had before the hand injury.

The team seemed to be coming together with the return of many familiar faces. With the return of Federov, Brown, Maltby, McCarty, Draper and Brent Gilchrist, Detroit was back on top of their game. The return of Gilchrist was the biggest surprise.

Brent Gilchrist scored in his first game back. He was greeted with a great ovation from the loyal fans at Joe Louis Arena. It took a great amount of dedication and commitment for Gilchrist to return to the lineup. He worked extremely hard to return to the game that he loves so much.

As the season was coming to a close, the Detroit Red Wings were at the top of their game. They got contributions from several players, something that eluded them against Colorado in the 1999 Stanley Cup playoffs. The 2000 playoffs looked promising for the Detroit Red Wings, whom their captain, Steve Yzerman, led.

The Red Wings entered the first round of the playoffs against the Los Angeles Kings. Detroit won the series in four games, but they were not getting production from some of their main players. The Red Wings had to step up their production on offense in the second round against the Colorado Avalanche.

Colorado won the first two games of the series, just as Detroit had done in the previous playoff season after they dropped the next four games to be eliminated by the Avalanche. Detroit hoped that they would win four straight and return the favor to the Avalanche one year later. The Red Wings won game three at home, but game four was the pivotal game in the series.

Everything was going well for the Wings in game four as Detroit took the lead in the third period with about five minutes remaining. Colorado tied the score late in the game and went on to beat Detroit. The Avalanche were heading back home with a 3-1 lead in the series. The loss in game four was a crushing blow for the Detroit Red Wings.

The Colorado Avalanche were one game away from eliminating the Detroit Red Wings for a second consecutive season. Detroit did not get production from their big name players. Brendan Shanahan was relatively quiet in the series and so was Steve Yzerman. Colorado did not get offensive help from their captain Joe Sakic. The Avalanche did not need any help from Sakic as they went on to win game five and eliminate the Wings from the Stanley Cup playoffs.

The Detroit Red Wings had a season that was filled with milestones. Brendan Shanahan scored career goal number 400 during the regular season. Pat Verbeek scored his 500th career goal in a game down the stretch. Sergei Federov scored goal number 300, and Larry Murphy added to his numerous records he has set during his career in the NHL. Only one player claimed all of his accomplishments with one team, the Detroit Red Wings (except for Federov).

Steve Yzerman enjoyed a season that was filled with many highlights. He needed just eight goals heading into the season to reach the 600-goal mark in his career. On December 6, 1999, Steve Yzerman scored goal number 600 in a game against the Edmonton Oilers. He played off the accomplishment as only he could do and he made no big deal out of the distinguished achievement.

Steve Yzerman passed several great players in goals scored during the 1999-2000 regular season. He escalated himself into the top seven in goals scored all-time in the NHL. He surpassed such great players as Bobby Hull, Mario Lemeiux, and Mark Messier in goals scored during his NHL career. With three years remaining on Yzerman's contract it was quite likely that he will surpass the 700 goal mark during his brilliant career with the Detroit Red Wings.

The captain of the Detroit Red Wings was no longer questioned in regard to his leadership qualities. *ESPN* hockey expert commentator, Barry Melrose, felt that Yzerman was a great leader in the NHL during the 1999-2000 season. The result of his great leadership led to continuous success for the Red Wings. Scotty Bowman was the leader behind the bench, but Steve Yzerman was clearly the leader on the ice due to his dedication and sacrifice game after game.

The hockey legacy in Detroit lived for a long time. Nobody ever replaced Gordie Howe as Mr. Hockey, but only one man will be remembered as Mr. Hockey Town: Steve Yzerman, #19, captain of the Detroit Red Wings.

He came here from Nepean, Ontario, at the tender age of 18. He was placed upon a pedestal to resurrect a team that had reached rock bottom in Detroit, a city that is proud of their Red Wings. He was the kid with all the answers in 1983.

As the team improved in Yzerman's early years, he was heralded as a franchise player. He put up great numbers offensively, and suddenly the Red Wings had hope of building the team into a realistic contender for the elusive Stanley Cup. Yzerman gave Detroit hope for the future.

After three seasons with the Detroit Red Wings, Steve Yzerman was selected by Jacques Demers to be the captain of the team. At the age of 21, he became the youngest captain ever to be selected by the Detroit Red Wings. Demers sensed that "Stevie Wonder," as Demers called him, would provide leadership by way of example. Demers was proud of his controversial decision to select Steve Yzerman as captain of the Red Wings for the 1986-87 season. He replaced Danny Gare as captain of a team that was improving, but not contending for the Cup.

In the early stages of his career, he provided the majority of offense for the Red Wings. He carried the team on his back, and when they failed, he took the blame. Yzerman was never one to make up excuses, but he remained focused and determined to capture the elusive dream – The Stanley Cup.

When Scotty Bowman arrived as coach, Yzerman changed his game to become a valuable all-around team player. His offensive numbers dropped drastically and until Detroit won the Stanley Cup his leadership qualities were constantly the topic of discussion.

Following the Stanley Cup victory against the Philadelphia Flyers in 1997, Yzerman finally had time to reflect back on his career with the Detroit Red Wings. He had grown up quickly because he was appointed team captain early in his career. When his career ends he will be remembered as #19 for the Detroit Red Wings. Yzerman will also be acknowledged by many people as a hero for all the lives he touched in a positive way.

CHAPTER NINETEEN

THE HUMBLE HERO, ACTIONS SPEAK LOUDER THAN WORDS

Quite often in life, a hero is someone who happens to be in the right place at the right time. Occasionally, a hero is someone who has a positive impact or influence upon a person during his or her lifetime. Rarely is a hero in the wrong place at the right time, but for one hero this was what happened in his life.

A celebrity is someone who is blessed with a gift, popular, wealthy, and famous. Celebrities are well known either in their community, regionally, nationally, or internationally. A celebrity is not necessarily a hero.

A hero does something voluntarily that betters the life of another human being. Some heroes happen to be in the right place at the right time. This type of hero is a hero of fate. An example would be someone who saves a person from death or injury.

Even though the hero of fate saves the person in danger, they reacted to the situation because they were present. They happened to be in the right place at the right time. Most all people would help another person whose life was in danger. None the less the hero of fate still decided to do the good deed and should never be mistaken as one who is not a hero.

Another type of hero is one who makes a positive impact upon a person within their lifetime. This type of hero differs from the hero of fate in that they are not placed in a situation that concerns life or death. This type of hero chooses to help others in a positive role model fashion. The name given for this type of hero is simply a role model.

A role model has a life long lasting affect on a person's life, not to be confused with a celebrity who is idolized and may have a short-term affect in a lifetime. A typical role model may be a grandparent, parent, aunt, uncle, brother, sister, teacher, and minister. Someone who touches the life of others in a positive manner and leaves a lasting impact of goodness upon one's life tends to be a positive role model.

One young man became a hero by being in the wrong place at the right time. He came to the Detroit Red Wings when they had reached rock bottom in the NHL. His career would have been much brighter in 1983 if the New York Islanders or any other team than the Red Wings had drafted him. Steve Yzerman found himself in the wrong place at the right time.

The timing was right, because the Red Wings had no where to go but upward in the standings. Steve Yzerman was given a chance to perform in the NHL at the age of 18 with the Red Wings. If Yzerman would have played on almost any other team, his talents may have been placed on hold for a few years until he made his leap to the NHL.

Detroit was the perfect fit for this talented youngster from Nepean, Ontario. The Red Wings were in desperate need of an offensive talented player who could lead the team back to respectability. Yzerman had speed and a scoring touch that may have been blemished if another team in the NHL drafted him. With Detroit, Steve Yzerman was in the wrong place at the right time. It took just three short years in the Red Wing sweater before he would be targeted as captain of the Detroit Red Wings.

197

In 1986, the Detroit Red Wings head coach, Jacques Demers, noticed that Steve Yzerman had a hidden talent as a leader. Demers appointed Yzerman as the captain of the Wings. His play on the ice was inspirational to the other players on his team. The Detroit Red Wings selection of Steve Yzerman helped to make him a well known celebrity, but being in the wrong place at the right time also helped to make him a hero.

Once Yzerman accepted his role as captain of the Red Wings he became more involved with the community in the Detroit area. He became a part of the city of Detroit. Yzerman did his charitable deeds as a nice gesture that he did not care to publicize.

Steve Yzerman was a humble person who let his actions speak louder than words. In his first years as captain, he led the Wings to the Campbell Conference Finals where they bowed out to the mighty Edmonton Oilers. The Red Wings were respectable and it was anticipated that they were on their way to a Stanley Cup championship following their defeat in the 1988 playoffs to Edmonton.

The move by Demers looked ingenious as Yzerman had led the Wings to the top of the pack in the NHL. Instant success helped Yzerman adjust to his role as captain at such a young age. Steve Yzerman was bringing success to the Detroit Red Wings instantaneously. He was performing beyond his expectations, which was a pleasant surprise for the rejuvenated Red Wings.

In 1989, the Red Wings took a step backwards, only the beginning of the firing squad for Steve Yzerman as the Red Wings lost to the Chicago Black Hawks in the first round of the Stanley Cup playoffs.

In 1990, Yzerman suffered an injury that led many to question not only his leadership but also some thought he was too fragile. In two short years, Steve Yzerman had seen a sudden twist of fate. When Detroit played Edmonton in the Campbell Conference Finals, many Red Wing fans believed that Yzerman was the correct choice as captain: when things went sour, he suddenly had critics with questions for him to answer.

Steve Yzerman bounced back in 1991 with one of his best seasons in the NHL. The fans and media questioned his leadership, but nobody could ever question his character. Detroit took an early first round exit in the playoffs as the frustration was building in Hockey Town.

In the 1992 playoffs, the Wings made it to the second round only to be swept by the Chicago Black Hawks. Steve Yzerman had to face the humiliating questions again, which he did with the utmost class and dignity. Yzerman accepted the blame for the early exits, and returned next season ready to lead his team by example, hopeful that one day his hard work would pay off for the Detroit Red Wings.

During the 1993 Stanley Cup playoffs, doubt set in as to the future of the Red Wings as they lost in the first round again. The good news was that Detroit was making the playoffs, but the bad news was they did not last very long in the second season. The Toronto Maple Leafs took the Wings out in seven games to end another disappointing season for Yzerman and the Red Wings.

Steve Yzerman changed his game dramatically when Scotty Bowman arrived in town to coach the Red Wings in the 1994 Stanley Cup playoffs. People expected big things from the Wings in the playoffs. Yzerman went down in the first round with an injury, and the number eight seeded San Jose Sharks eliminated the Red Wings in the first round. The number one seeded Red Wings were embarrassed and eliminated in seven games by the expansion San Jose Sharks. Changes were in the making for the Wings, would Yzerman survive the shakedown and return for next season?

The 1995 playoff run was the best to date under the leadership of Steve Yzerman. Detroit made it to the Stanley Cup Finals, only to be ousted in four straight games by the New Jersey Devils. The question still lingered, would the Wings win the Cup under the leadership of Yzerman?

In the 1996 Stanley Cup playoffs, Detroit was the best team in the league during the regular season. They recorded the most victories (62) by any NHL team. In the second round of the playoffs against the St. Louis Blues, Steve Yzerman delivered the biggest goal of his career. In game seven, in double overtime, Yzerman whistled a shot over the right shoulder of Jon Casey to end the marathon game and series.

The goal by Yzerman against St. Louis put an end to questioning his leadership qualities even though Detroit did not win the Cup. The Red Wings lost in the Western Conference Finals against the Colorado Avalanche to end another long season in disappointment. Many fans sensed that it was just a matter of time before the Red Wings won the elusive Stanley Cup.

Everything came together for Detroit in the 1997 Stanley Cup playoffs. The Red Wings returned to the Finals and captured the Cup after a 42-year drought in Detroit. The critics put the leadership question of Steve Yzerman to rest once and for all. Yzerman reached the end of his roller coaster ride.

The Stanley Cup playoffs were played to the theme of BELIEVE for the Red Wings in 1998. The team dedicated the repeat championship to two men, Sergei Mnatsakanov and Vladimir Konstantinov. The two Red Wings were severely injured in an auto accident just a short time after the team won the Cup in 1997.

Detroit recaptured the Cup in 1998, and Steve Yzerman led the way. Yzerman won the Conn-Smythe Trophy as the most valuable player during the Stanley Cup playoffs. At last the criticism had ended, and he was proclaimed the unquestionable leader of the Detroit Red Wings. Even though his career did not officially end in 1998, he put an end to his critics questioning him as to what went wrong, and was he the man to lead his team to the top?

During the past few seasons Detroit enjoyed success even though they did not win the Stanley Cup. The questions and humiliation were gone for Steve Yzerman. He did what Wayne Gretzky and Mario Lemeuix had done that placed them one notch above Yzerman – won the Stanley Cup.

The captain, Yzerman, entered the 2000-01 season with optimism, but a freak injury to his right knee during the pre-season would require arthroscopic surgery to repair cartilage damage. The team played relatively well during the absence of Steve Yzerman. He missed a good portion of the beginning of the regular season. Upon his return, the team improved in the standings to finish second overall in the NHL.

The Red Wings were confident going into the first round of the playoffs against the Los Angeles Kings. Detroit was optimistic about their chances of winning back the Stanley Cup in 2000-01. All hopes diminished when Steve Yzerman was sidelined with a leg injury. Detroit hoped that they could eliminate the Kings in the first round to give Yzerman time to heal for the next round of the playoffs. Injuries hampered the Wings quest for the Cup.

The Wings jumped out to a two game lead in the series against Los Angeles. Brendan Shanahan and Sergei Federov provided leadership in the absence of Yzerman. When Shanahan went down with an injury, the Wings suffered for the remainder of the series. Los Angeles won four straight games and eliminated the Detroit Red Wings in the first round of the playoffs.

Without Yzerman and Shanahan, the team lacked leadership to carry them forward in the playoffs. Once again, the importance of Steve

Yzerman to his team was reaffirmed. The Detroit Red Wings failed without Yzerman on the ice.

As a player, Steve Yzerman enjoyed early success with the Red Wings. He came into the NHL at the young age of 18. He was an instant success offensively.

When he was 21, he was named captain of the Red Wings. He took on responsibility beyond his years. Yzerman was not vocal. He let his actions speak for him on the ice. Some fans and some of the media were constantly questioning his leadership and health until Detroit captured the Cup. Steve Yzerman was a quiet and humble man who performed heroic actions off the ice where he made his mark as a hero.

To be a humble person was difficult for a celebrity. Every good deed done was publicized with the mass media of the world. Steve Yzerman was a man who tended to keep his charitable actions unpronounced. His peaceful and reserved behavior made him a humble hero.

Steve Yzerman was a hero for the many lives that he touched in a positive way and for way he conducted himself in a humbling manner. He did not want the attention for all the good things he has done. He responded for others out of the kindness of his heart. The time that Yzerman spent with Elysia Pefley was not for show. It was his time and he was sincere and genuine in his actions. Elysia loved Steve Yzerman for the person he was not because he played for the Detroit Red Wings.

The way in which Steve Yzerman lived was magnetic. He attracted people to react upon his actions and not his words. His heroism was not limited to just children. Adults have openly admitted that this man was their hero.

The Detroit Red Wings team trainer, John Wharton, went through numerous injuries with Yzerman. He watched Yzerman persevere and overcome injuries through hard work and determination. Wharton was not ashamed to claim Steve Yzerman as his hero.

Kevin Hodson, who was known as "Ticker" played goalie with the Red Wings before he was dealt away to Tampa Bay. He treasured the moments he shared on the ice with Steve Yzerman. Kevin Hodson was another Red Wing player who looked up to Yzerman during his days with the Wings.

Steve Yzerman was admired because he played his heart out every season for the Red Wings. He dragged himself onto the ice because of numerous injuries playoff season after playoff season. He led his team quietly, never complained, earned the respect of his teammates, and still answered the media onslaught after every last game of the season. With his head held high and his eyes staring blankly into space, in his soft tone, and with disappointment in his voice, he always had the courage to explain what went wrong.

This man had class, this man had character, and Red Wing fans knew it. One day the whole world will realize that this man, Steve Yzerman, never sold anybody short. He never gave up, win or lose game seven of any playoff series.

He had not fulfilled his lifelong dream, and until he did, he would not give up pursuit of his ultimate goal – Lord Stanley's Cup.

Mitch Albom, *The Detroit Free Press*, April 22, 1998, shared in a column written for one of Steve Yzerman's daughters that, "your dear old Dad is a real hero, the kind where courage and patience is rewarded with the ultimate prize." The ultimate prize being the Stanley Cup. Albom continued to share his feelings about Yzerman when he wrote, "You see a lot of us in Detroit have come to know your father over the years. We call him "The Captain" or "Stevie Y." He symbolizes many of us in this city of hard working people who don't always get rewarded when we deserve it. Who don't complain, who just go back to work and believe in the future." (© Tribune Media Services, Inc. All Rights Reserved. Reprinted with permission.)

Steve Yzerman may not have been a hero for all of his teammates, but he was respected as the leader of the Detroit Red Wings. He reached out to the community and expected nothing in return. He displayed a magnetic personality that children and adults sensed to be sincere. This was truly one nice guy who did not finish last.

Steve Yzerman just finished a skating session at training camp in Traverse City, Michigan, during the 2000 pre-season. Perhaps he was anxious to get back to the hotel and relax, and participate in his hobby playing golf. On the way out from the Center Ice Arena, Yzerman stopped at the attention of a young boy who suffered from Cerebral Palsy.

The boy, Robbie Heska, was anxious to get a picture taken with his hero, Steve Yzerman. Robbie wrote a hero paper in class at his school about Steve Yzerman. As usual, Yzerman lived up to his hero status and posed in the picture with Robbie. It cost Steve Yzerman a little bit of his time, but it meant the world to Robbie Heska.

Steve Yzerman captured the heart of Robbie Heska and Elysia Pefley, won the respect of Marc Marzullo, and helped Breanna Morrison persevere in times of trouble. He did not gain their respect with his words, but rather he gained their attention with his caring and humble personality. Yzerman will be remembered primarily for his accomplishments on the ice with the Detroit Red Wings.

Steve Yzerman should not be concerned about being compared to Gordie Howe, Wayne Gretzky or Mario Lemeuix. He should not be remembered for his individual accomplishments on the ice, but he should be remembered as a Detroit Red Wing.

The thing that Steve Yzerman should be remembered for was the way he willingly reached out to touch the lives of others. The way he stuck to his guns, and did things his way to overcome obstacles. Steve Yzerman the soft spoken, humble and caring man will forever be a Wing...and a hero!

INDEX

Abel, Sid, 16, 18, 28
Adams, Jack, 15, 16, 64, 72
Albom, Mitch, 77, 202
Anderson, Sparky, 11
Arbour, Al, 22, 41, 68, 69
Aristotle, 2
Ashton, Brent, 34
Askey, Tom, 180
Audet, Philipe, 177
Barney, Lem, 13
Barr, Dave, 34
Barrasso, Tom, 28, 67
Bellows, Brian, 128, 168, 169
Berenson, Red, 71
Bergevin, Marc, 121
Bettman, Gary, 7, 140, 143, 171, 172
Bing, Dave, 14, 15
Bird, Larry, 14, 38
Blake, Toe, 62, 63, 67
Bossy, Mike, 41
Bowman, Scotty, xiv, 9, 11, 21, 41, 42,
   61, 62, 63, 64, 65, 66, 67, 68, 69, 70,
   71, 72, 74, 78, 90, 91, 94, 95, 98,
   101, 103, 104, 105, 106, 112, 117,
   118, 119, 120, 121, 124, 126, 127,
   132, 142, 148, 152, 167, 169, 171,
   173, 174, 175, 177, 179, 181, 189,
   190, 191, 194, 195, 199
Bridgeman, Mel, 34
Brind'Amour, Rob, 135, 136, 137
Brodeur, Martin, 99
Brown, Doug, 90, 115, 116, 125, 127,
   128, 156, 167, 168, 169, 170, 180,
   181, 191
Brown, Gates, 11
Burr, Shawn, 29, 77
Butsayev, Yuri, 191, 192
Campbell, Jim, 123, 152, 153, 155, 157
Carkner, Terry, 9
Carson, Jimmy, 50, 58, 59
Casey, Jon, 110, 111, 199
Cashman, Wayne, 41
Chaisson, Steve, 35, 77, 91

Chamberlain, Wilt, 38
Chelios, Chris, xiv, 178, 184, 190
Cherry, Don, 41
Churchill, Winston, 3
Ciccarelli, Dino, 58, 59, 94, 112, 115
Clark, Dutch, 13
Clark, Wendal, 178, 179, 180, 185
Clemente, Roberto, 2
Cobb, Ty, 10, 12
Cochrane, Mickey, 12
Coffey, Paul, 42, 59, 67, 68, 97, 98,
   103, 109, 112, 113, 114, 115, 116,
   117, 118
Constantine, Kevin, 73
Cornoyer, Yvan, 41
Courtnall, Geoff, 120, 122, 156
Daly, Chuck, 14, 15
Dandenault, Matheiu, 119
Deadmarsh, Adam, 113, 115, 184, 186,
   187
Delvecchio, Alex, 40, 176
Demers, Jacques, 34, 35, 44, 45, 46, 52,
   180, 194, 198
Devellano, Jimmy, xii, 22, 23, 29, 45,
   61, 63, 68, 69
Dollas, Bobby, 52
Domi, Tie, 9
Drake, Dallas, 58
Draper, Kris, 71, 94, 117, 121, 129,
   142, 155, 156, 167, 172, 191
Drury, Chris, 186, 188
Drury, Ted, 127
Dryden, Ken, 41, 63
Dugay, Ron, 26, 31
Dumars, Joe, 14
Edison, Thomas, 2, 3
Elway, John, 40
Eriksson, Anders, 102, 177, 178
Errey, Bob, 9, 67, 118
Esposito, Phil, 41
Essena, Bob, 73
Federko, Bernie, 50

I

Federov, Sergei, xiv, 52, 53, 56, 73, 76, 90, 94, 103, 104, 105, 111, 114, 115, 116, 117, 124, 125, 127, 131, 133, 134, 137, 146, 147, 148, 149, 150, 151, 152, 153, 155, 162, 164, 168, 169, 170, 181, 182, 191, 193, 200
Ferguson, John, 62
Fetisov, Slava, 91, 103, 104, 142, 144, 172, 175, 177
Fidrych, Mark, 12
Fischer, Jiri, 190
Fleury, Theo, 185
Ford, Henry, 3
Forsberg, Peter, 112, 115, 187, 188
Frances, Ron, 67
Fuhr, Grant, 42, 107, 110, 120, 121, 122, 123, 152, 153, 154, 155, 156, 157
Gallant, Gerard, 29, 32, 45, 46, 48, 59
Gare, Danny, xiii, 22, 26, 34, 194
Gave, Keith, 73
Gibson, Kirk, 12
Goloubovsky, Yan, 177
Gordon, Jeff, 86, 87
Goslin, Goose, 12
Graves, Adam, 45, 50, 68
Gretzky, Wayne, 42, 47, 48, 50, 66, 77, 94, 107, 109, 111, 147, 189, 200, 203
Grimson, Stu, 90
Hall, Glenn, 63
Harkness, Ned, 22
Harwell, Ernie, 12, 116
Havlechek, John, 38
Hejduk, Milan, 186, 188
Herbert, Guy, 181, 182
Heska, Robbie, 202
Hextall, Ron, 136, 137, 139
Hill, Grant, 15
Hiller, Jim, 59
Hodson, Kevin, 102
Holmstrom, Tomas Homer, 119, 151, 153, 154, 157, 161, 164, 168, 170, 181, 182, 183, 186
Horton, Willie, 11

Howe, Gordie, xi, 3, 8, 16, 17, 18, 19, 21, 28, 40, 58, 118, 138, 139, 176, 194, 203
Howe, Mark, 58, 59
Hull, Brett, 32, 107, 109, 122, 124, 153
Hunter, Dale, 184, 186
Irbe, Artes, 73
Irvan, Dick, 72
Isbell, Frances T., vii, 79
Ivan, Tommy, 16
Jackson, Janet, 86
Jackson, Reggie, 37
Jagr, Jamr, 42
Jenning, Grant, 67
John Paul II, Pope, 87
Johnson, Eddie, 67, 68
Johnson, Greg, 70, 105, 116, 118
Johnson, Magic, 14, 38
Johnson, Vinnie, 14, 15
Jordan, Michael, 39, 86, 87
Juneau, Joe, 167
Kaline, Al, 11, 12
Kamensky, Valarie, 187
Kariya, Paul, 124, 125, 126, 179, 180
Karras, Alex, 13
Keane, Mike, 113, 161
Keenan, Mike, 59, 69
Kell, George, 12
Keller, Helen, 2
Kelly, Jim, 40
Kidd, Trevor, 91, 103
King, Kris, 9, 45
King, Martin Luther Jr, 2
Kisio, Kelly, 32
Knuble, Mike, 119
Konstantinov, Vladimir, 55, 56, 81, 90, 103, 104, 111, 116, 127, 144, 145, 146, 165, 172, 173, 200
Kournikova, Anna, 53
Kozlov, Slava, 55, 56, 94, 97, 103, 107, 115, 116, 123, 124, 126, 127, 132, 133, 151, 155, 158, 168, 182, 183, 184, 186, 187
Kromm, Bobby, 21, 22
Krupp, Uwe, 115, 177
Krushelnyski, Mike, 90

Kuenn, Harvey, 12
LaFontaine, Pat, 24, 28, 29, 31, 54
Lambert, Cynthia, 73
Lambert, Lane, 33
Lambier, Bill, 14, 15
Langenbrunner, Jamie, 9, 162
Lanier, Bob, 14, 15
LaPlante, Darryl, 177
Lapointe, Martin, 55, 148, 152, 153, 156, 164, 167, 169
Larionov, Igor, xiv, 91, 103, 116, 124, 127, 131, 132, 134, 142, 149, 150, 161, 187
Larry, Yale, 13
Larson, Reed, 21, 22, 26
Lawton, Brian, 23, 28
Layne, Bobby, 13
LeClair, John, 135, 137
Lefebvre, Sylvain, 117
Lemeuix, Claude, 117, 130, 131, 133
Lemeuix, Mario, 200, 203
Lewis, Dave, 34, 177
Lidstrom, Nicklas, xiv, 55, 56, 95, 114, 147, 150, 159, 177, 183
Lincoln, Abraham, 2
Lindros, Eric, 54, 135, 139
Lindsay, Ted, 16, 18, 22, 28, 40, 176
Lolich, Mickey, 11
Lombardi, Vince, 39
Lowe, Kevin, 42
MacInnis, Al, 123, 154, 192
Mahorn, Rick, 14
Mahovolich, Pete, 64
Makarov, Sergei, 75, 91
Maltby, Kirk, 102, 118, 124, 133, 135, 136, 148, 154, 160, 184, 191
Mantle, Mickey, 3, 12, 37
Marino, Dan, 40
Marshall, Jason, 182
Marzullo, Marc, v, viii, 79, 86, 87, 88, 89, 202
Marzullo, Nancy, 88
Marzullo, Peter, 87, 88
Maxner, Wayne, 22

McCarty, Darren, 71, 90, 94, 123, 130, 131, 139, 142, 148, 154, 156, 188, 191
McClain, Denny, 11
McClleland, Kevin, 50
McCourt, Dale, 21
McInnis, Marty, 179, 182
Melrose, Barry, 194
Messier, Mark, 42, 194
Millen, Greg, 54
Miller, Aaron, 186
Miracle, Norm, 186
Montana, Joe, 39, 40
Morrison, Breanna, 79, 81, 84, 89, 202
Mother Teresa, 2, 3
Murphy, Joe, 35, 50, 122
Murphy, Larry, xiv, 67, 118, 121, 123, 127, 148, 154, 162, 169, 177, 190, 193
Murray, Bryan, 52, 60, 61, 69, 72, 91
Murray, Terry, 136
Namath, Joe, 39
Neale, Harry, 31, 32, 33, 34
Newhouser, Hal, 11, 12
Oates, Adam, 32, 48, 103, 166
Odgers, Jeff, 187
Ogrodnick, John, 22, 26, 31, 32, 34
Orr, Bobby, 41
Osgood, Chris, 71, 73, 76, 91, 104, 106, 110, 113, 114, 115, 116, 117, 120, 142, 146, 149, 150, 152, 153, 154, 156, 157, 158, 160, 162, 164, 166, 168, 169, 170, 173, 180, 181, 183, 184, 186, 187, 188, 190, 191, 192
Ozolinsh, Sandis, 114, 116
Pang, Darren, 172
Park, Brad, xii, 22, 26, 27, 34
Parks, Rosa, 2
Patrick, Craig, 67
Pefley, Elysia, 4, 80, 88, 89, 201, 202
Plato, 2
Polano, Nick, 22, 31
Primeau, Keith, 52, 80, 94, 117, 118
Probert, Bob, 33, 45, 46, 48, 49, 52, 77
Pronger, Chris, 9
Pronovost, Marcel, 22

Ranford, Bill, 183, 184, 185, 186
Recchi, Mark, 67
Ricchi, Mike, 113, 114, 116, 130
Richard, Henri, 41
Riendeau, Vincent, 55
Roberts, Gordie, 67
Robinson, Larry, 64
Robinson, Smokey, 17
Rodman, Dennis, 14, 15
Roest, Stacey, 177
Roosevelt, Franklin, D., 3
Ross, Diana, 17
Rouse, Bob, 91, 177
Roy, Patrick, 80, 105, 112, 114, 115,
   116, 117, 130, 131, 134, 183, 184,
   186, 187, 188
Ruth, Babe, 2, 37
Rychel, Warren, 114
Sacco, Joe, 128
Sakic, Joe, 112, 114, 115, 117, 130,
   132, 133, 188, 193
Sallie, John, 15
Samuelson, Ulf, 67, 178
Sanders, Barry, 13, 40
Sandstrom, Tomas, 118
Sather, Glen, 42
Sawchuk, Terry, 16
Schmidt, Joe, 13
Schonfield, Jim, 22
Schultz, Dave, 41
Selanne, Teemu, 124, 125, 126, 179,
   180, 181
Shanahan, Brendan, xiv, 118, 119, 122,
   123, 124, 130, 134, 136, 137, 147,
   150, 151, 152, 154, 181, 183, 186,
   191, 192, 193, 200
Sheppard, Ray, 54, 56, 73, 94, 103
Simon, Chris, 166
Sims, Billy, 13
Sittler, Darryl, 29
Skinner, Jimmy, 16
Smith, Barry, 68, 99, 177
Smith, Billy, 41
Snepts, Harold, 33
Snow, Garth, 136
Socrates, 2

Stalenkov, Mikhail, 126
Stanley, Mickey, 11
Steffan, Greg, 22
Stewart, Bill, 67
Thomas, Isiah, 14, 15, 38, 101
Tocchet, Rick, 68, 148, 149, 150, 151
Torrey, Bill, 31
Trammel, Alan, 11
Trottier, Bryan, xi, 8, 22, 26, 41, 67, 85
Turgeon, Pierre, 120, 155
Turgeon, Sylvain, 23, 28
Vachon, Rogie, 62
Verbeek, Pat, xiv, 160, 191, 192, 193
Vernon, Mike, 91, 92, 95, 99, 104, 106,
   120, 121, 122, 124, 126, 128, 130,
   132, 133, 134, 136, 139, 142, 146,
   164
Waite, Jimmy, 73, 150, 151
Walker, Doak, 13
Walker, Wayne, 13
Ward, Aaron, 71, 177, 185, 190, 192
West, Jerry, 38
Wharton, John, 173, 201
Whitaker, Lou, 12
Williams, Dave, 29
Wilson, Earl, 11
Worsley, Gump, 41
Wregget, Ken, 190, 192
Wyatt, John, 11
Yardley, George, 15
Yelle, Stephane, 113, 114, 133
Young, Scott, 131, 133, 134
Ysabaert, Paul, 52
Yzerman, Jean, xi, 7, 8
Yzerman, Mike, 7
Yzerman, Ron, xi, 7, 8
Yzerman, Steve, 1, vii, xi, xii, xiii, xiv,
   3, 4, 6, 7, 8, 9, 12, 17, 24, 26, 27, 28,
   29, 30, 31, 32, 33, 34, 35, 43, 44, 45,
   46, 47, 48, 49, 51, 52, 53, 54, 56, 57,
   59, 61, 69, 71, 73, 74, 75, 76, 77, 80,
   81, 82, 83, 84, 85, 86, 87, 88, 89, 92,
   94, 95, 96, 98, 99, 100, 101, 103,
   104, 105, 107, 108, 109, 111, 112,
   113, 114, 116, 117, 118, 119, 121,
   123, 125, 131, 132, 134, 136, 137,

138, 139, 140, 141, 142, 143, 145,
146, 147, 148, 151, 153, 154, 156,
157, 159, 160, 161, 164, 165, 166,
167, 168, 170, 171, 172, 173, 176,
179, 180, 181, 182, 183, 185, 188,

189, 190, 191, 192, 193, 194, 197,
198, 199, 200, 201, 202, 203
Zednik, Richard, 166
Zubov, Sergei, 160

ACKNOWLEDGEMENTS

The purpose in writing this book is to assist in the need of helping others less fortunate. Steve Yzerman and several other professional athletes have taken time out from their busy schedules to help children who have been stricken with an illness. There truly is no better reward than to place a smile upon the face of a child who is suffering from an illness.

I would like to personally thank each and every person who purchased this book. Your generosity has helped children who are in need, and that are grateful for the contributions provided from a proceeds of sales from this book. Without you, the reader, my dream of helping a child in need would not be possible.

This book would not be possible without the expertise of the following authors who assisted me in gathering together my thoughts to put together the story of a true modern day hero in the likes of Steve Yzerman. I would like to thank Mr. Douglas Hunter, *Scotty Bowman – A Life in Hockey*, TRUIMPH Books, Chicago, 1998; Mr. Bruce Dowbiggin, *Of Ice And Men*; MacFarlane, Walter and Ross, Toronto, 1998; Ms. Yitta Halberstam and Judith Levanthal, *Small Miracles*, Adams Media Corporation, Holbrook, Mass., 1997. The following members of *The Detroit News* for their contribution to *Heart of A Champion*, edited by Frances J. Fitzgerald: Mr. Joe Falls, Vartan Kupelian, Cynthia Lambert, John U. Bacon, Terry Foster, Ad-Craft, Louisville, Kentucky, 1996.

This book could not have been written without the hockey experts who work for *ESPN*. A special thank you goes out to Barry Melrose and Darren Pang, and to *Hockey Night in Canada*, and the coverage of *WDIV* television in Detroit; the writers from *The Detroit News* (Keith Gave, Jerry Green, Paul Harris, Cynthia Lambert, Vartan Kupelian, and Bob Wojonowski); *The Detroit Free Press* (Mitch Albom and Jason LaCanfora); *USA Today*, who provided great insight to this book with their professionalism that they display daily on the job. Thank You to *Make-A-Wish Foundation* and their wonderful website at: http://www.wish.org/ - a valuable source of giving.

A special thanks goes out to Mr. J. P. Delaney, Mr. Bobby Lewis, Mrs. Nancy Marzullo, and Dr. Gordon Isbell, III, D.M.D., P.A., for their kindness and brilliant photography they contributed to this book. Thanks to all who lent their support in making this project possible: Fr.

Mark Lamprich, Ms. Roberta Hutchcraft, Ms. Erin Key (editor), I am grateful for your efforts in assisting me in different aspects of writing this book. A special thanks goes out to William Anderson for proofreading. Thanks to Donald Morrison, Sr., Patricia Morrison (Dad and Mom), Rita Mayrand, Bobby McCollouch, and my lovely wife, Teresa, for your support to see me through this endeavor. A special thanks to my children; Breanna, Ryan, Crystal, and Tinesha thanks for believing in me. Thanks to Ryan P. Morrison for designing the cover for my book: A job well done!

A special thanks goes out to Mr. Ralph Slater, who spent countless hours developing the *Internet HOCKEY Database* website at: http://www.slater.alabanza.com/idhb/stats/leagues/seasons/teams/00003484/html an excellent resource that provides statistics that were used to compile this book.

I would like to thank Mr. Mike Yzerman, the elder brother of Steve, for speaking to me at the Ice Chalet in Greensboro, North Carolina, in attempting to assist me for a proposed interview with Mr. Steve Yzerman. A special thanks for gathering together my paperwork to be sent to Steve Yzerman for proposed authorization of this biography. I never could directly contact Steve Yzerman for authorization of this book, this is an unauthorized biography.

I did, however, have the opportunity to speak briefly with Steve Yzerman about Marc Marzullo. Steve Yzerman agreed to autograph a photo for the Marzullo family following Marc's death in July 1999. Mr. Yzerman signed the photo in Nashville, Tennessee, before boarding the team bus. Steve Yzerman again proved that he truly is a class act. Thanks, Mr. Steve Yzerman, for brightening the lives of so many children.

In conclusion, I would like to thank the children who need our help and prayers. Thanks to Frances Isbell and her father Gordon for sharing information on Spinal Muscular Atrophy, and I pray that everything goes well on her operation in September, 2001. Thank you to the late Marc Marzullo, who blessed me with an interview to better understand the Make-A-Wish Foundation and the true meaning of a hero. Thank you, Marc, for touching my life and the lives of so many others.

ABOUT THE AUTHOR

Gary L. Morrison was born in Detroit, Michigan (1958). He resided in Farmington Hills, Michigan for thirty-five years. He currently resides in Alabama. He has written multiple articles that appear in encyclopedias. He was also the President of the History Club at Jacksonville State University. Mr. Morrison graduated from Farmington Hills Harrison High School (1976). He earned his B.A. in History from the University of Detroit in 1991. He earned his M.A. in History from Jacksonville State University in Jacksonville, Alabama in 1996. He taught Social Studies for two years in Greensboro, North Carolina at Our Lady of Grace School.

Printed in the United States
4023